Born to a Kree mother and human father, former U.S. Air Force pilot
CAROL DANVERS became a super hero when a Kree device activated her latent powers.

NOW SHE'S AN AVENGER AND EARTH'S MIGHTIEST HERO.

CAPTAIN MARVEL
DARK TEMPEST

ANN NOCENTI
WRITER

PAOLO VILLANELLI
ARTIST

JAVA TARTAGLIA
COLOR ARTIST

VC's ARIANA MAHER
LETTERER

MIKE McKONE & JESUS ABURTOV
COVER ART

SARAH BRUNSTAD
EDITOR

TOM BREVOORT
EXECUTIVE EDITOR

SPECIAL THANKS TO **ANITA OKOYE** & **LINDSEY COHICK**

COLLECTION EDITOR: **JENNIFER GRÜNWALD**
ASSISTANT EDITOR: **DANIEL KIRCHHOFFER**
ASSOCIATE MANAGER, TALENT RELATIONS: **LISA MONTALBANO**
VP PRODUCTION & SPECIAL PROJECTS: **JEFF YOUNGQUIST**
LOGO & BOOK DESIGNER: **SARAH SPADACCINI**

MANAGER & SENIOR DESIGNER: **ADAM DEL RE**
LEAD DESIGNER: **JAY BOWEN**
SVP PRINT, SALES & MARKETING: **DAVID GABRIEL**
EDITOR IN CHIEF: **C.B. CEBULSKI**

CAPTAIN MARVEL: DARK TEMPEST. Contains material originally published in magazine form as CAPTAIN MARVEL: DARK TEMPEST (2023) #1-5. First printing 2023. ISBN 978-1-302-95121-4. Published by MARVEL WORLDWIDE, INC., a subsidiary of MARVEL ENTERTAINMENT, LLC. OFFICE OF PUBLICATION: 1290 Avenue of the Americas, New York, NY 10104. © 2023 MARVEL. No similarity between any of the names, characters, persons, and/or institutions in this book with those of any living or dead person or institution is intended, and any such similarity which may exist is purely coincidental. **Printed in the U.S.A.** KEVIN FEIGE, Chief Creative Officer; DAN BUCKLEY, President, Marvel Entertainment; DAVID BOGART, Associate Publisher & SVP of Talent Affairs; TOM BREVOORT, VP, Executive Editor; NICK LOWE, Executive Editor, VP of Content, Digital Publishing; DAVID GABRIEL, VP of Print & Digital Publishing; SVEN LARSEN, VP of Licensed Publishing; MARK ANNUNZIATO, VP of Planning & Forecasting; JEFF YOUNGQUIST, VP of Production & Special Projects; ALEX MORALES, Director of Publishing Operations; DAN EDINGTON, Director of Editorial Operations; RICKEY PURDIN, Director of Talent Relations; JENNIFER GRÜNWALD, Director of Production & Special Projects; SUSAN CRESPI, Production Manager; STAN LEE, Chairman Emeritus. For information regarding advertising in Marvel Comics or on Marvel.com, please contact Vit DeBellis, Custom Solutions & Integrated Advertising Manager, at vdebellis@marvel.com. For Marvel subscription inquiries, please call 888-511-5480. Manufactured between 11/24/2023 and 1/2/2024 by SEAWAY PRINTING, GREEN BAY, WI, USA.

10 9 8 7 6 5 4 3 2 1

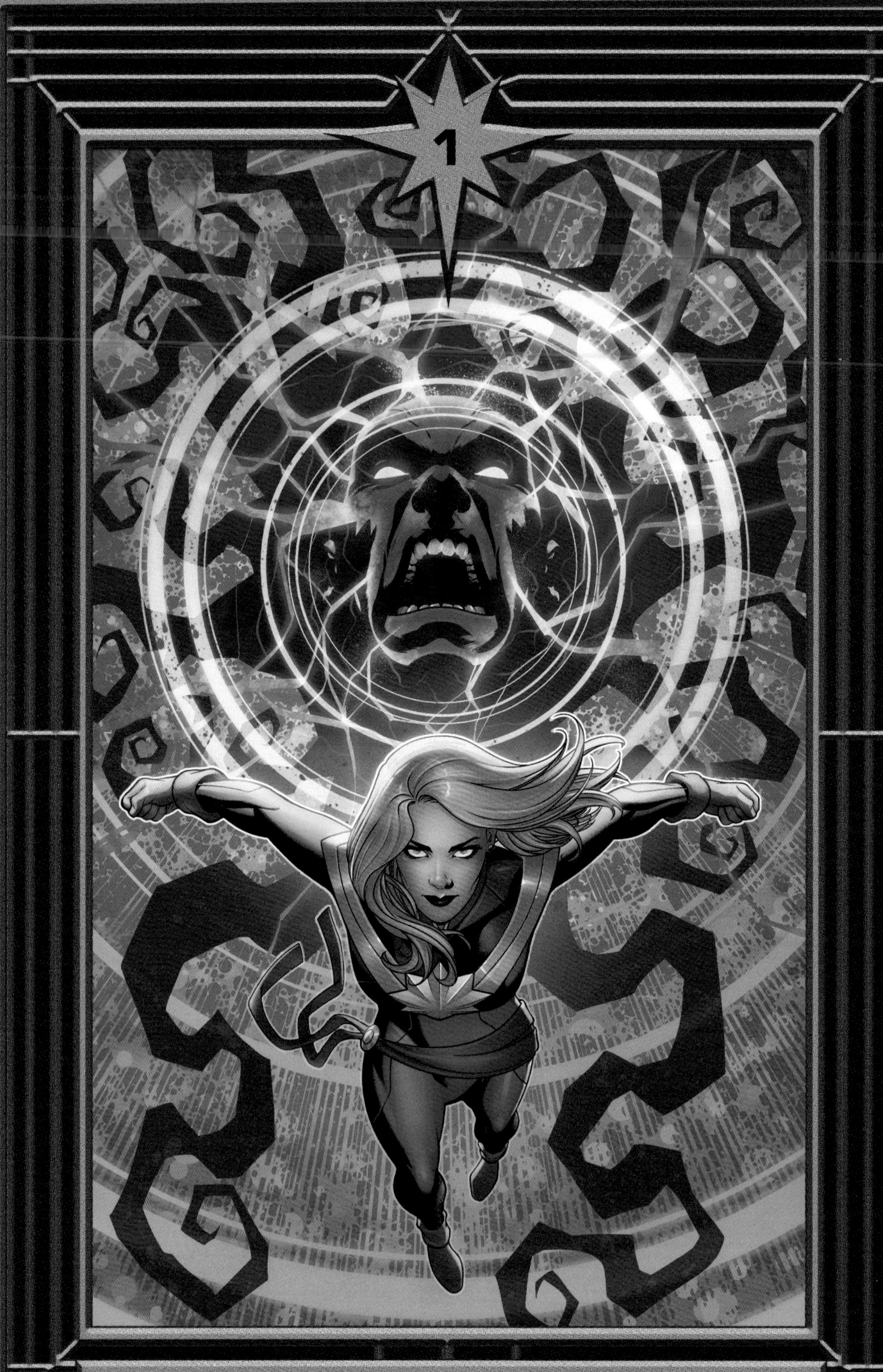
1

THE CURIOUS CASE OF THE EXPLODING MAN

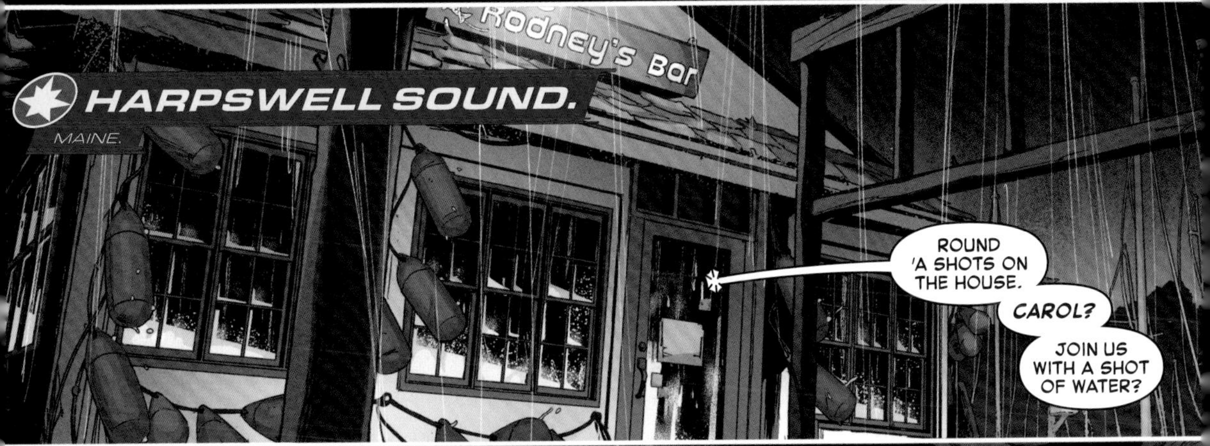
Rodney's Bar
HARPSWELL SOUND.
MAINE.
ROUND 'A SHOTS ON THE HOUSE.
CAROL?
JOIN US WITH A SHOT OF WATER?

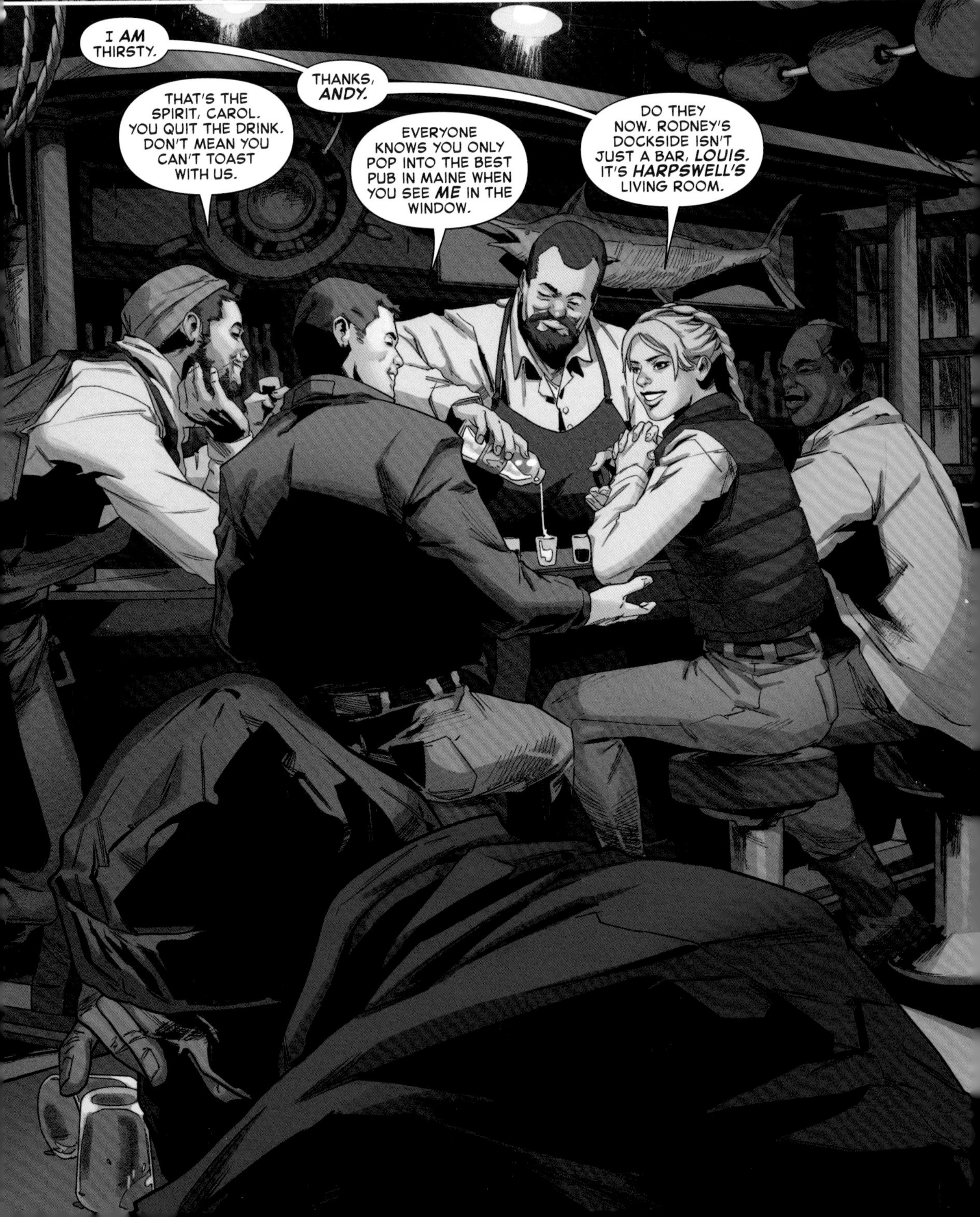
I AM THIRSTY.
THANKS, ANDY.
THAT'S THE SPIRIT, CAROL. YOU QUIT THE DRINK. DON'T MEAN YOU CAN'T TOAST WITH US.
EVERYONE KNOWS YOU ONLY POP INTO THE BEST PUB IN MAINE WHEN YOU SEE ME IN THE WINDOW.
DO THEY NOW. RODNEY'S DOCKSIDE ISN'T JUST A BAR, LOUIS. IT'S HARPSWELL'S LIVING ROOM.

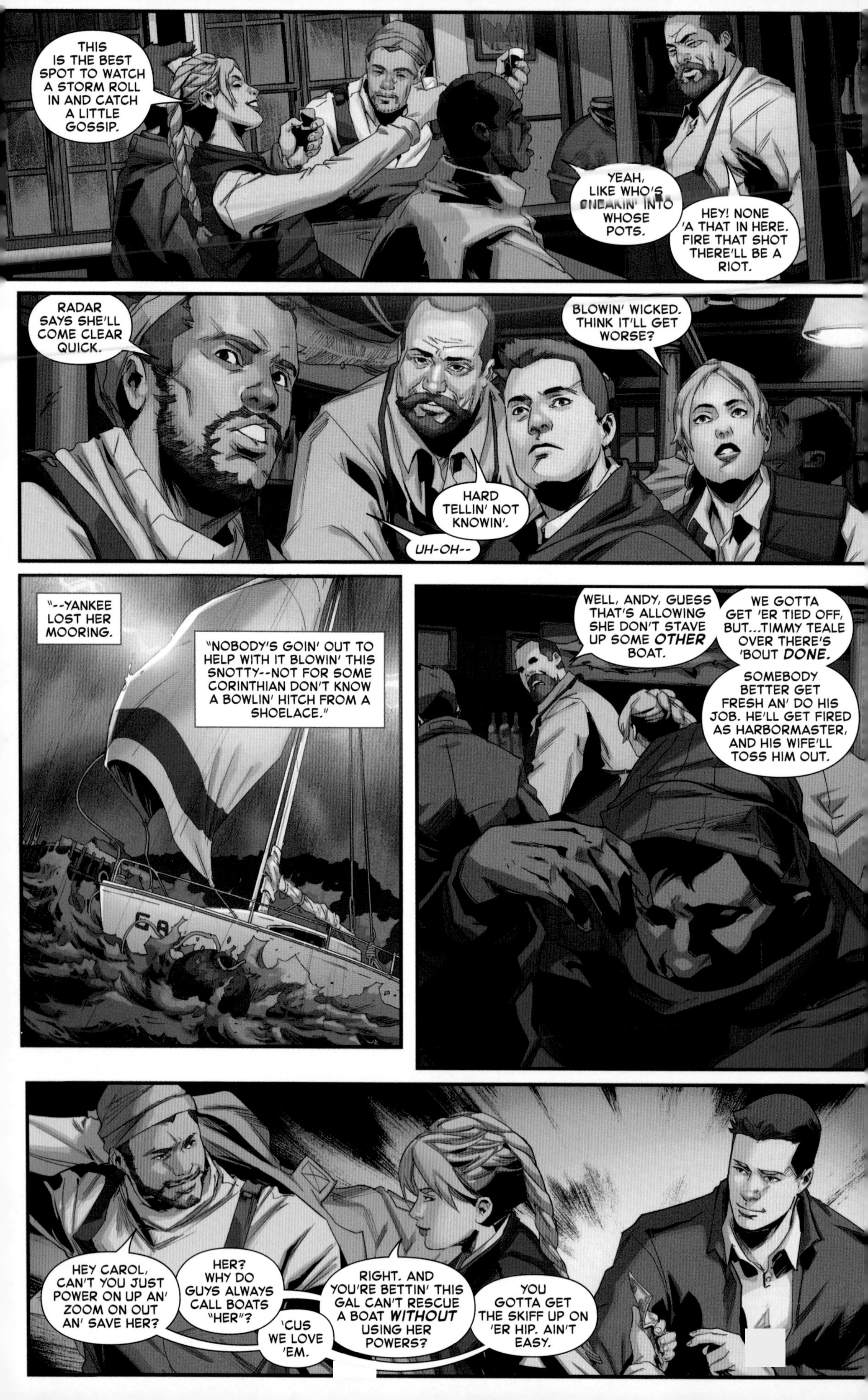
THIS IS THE BEST SPOT TO WATCH A STORM ROLL IN AND CATCH A LITTLE GOSSIP.
YEAH, LIKE WHO'S SNEAKIN' INTO WHOSE POTS.
HEY! NONE 'A THAT IN HERE. FIRE THAT SHOT THERE'LL BE A RIOT.
RADAR SAYS SHE'LL COME CLEAR QUICK.
BLOWIN' WICKED. THINK IT'LL GET WORSE?
HARD TELLIN' NOT KNOWIN'.
UH-OH--
"--YANKEE LOST HER MOORING.
"NOBODY'S GOIN' OUT TO HELP WITH IT BLOWIN' THIS SNOTTY--NOT FOR SOME CORINTHIAN DON'T KNOW A BOWLIN' HITCH FROM A SHOELACE."
WELL, ANDY, GUESS THAT'S ALLOWING SHE DON'T STAVE UP SOME *OTHER* BOAT.
WE GOTTA GET 'ER TIED OFF, BUT...TIMMY TEALE OVER THERE'S 'BOUT *DONE.*
SOMEBODY BETTER GET FRESH AN' DO HIS JOB. HE'LL GET FIRED AS HARBORMASTER, AND HIS WIFE'LL TOSS HIM OUT.
HEY CAROL, CAN'T YOU JUST POWER ON UP AN' ZOOM ON OUT AN' SAVE HER?
HER? WHY DO GUYS ALWAYS CALL BOATS "HER"?
'CUS WE LOVE 'EM.
RIGHT. AND YOU'RE BETTIN' THIS GAL CAN'T RESCUE A BOAT *WITHOUT* USING HER POWERS?
YOU GOTTA GET THE SKIFF UP ON 'ER HIP. AIN'T EASY.

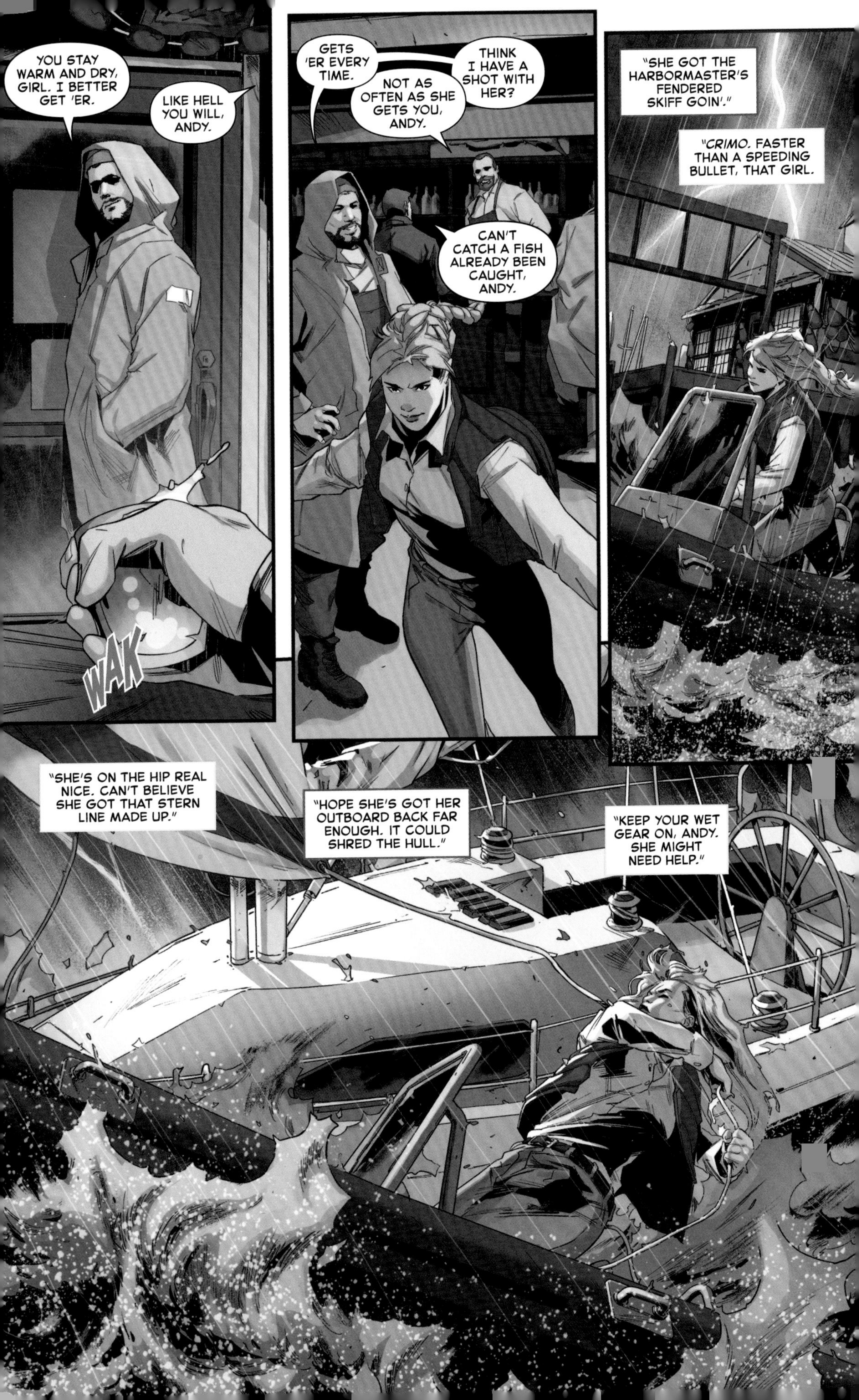
YOU STAY WARM AND DRY, GIRL. I BETTER GET 'ER.
LIKE HELL YOU WILL, ANDY.
WAK
GETS 'ER EVERY TIME.
THINK I HAVE A SHOT WITH HER?
NOT AS OFTEN AS SHE GETS YOU, ANDY.
CAN'T CATCH A FISH ALREADY BEEN CAUGHT, ANDY.
"SHE GOT THE HARBORMASTER'S FENDERED SKIFF GOIN'."
"CRIMO. FASTER THAN A SPEEDING BULLET, THAT GIRL.
"SHE'S ON THE HIP REAL NICE. CAN'T BELIEVE SHE GOT THAT STERN LINE MADE UP."
"HOPE SHE'S GOT HER OUTBOARD BACK FAR ENOUGH. IT COULD SHRED THE HULL."
"KEEP YOUR WET GEAR ON, ANDY. SHE MIGHT NEED HELP."

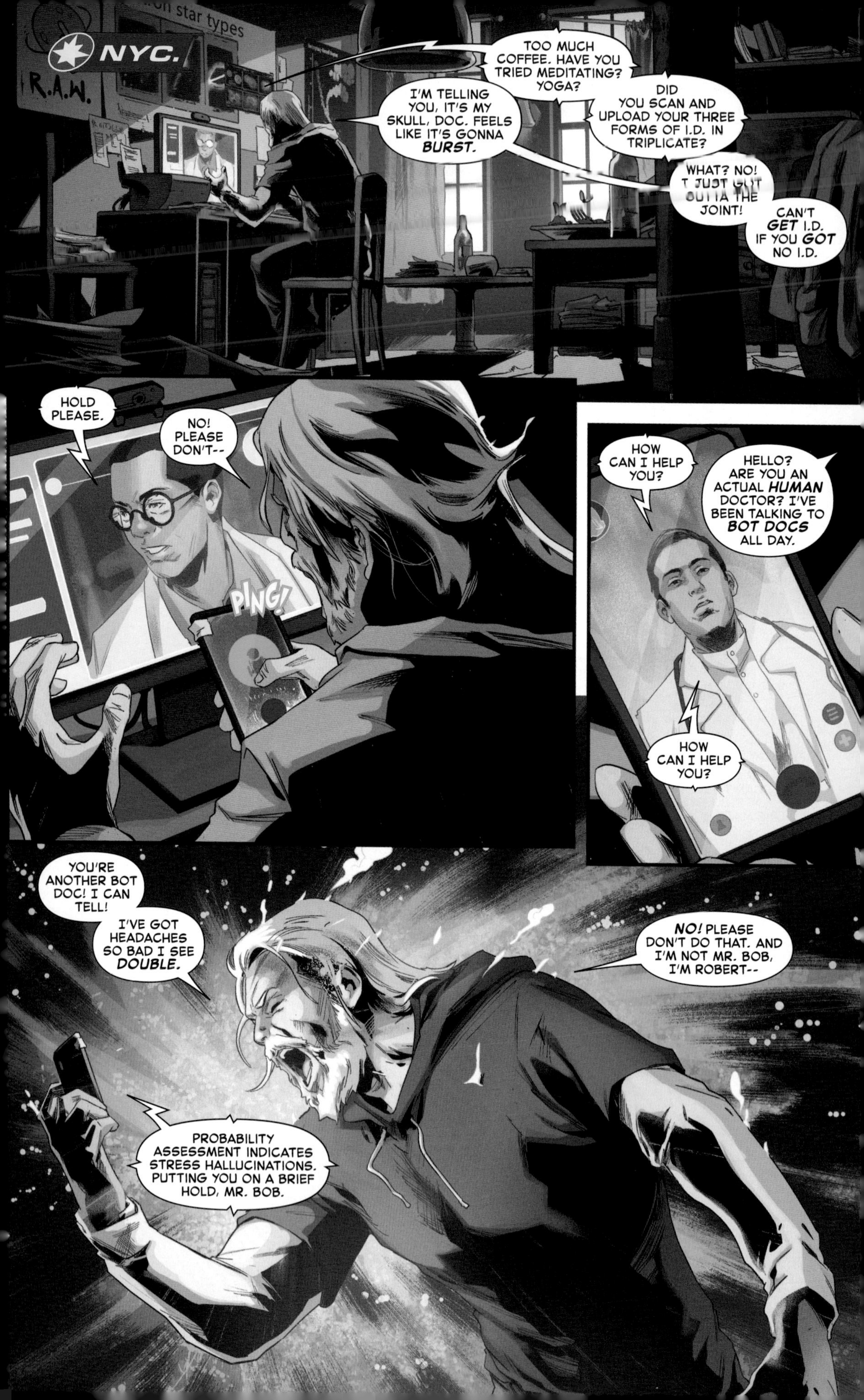
NYC.
TOO MUCH COFFEE. HAVE YOU TRIED MEDITATING? YOGA?
I'M TELLING YOU, IT'S MY SKULL, DOC. FEELS LIKE IT'S GONNA BURST.
DID YOU SCAN AND UPLOAD YOUR THREE FORMS OF I.D. IN TRIPLICATE?
WHAT? NO! I JUST GOT OUTTA THE JOINT!
CAN'T GET I.D. IF YOU GOT NO I.D.
HOLD PLEASE.
NO! PLEASE DON'T--
PING!
HOW CAN I HELP YOU?
HELLO? ARE YOU AN ACTUAL HUMAN DOCTOR? I'VE BEEN TALKING TO BOT DOCS ALL DAY.
HOW CAN I HELP YOU?
YOU'RE ANOTHER BOT DOC! I CAN TELL!
I'VE GOT HEADACHES SO BAD I SEE DOUBLE.
PROBABILITY ASSESSMENT INDICATES STRESS HALLUCINATIONS. PUTTING YOU ON A BRIEF HOLD, MR. BOB.
NO! PLEASE DON'T DO THAT. AND I'M NOT MR. BOB, I'M ROBERT--

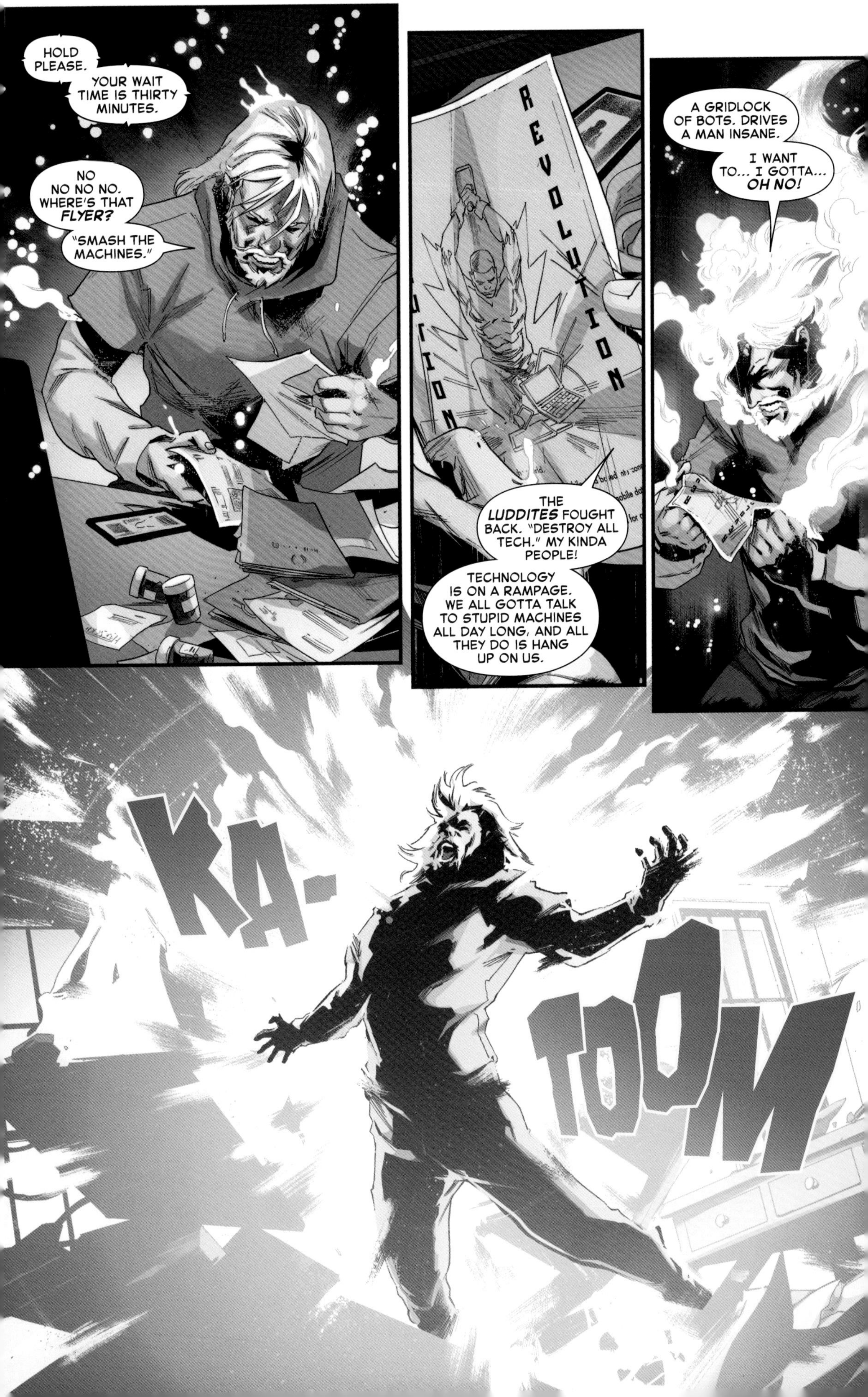
HOLD PLEASE.
YOUR WAIT TIME IS THIRTY MINUTES.
NO NO NO NO. WHERE'S THAT FLYER?
"SMASH THE MACHINES."
REVOLUTION
THE LUDDITES FOUGHT BACK. "DESTROY ALL TECH." MY KINDA PEOPLE!
TECHNOLOGY IS ON A RAMPAGE. WE ALL GOTTA TALK TO STUPID MACHINES ALL DAY LONG, AND ALL THEY DO IS HANG UP ON US.
A GRIDLOCK OF BOTS. DRIVES A MAN INSANE.
I WANT TO... I GOTTA... OH NO!
KA-
TOOM

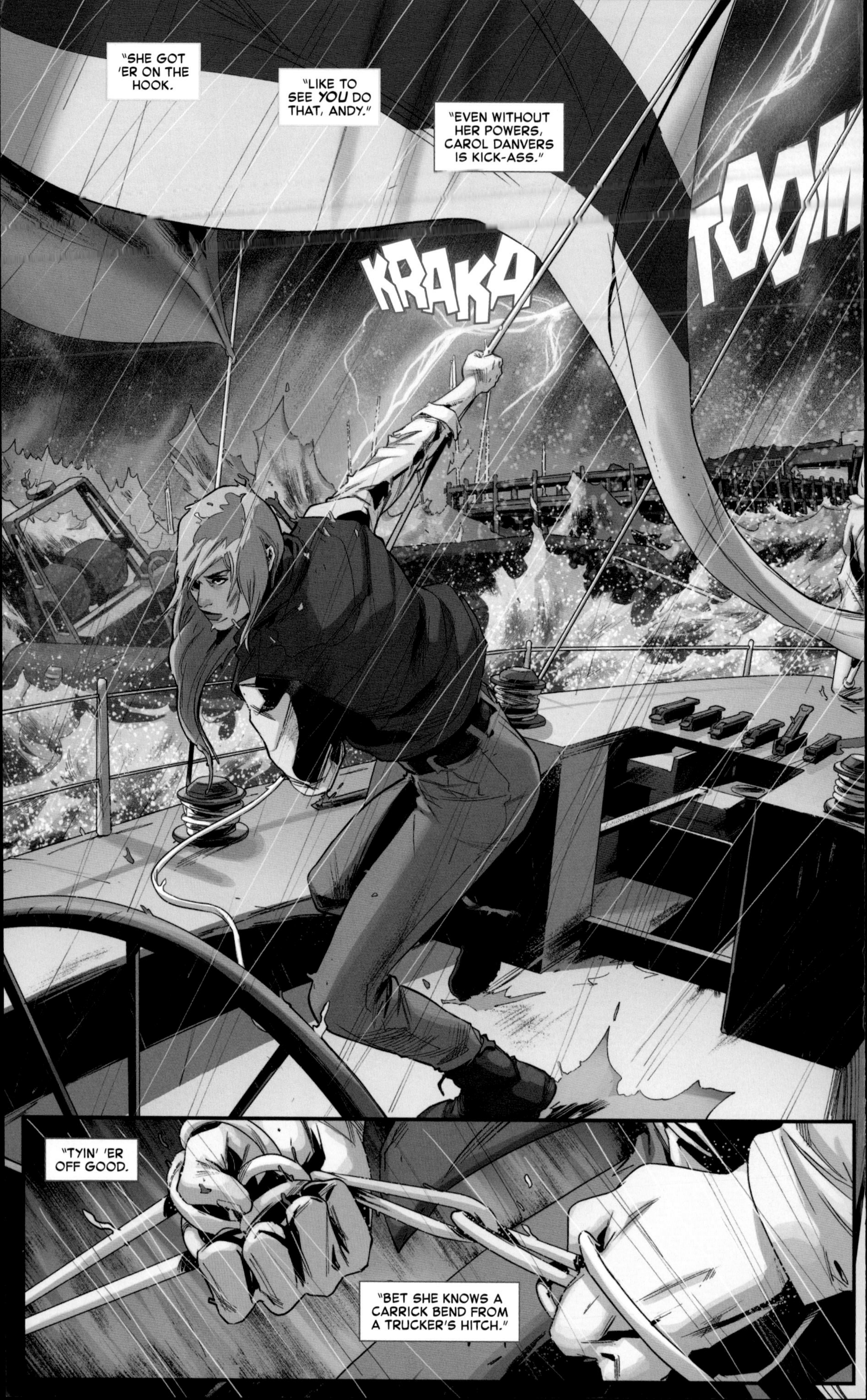
"SHE GOT 'ER ON THE HOOK.
"LIKE TO SEE YOU DO THAT, ANDY."
"EVEN WITHOUT HER POWERS, CAROL DANVERS IS KICK-ASS."
KRAKA
TOOM
"TYIN' 'ER OFF GOOD.
"BET SHE KNOWS A CARRICK BEND FROM A TRUCKER'S HITCH."

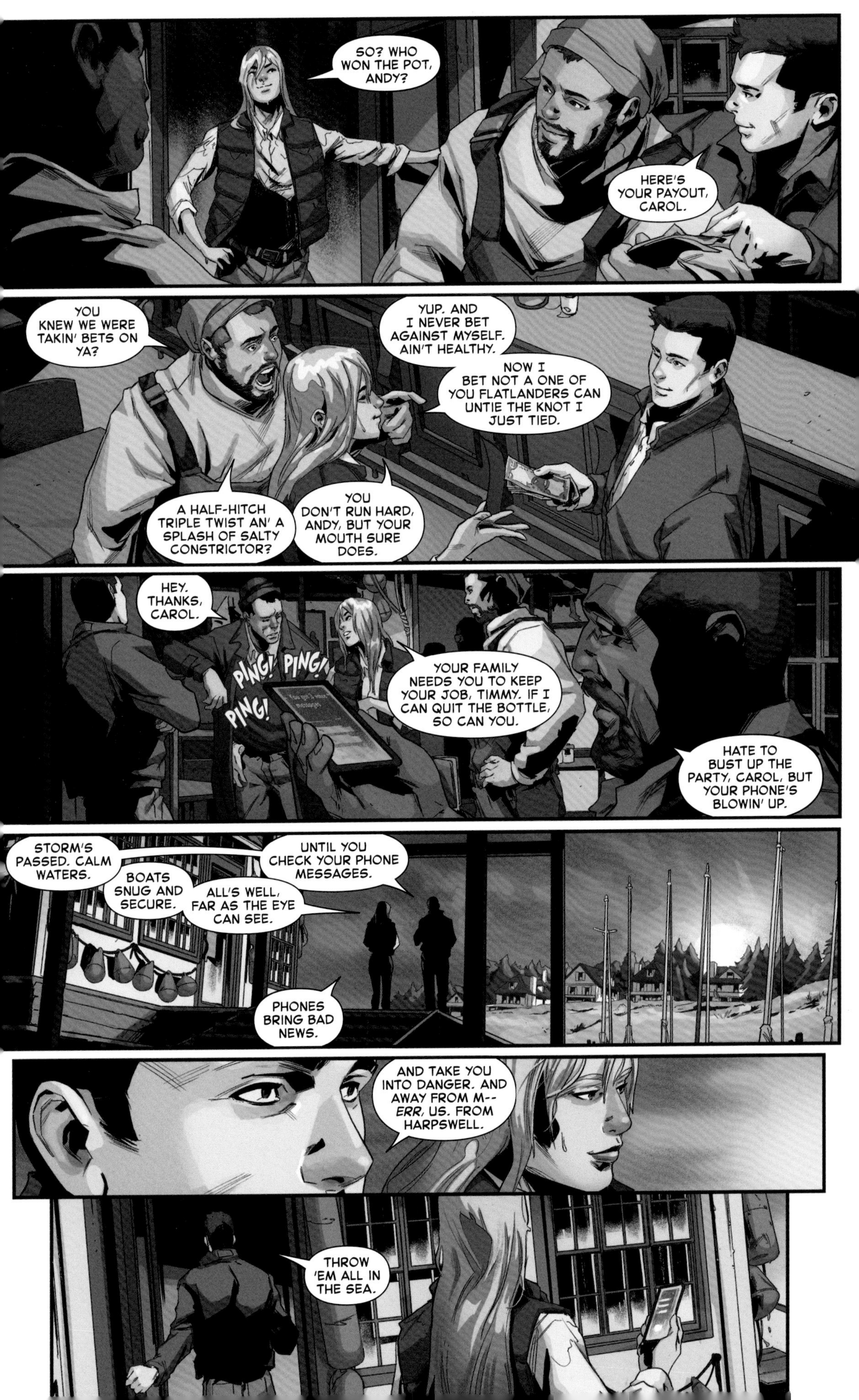

SO? WHO WON THE POT, ANDY?
HERE'S YOUR PAYOUT, CAROL.
YOU KNEW WE WERE TAKIN' BETS ON YA?
YUP. AND I NEVER BET AGAINST MYSELF. AIN'T HEALTHY.
NOW I BET NOT A ONE OF YOU FLATLANDERS CAN UNTIE THE KNOT I JUST TIED.
A HALF-HITCH TRIPLE TWIST AN' A SPLASH OF SALTY CONSTRICTOR?
YOU DON'T RUN HARD, ANDY, BUT YOUR MOUTH SURE DOES.
HEY. THANKS, CAROL.
PING! PING!! PING!
YOUR FAMILY NEEDS YOU TO KEEP YOUR JOB, TIMMY. IF I CAN QUIT THE BOTTLE, SO CAN YOU.
HATE TO BUST UP THE PARTY, CAROL, BUT YOUR PHONE'S BLOWIN' UP.
STORM'S PASSED. CALM WATERS.
UNTIL YOU CHECK YOUR PHONE MESSAGES.
BOATS SNUG AND SECURE.
ALL'S WELL, FAR AS THE EYE CAN SEE.
PHONES BRING BAD NEWS.
AND TAKE YOU INTO DANGER. AND AWAY FROM M-- *ERR,* US. FROM HARPSWELL.
THROW 'EM ALL IN THE SEA.

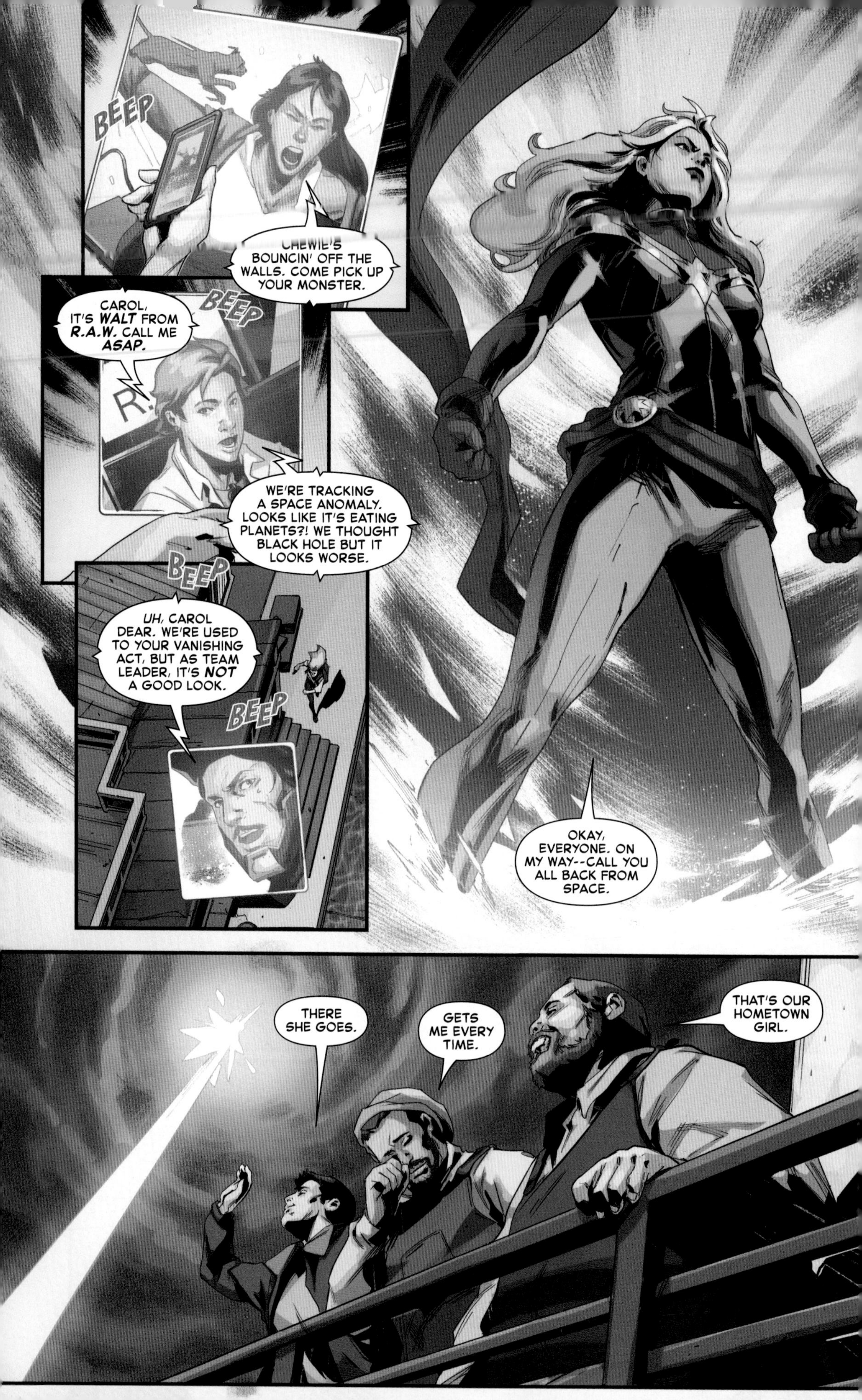
BEEP
CHEWIE'S BOUNCIN' OFF THE WALLS. COME PICK UP YOUR MONSTER.
BEEP
CAROL, IT'S WALT FROM R.A.W. CALL ME ASAP.
WE'RE TRACKING A SPACE ANOMALY. LOOKS LIKE IT'S EATING PLANETS?! WE THOUGHT BLACK HOLE BUT IT LOOKS WORSE.
BEEP
UH, CAROL DEAR. WE'RE USED TO YOUR VANISHING ACT, BUT AS TEAM LEADER, IT'S NOT A GOOD LOOK.
BEEP
OKAY, EVERYONE. ON MY WAY--CALL YOU ALL BACK FROM SPACE.
THERE SHE GOES.
GETS ME EVERY TIME.
THAT'S OUR HOMETOWN GIRL.

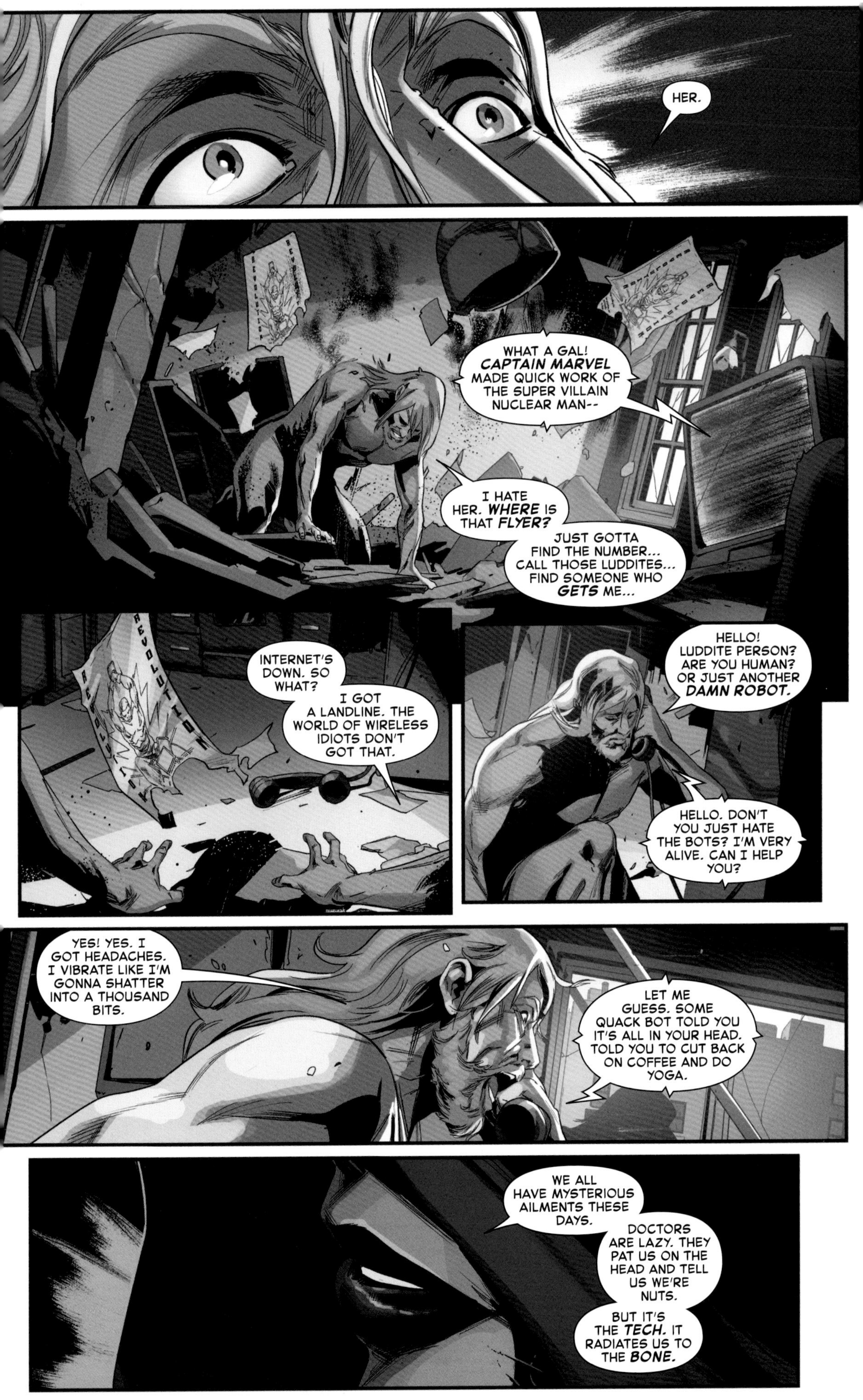

HER.
WHAT A GAL! *CAPTAIN MARVEL* MADE QUICK WORK OF THE SUPER VILLAIN NUCLEAR MAN--
I HATE HER. ***WHERE*** IS THAT ***FLYER?***
JUST GOTTA FIND THE NUMBER... CALL THOSE LUDDITES... FIND SOMEONE WHO ***GETS*** ME...
REVOLUTION
INTERNET'S DOWN. SO WHAT?
I GOT A LANDLINE. THE WORLD OF WIRELESS IDIOTS DON'T GOT THAT.
HELLO! LUDDITE PERSON? ARE YOU HUMAN? OR JUST ANOTHER ***DAMN ROBOT.***
HELLO. DON'T YOU JUST HATE THE BOTS? I'M VERY ALIVE. CAN I HELP YOU?
YES! YES. I GOT HEADACHES. I VIBRATE LIKE I'M GONNA SHATTER INTO A THOUSAND BITS.
LET ME GUESS. SOME QUACK BOT TOLD YOU IT'S ALL IN YOUR HEAD. TOLD YOU TO CUT BACK ON COFFEE AND DO YOGA.
WE ALL HAVE MYSTERIOUS AILMENTS THESE DAYS.
DOCTORS ARE LAZY. THEY PAT US ON THE HEAD AND TELL US WE'RE NUTS.
BUT IT'S THE ***TECH.*** IT RADIATES US TO THE ***BONE.***

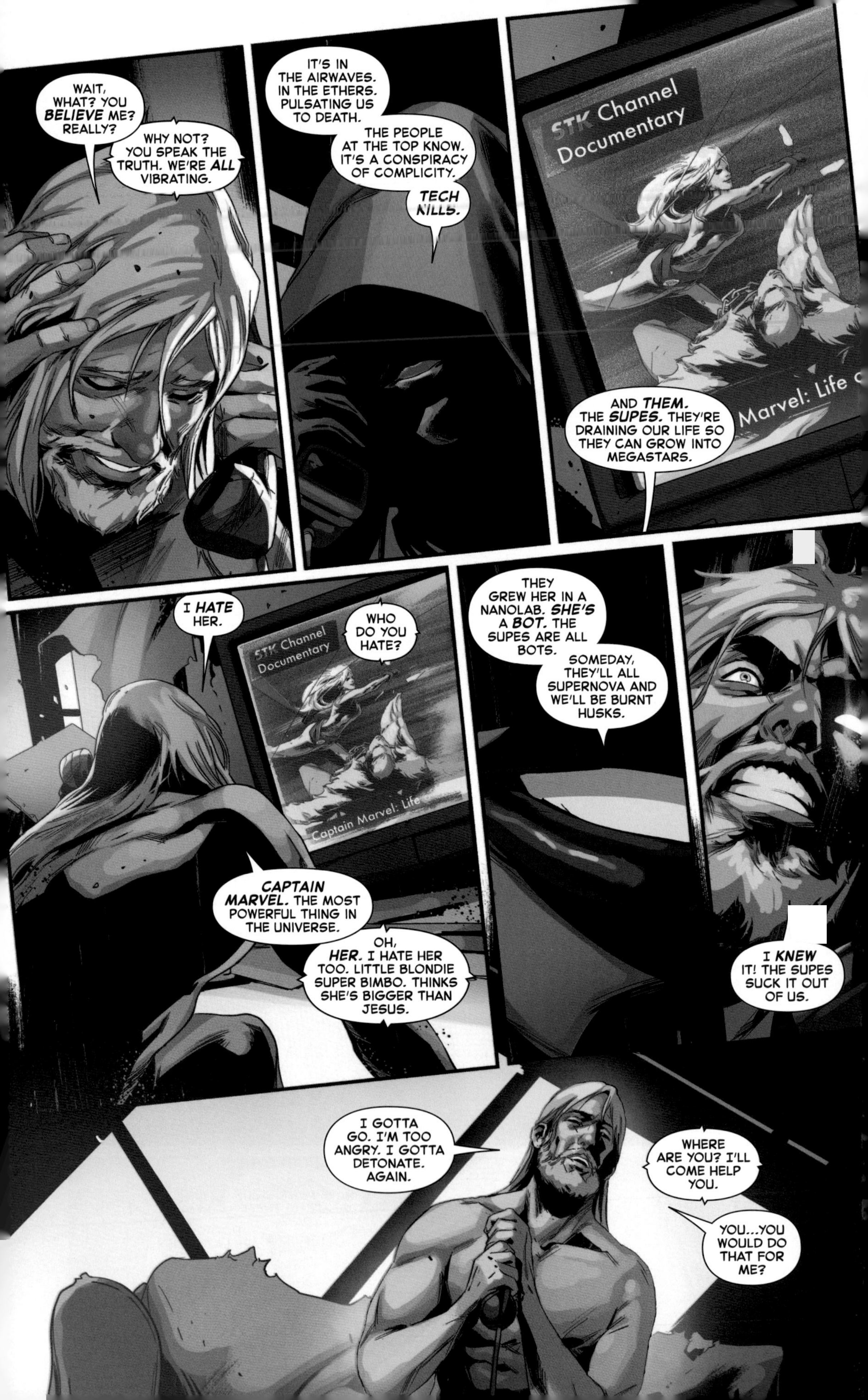
WAIT, WHAT? YOU BELIEVE ME? REALLY?
WHY NOT? YOU SPEAK THE TRUTH. WE'RE ALL VIBRATING.
IT'S IN THE AIRWAVES. IN THE ETHERS. PULSATING US TO DEATH.
THE PEOPLE AT THE TOP KNOW. IT'S A CONSPIRACY OF COMPLICITY.
TECH KILLS.
STK Channel Documentary
Marvel: Life
AND THEM. THE SUPES. THEY'RE DRAINING OUR LIFE SO THEY CAN GROW INTO MEGASTARS.
I HATE HER.
WHO DO YOU HATE?
STK Channel Documentary
Captain Marvel: Life
CAPTAIN MARVEL. THE MOST POWERFUL THING IN THE UNIVERSE.
OH, HER. I HATE HER TOO. LITTLE BLONDIE SUPER BIMBO. THINKS SHE'S BIGGER THAN JESUS.
THEY GREW HER IN A NANOLAB. SHE'S A BOT. THE SUPES ARE ALL BOTS.
SOMEDAY, THEY'LL ALL SUPERNOVA AND WE'LL BE BURNT HUSKS.
I KNEW IT! THE SUPES SUCK IT OUT OF US.
I GOTTA GO. I'M TOO ANGRY. I GOTTA DETONATE. AGAIN.
WHERE ARE YOU? I'LL COME HELP YOU.
YOU...YOU WOULD DO THAT FOR ME?

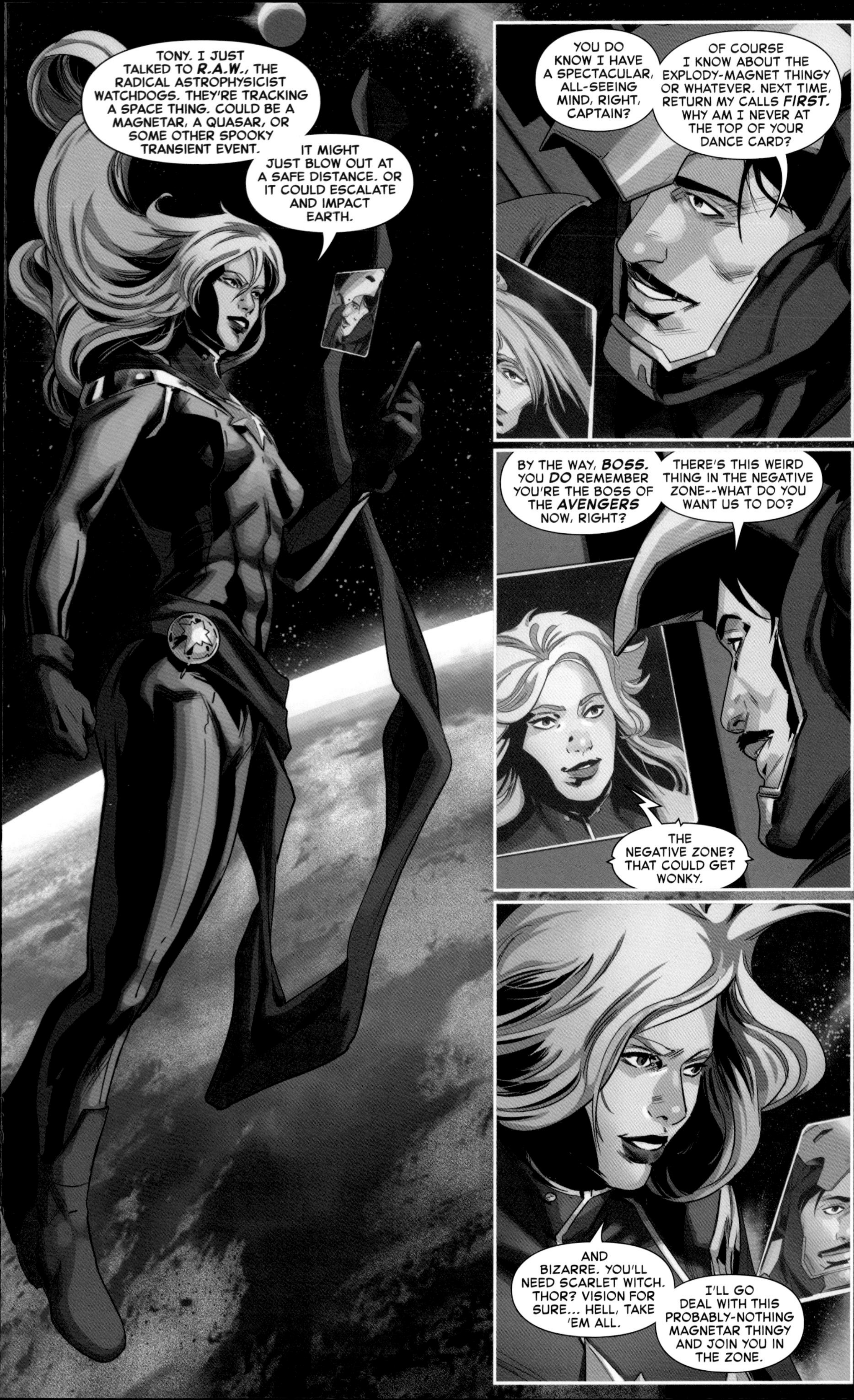
TONY. I JUST TALKED TO R.A.W., THE RADICAL ASTROPHYSICIST WATCHDOGS. THEY'RE TRACKING A SPACE THING. COULD BE A MAGNETAR, A QUASAR, OR SOME OTHER SPOOKY TRANSIENT EVENT.
IT MIGHT JUST BLOW OUT AT A SAFE DISTANCE. OR IT COULD ESCALATE AND IMPACT EARTH.
YOU DO KNOW I HAVE A SPECTACULAR, ALL-SEEING MIND, RIGHT, CAPTAIN?
OF COURSE I KNOW ABOUT THE EXPLODY-MAGNET THINGY OR WHATEVER. NEXT TIME, RETURN MY CALLS FIRST. WHY AM I NEVER AT THE TOP OF YOUR DANCE CARD?
BY THE WAY, BOSS. YOU DO REMEMBER YOU'RE THE BOSS OF THE AVENGERS NOW, RIGHT?
THERE'S THIS WEIRD THING IN THE NEGATIVE ZONE--WHAT DO YOU WANT US TO DO?
THE NEGATIVE ZONE? THAT COULD GET WONKY.
AND BIZARRE. YOU'LL NEED SCARLET WITCH. THOR? VISION FOR SURE... HELL, TAKE 'EM ALL.
I'LL GO DEAL WITH THIS PROBABLY-NOTHING MAGNETAR THINGY AND JOIN YOU IN THE ZONE.

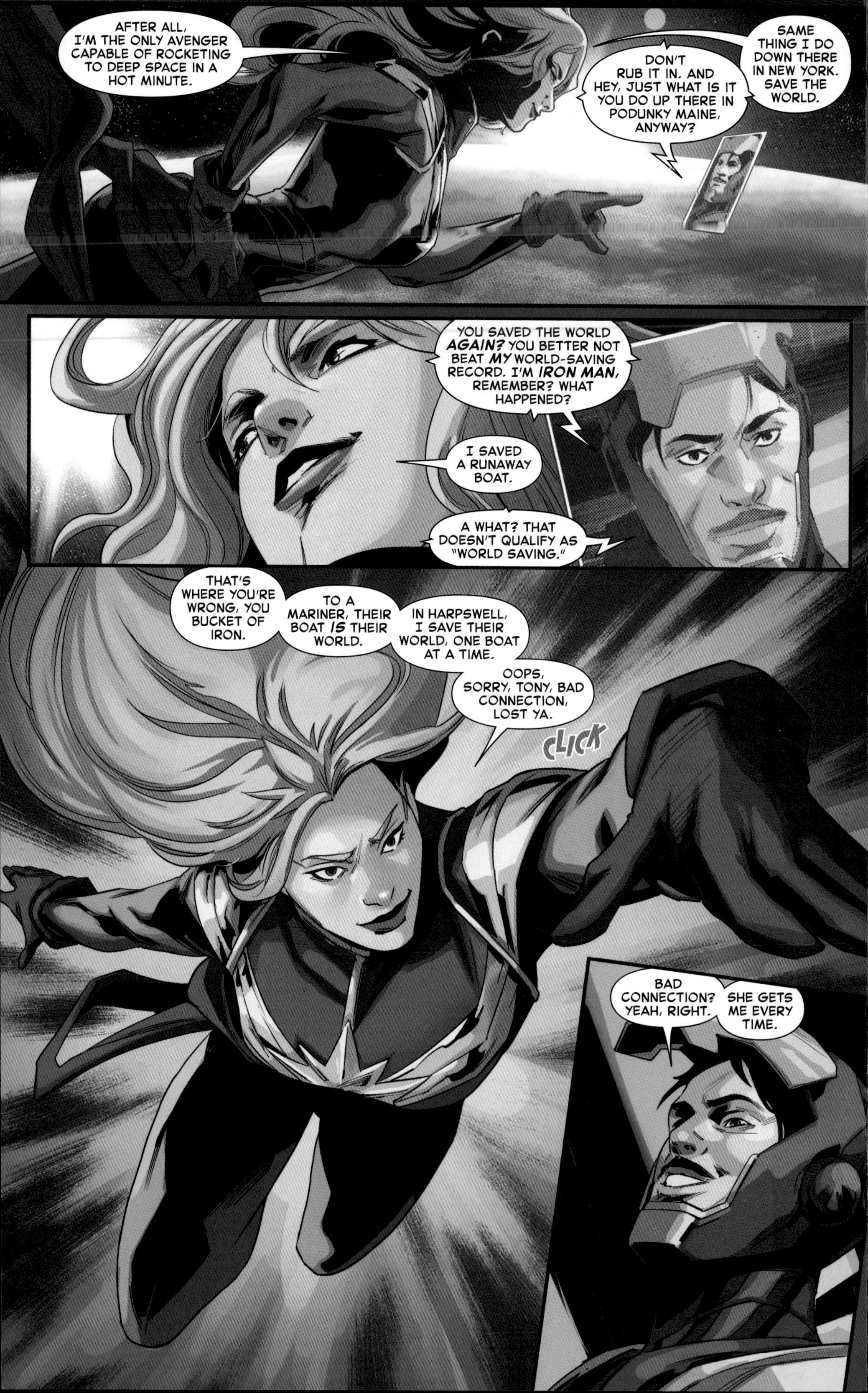
AFTER ALL, I'M THE ONLY AVENGER CAPABLE OF ROCKETING TO DEEP SPACE IN A HOT MINUTE.
DON'T RUB IT IN. AND HEY, JUST WHAT IS IT YOU DO UP THERE IN PODUNKY MAINE, ANYWAY?
SAME THING I DO DOWN THERE IN NEW YORK. SAVE THE WORLD.
YOU SAVED THE WORLD **AGAIN?** YOU BETTER NOT BEAT **MY** WORLD-SAVING RECORD. I'M ***IRON MAN,*** REMEMBER? WHAT HAPPENED?
I SAVED A RUNAWAY BOAT.
A WHAT? THAT DOESN'T QUALIFY AS "WORLD SAVING."
THAT'S WHERE YOU'RE WRONG, YOU BUCKET OF IRON.
TO A MARINER, THEIR BOAT ***IS*** THEIR WORLD.
IN HARPSWELL, I SAVE THEIR WORLD, ONE BOAT AT A TIME.
OOPS, SORRY, TONY, BAD CONNECTION, LOST YA.
CLICK
BAD CONNECTION? YEAH, RIGHT.
SHE GETS ME EVERY TIME.

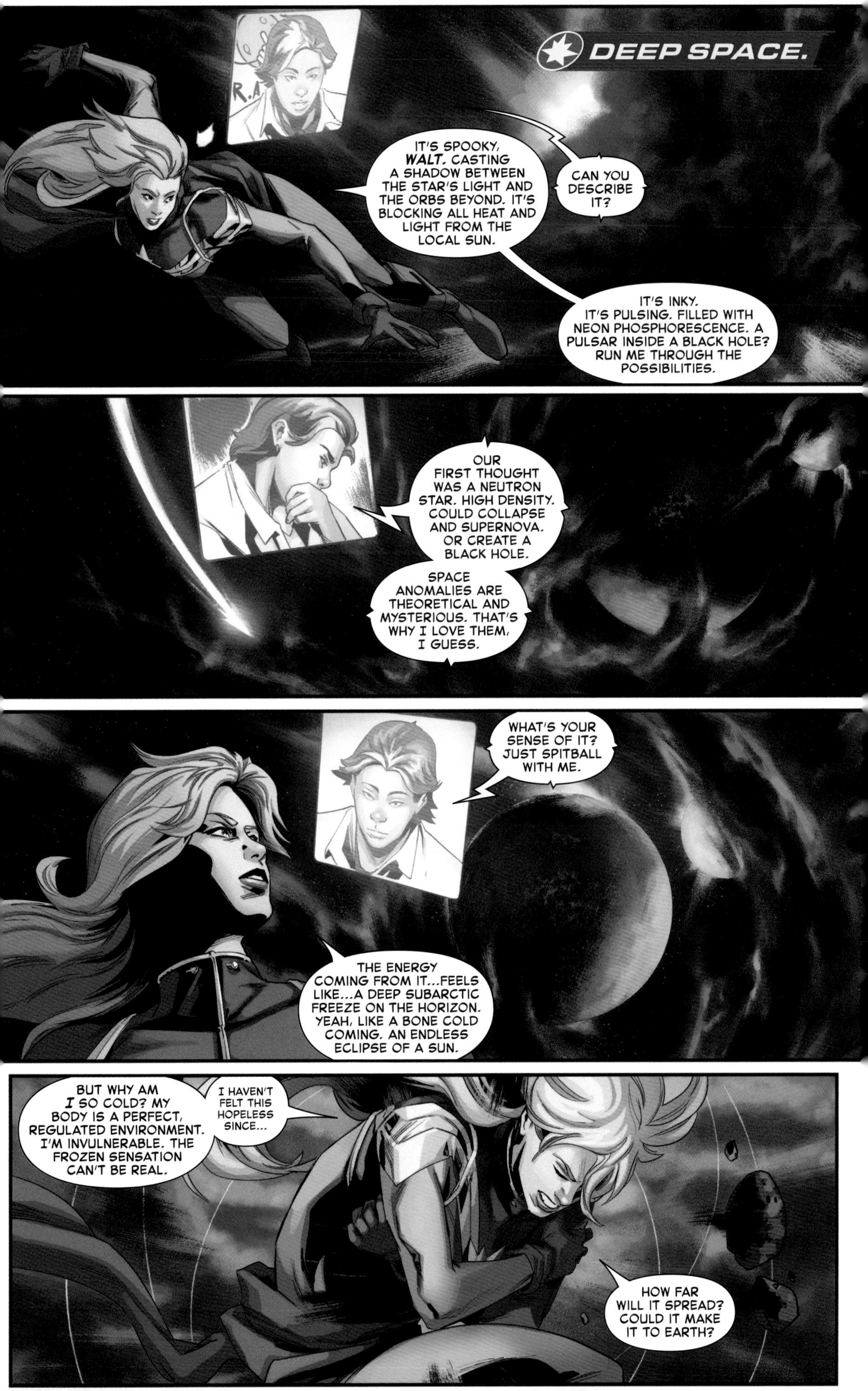
DEEP SPACE.
R.A.
IT'S SPOOKY, WALT. CASTING A SHADOW BETWEEN THE STAR'S LIGHT AND THE ORBS BEYOND. IT'S BLOCKING ALL HEAT AND LIGHT FROM THE LOCAL SUN.
CAN YOU DESCRIBE IT?
IT'S INKY. IT'S PULSING. FILLED WITH NEON PHOSPHORESCENCE. A PULSAR INSIDE A BLACK HOLE? RUN ME THROUGH THE POSSIBILITIES.
OUR FIRST THOUGHT WAS A NEUTRON STAR. HIGH DENSITY. COULD COLLAPSE AND SUPERNOVA. OR CREATE A BLACK HOLE.
SPACE ANOMALIES ARE THEORETICAL AND MYSTERIOUS. THAT'S WHY I LOVE THEM, I GUESS.
WHAT'S YOUR SENSE OF IT? JUST SPITBALL WITH ME.
THE ENERGY COMING FROM IT...FEELS LIKE...A DEEP SUBARCTIC FREEZE ON THE HORIZON. YEAH, LIKE A BONE COLD COMING. AN ENDLESS ECLIPSE OF A SUN.
BUT WHY AM I SO COLD? MY BODY IS A PERFECT, REGULATED ENVIRONMENT. I'M INVULNERABLE. THE FROZEN SENSATION CAN'T BE REAL.
I HAVEN'T FELT THIS HOPELESS SINCE...
HOW FAR WILL IT SPREAD? COULD IT MAKE IT TO EARTH?

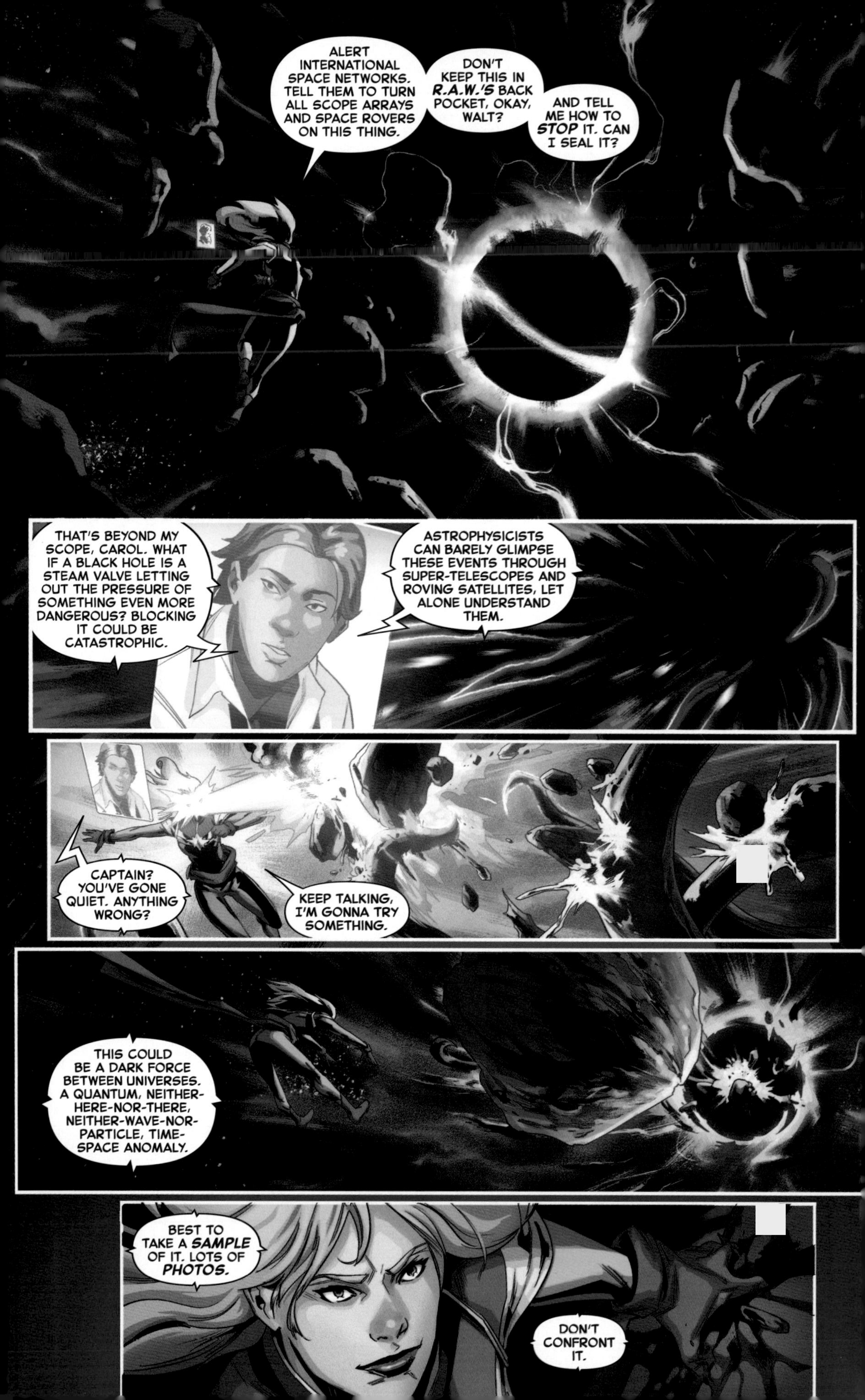
ALERT INTERNATIONAL SPACE NETWORKS. TELL THEM TO TURN ALL SCOPE ARRAYS AND SPACE ROVERS ON THIS THING.
DON'T KEEP THIS IN R.A.W.'S BACK POCKET, OKAY, WALT?
AND TELL ME HOW TO STOP IT. CAN I SEAL IT?
THAT'S BEYOND MY SCOPE, CAROL. WHAT IF A BLACK HOLE IS A STEAM VALVE LETTING OUT THE PRESSURE OF SOMETHING EVEN MORE DANGEROUS? BLOCKING IT COULD BE CATASTROPHIC.
ASTROPHYSICISTS CAN BARELY GLIMPSE THESE EVENTS THROUGH SUPER-TELESCOPES AND ROVING SATELLITES, LET ALONE UNDERSTAND THEM.
CAPTAIN? YOU'VE GONE QUIET. ANYTHING WRONG?
KEEP TALKING, I'M GONNA TRY SOMETHING.
THIS COULD BE A DARK FORCE BETWEEN UNIVERSES. A QUANTUM, NEITHER-HERE-NOR-THERE, NEITHER-WAVE-NOR-PARTICLE, TIME-SPACE ANOMALY.
BEST TO TAKE A SAMPLE OF IT. LOTS OF PHOTOS.
DON'T CONFRONT IT.

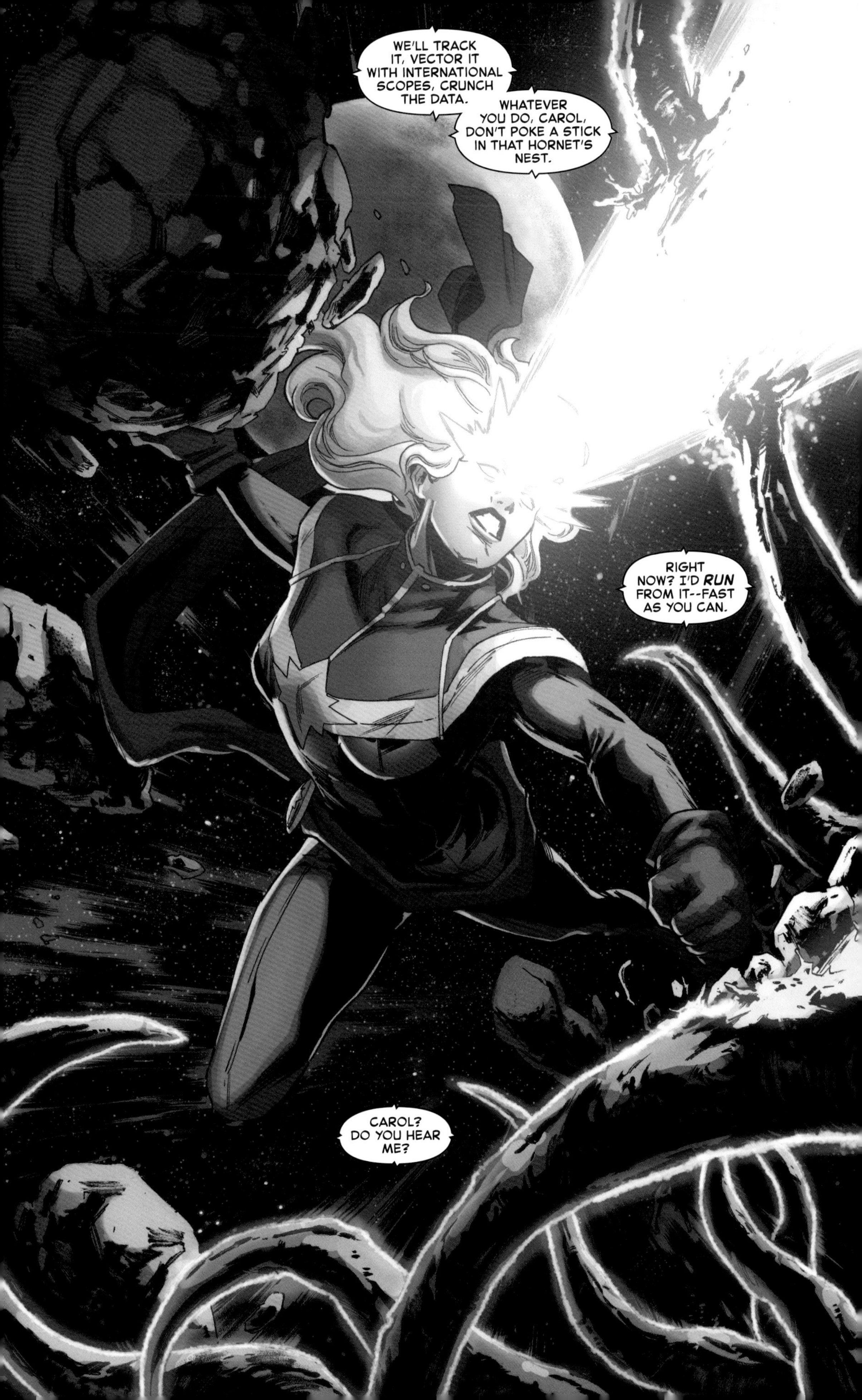
WE'LL TRACK IT, VECTOR IT WITH INTERNATIONAL SCOPES, CRUNCH THE DATA.
WHATEVER YOU DO, CAROL, DON'T POKE A STICK IN THAT HORNET'S NEST.
RIGHT NOW? I'D RUN FROM IT--FAST AS YOU CAN.
CAROL? DO YOU HEAR ME?

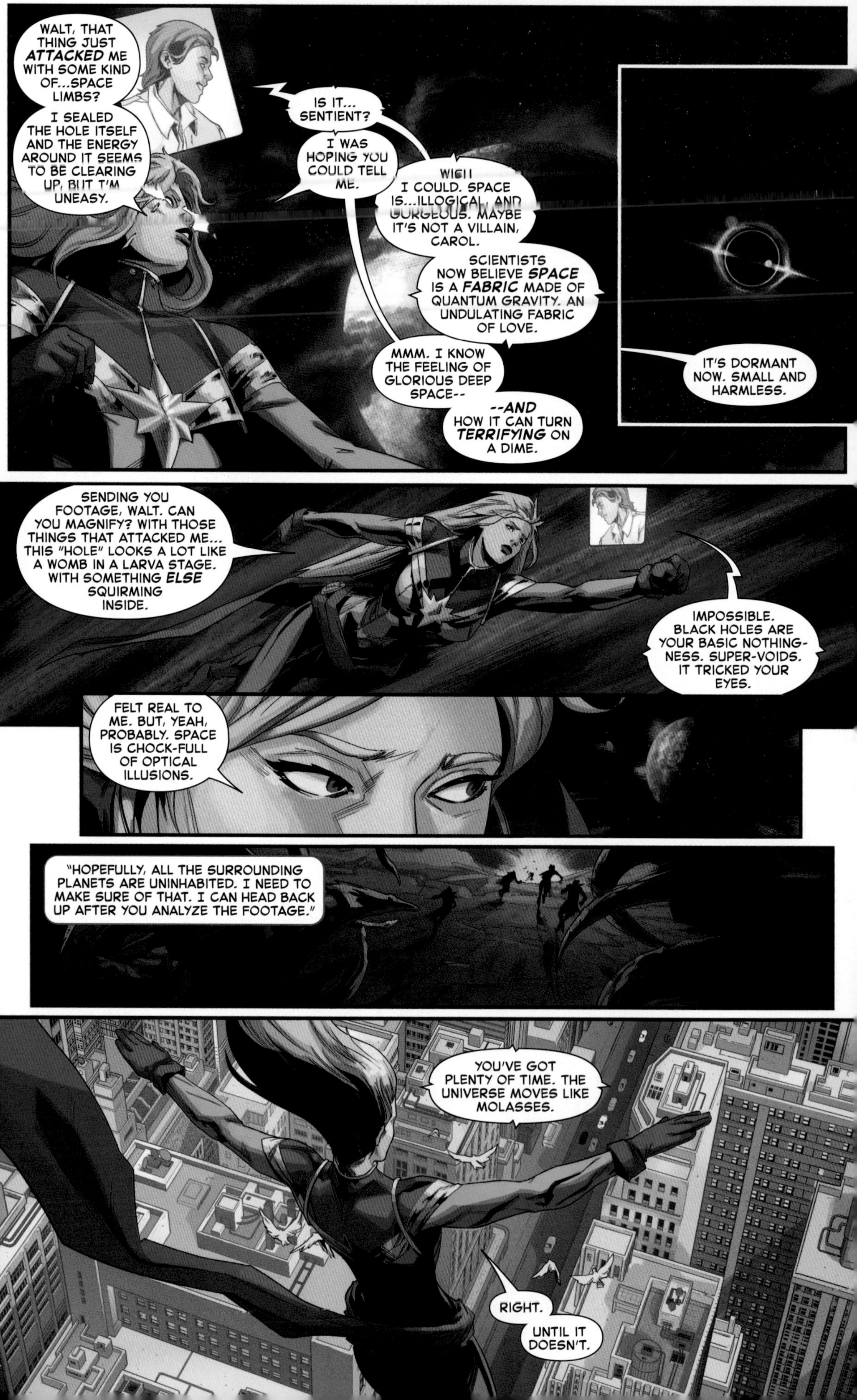

WALT, THAT THING JUST ATTACKED ME WITH SOME KIND OF...SPACE LIMBS?
I SEALED THE HOLE ITSELF AND THE ENERGY AROUND IT SEEMS TO BE CLEARING UP, BUT I'M UNEASY.
IS IT... SENTIENT?
I WAS HOPING YOU COULD TELL ME.
WISH I COULD. SPACE IS...ILLOGICAL, AND GORGEOUS. MAYBE IT'S NOT A VILLAIN, CAROL.
SCIENTISTS NOW BELIEVE SPACE IS A FABRIC MADE OF QUANTUM GRAVITY. AN UNDULATING FABRIC OF LOVE.
MMM. I KNOW THE FEELING OF GLORIOUS DEEP SPACE--
--AND HOW IT CAN TURN TERRIFYING ON A DIME.
IT'S DORMANT NOW. SMALL AND HARMLESS.
SENDING YOU FOOTAGE, WALT. CAN YOU MAGNIFY? WITH THOSE THINGS THAT ATTACKED ME... THIS "HOLE" LOOKS A LOT LIKE A WOMB IN A LARVA STAGE. WITH SOMETHING ELSE SQUIRMING INSIDE.
IMPOSSIBLE. BLACK HOLES ARE YOUR BASIC NOTHINGNESS. SUPER-VOIDS. IT TRICKED YOUR EYES.
FELT REAL TO ME. BUT, YEAH, PROBABLY. SPACE IS CHOCK-FULL OF OPTICAL ILLUSIONS.
"HOPEFULLY, ALL THE SURROUNDING PLANETS ARE UNINHABITED. I NEED TO MAKE SURE OF THAT. I CAN HEAD BACK UP AFTER YOU ANALYZE THE FOOTAGE."
YOU'VE GOT PLENTY OF TIME. THE UNIVERSE MOVES LIKE MOLASSES.
RIGHT.
UNTIL IT DOESN'T.

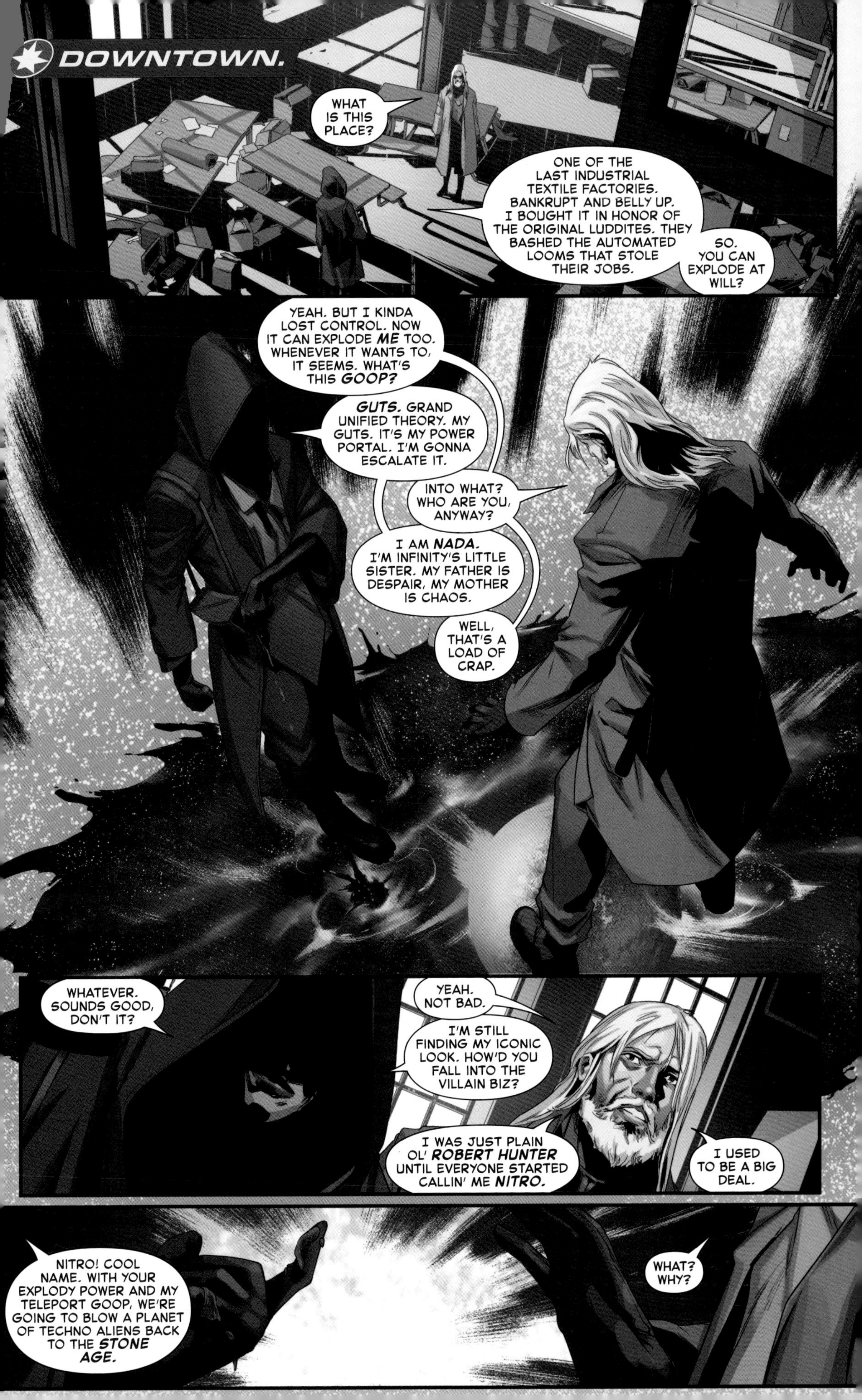
DOWNTOWN.
WHAT IS THIS PLACE?
ONE OF THE LAST INDUSTRIAL TEXTILE FACTORIES. BANKRUPT AND BELLY UP. I BOUGHT IT IN HONOR OF THE ORIGINAL LUDDITES. THEY BASHED THE AUTOMATED LOOMS THAT STOLE THEIR JOBS.
SO. YOU CAN EXPLODE AT WILL?
YEAH. BUT I KINDA LOST CONTROL. NOW IT CAN EXPLODE ME TOO. WHENEVER IT WANTS TO, IT SEEMS. WHAT'S THIS GOOP?
GUTS. GRAND UNIFIED THEORY. MY GUTS. IT'S MY POWER PORTAL. I'M GONNA ESCALATE IT.
INTO WHAT? WHO ARE YOU, ANYWAY?
I AM NADA. I'M INFINITY'S LITTLE SISTER. MY FATHER IS DESPAIR, MY MOTHER IS CHAOS.
WELL, THAT'S A LOAD OF CRAP.
WHATEVER. SOUNDS GOOD, DON'T IT?
YEAH. NOT BAD.
I'M STILL FINDING MY ICONIC LOOK. HOW'D YOU FALL INTO THE VILLAIN BIZ?
I WAS JUST PLAIN OL' ROBERT HUNTER UNTIL EVERYONE STARTED CALLIN' ME NITRO.
I USED TO BE A BIG DEAL.
NITRO! COOL NAME. WITH YOUR EXPLODY POWER AND MY TELEPORT GOOP, WE'RE GOING TO BLOW A PLANET OF TECHNO ALIENS BACK TO THE STONE AGE.
WHAT? WHY?

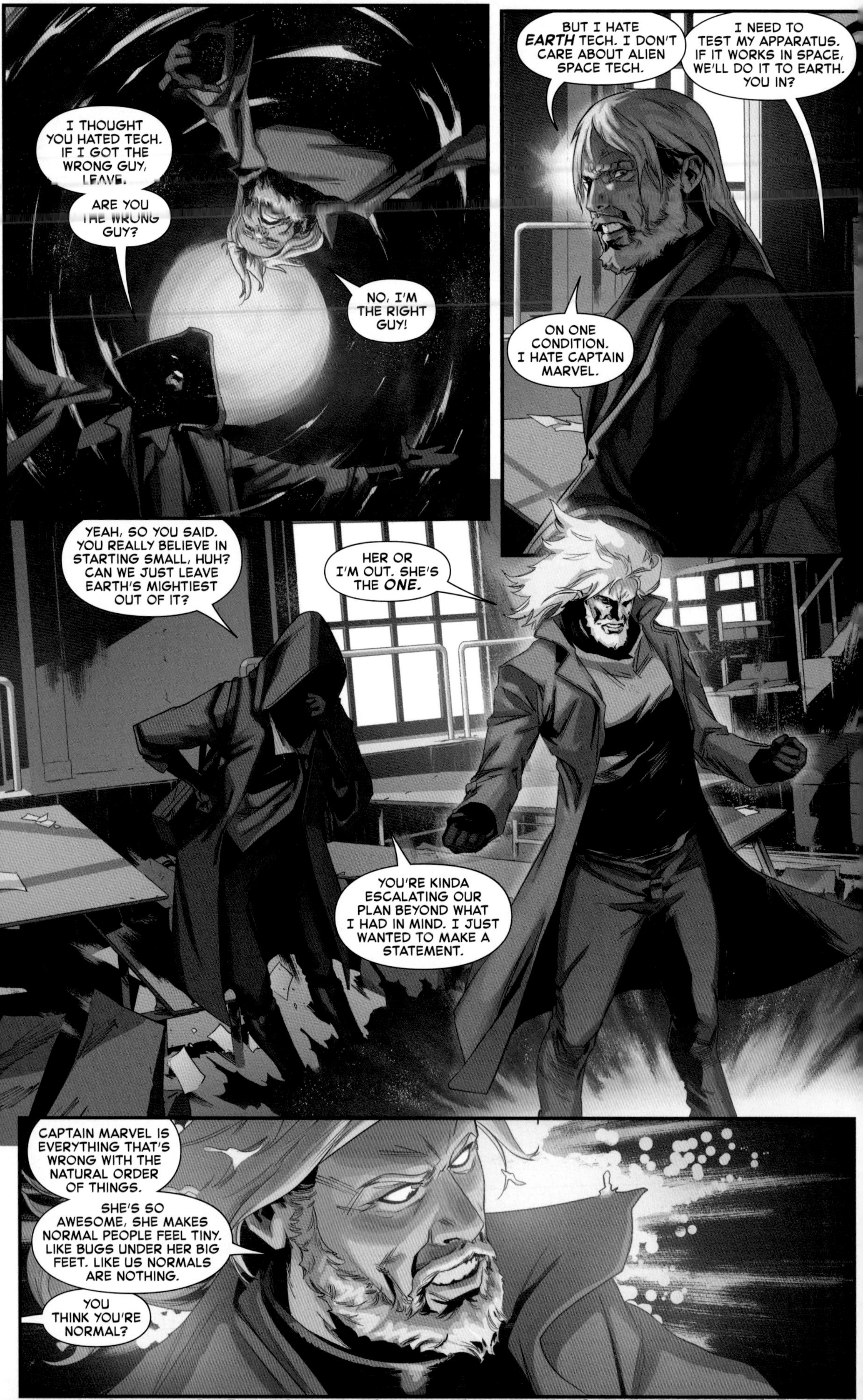
I THOUGHT YOU HATED TECH. IF I GOT THE WRONG GUY, LEAVE.
ARE YOU THE WRONG GUY?
NO, I'M THE RIGHT GUY!
BUT I HATE *EARTH* TECH. I DON'T CARE ABOUT ALIEN SPACE TECH.
I NEED TO TEST MY APPARATUS. IF IT WORKS IN SPACE, WE'LL DO IT TO EARTH. YOU IN?
ON ONE CONDITION. I HATE CAPTAIN MARVEL.
YEAH, SO YOU SAID. YOU REALLY BELIEVE IN STARTING SMALL, HUH? CAN WE JUST LEAVE EARTH'S MIGHTIEST OUT OF IT?
HER OR I'M OUT. SHE'S THE *ONE.*
YOU'RE KINDA ESCALATING OUR PLAN BEYOND WHAT I HAD IN MIND. I JUST WANTED TO MAKE A STATEMENT.
CAPTAIN MARVEL IS EVERYTHING THAT'S WRONG WITH THE NATURAL ORDER OF THINGS.
SHE'S SO AWESOME, SHE MAKES NORMAL PEOPLE FEEL TINY. LIKE BUGS UNDER HER BIG FEET. LIKE US NORMALS ARE NOTHING.
YOU THINK YOU'RE NORMAL?

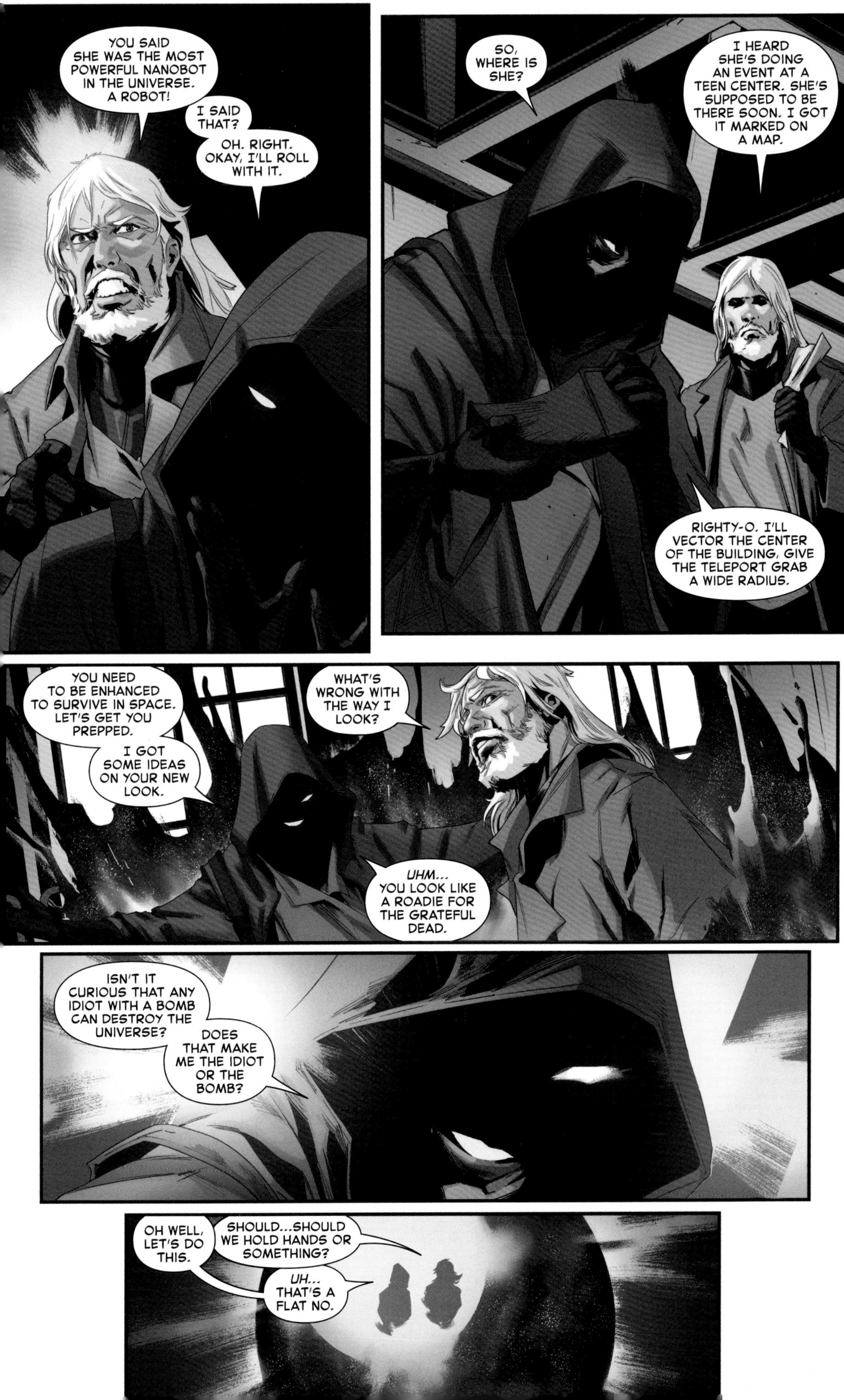
YOU SAID SHE WAS THE MOST POWERFUL NANOBOT IN THE UNIVERSE. A ROBOT!
I SAID THAT?
OH. RIGHT. OKAY, I'LL ROLL WITH IT.
SO, WHERE IS SHE?
I HEARD SHE'S DOING AN EVENT AT A TEEN CENTER. SHE'S SUPPOSED TO BE THERE SOON. I GOT IT MARKED ON A MAP.
RIGHTY-O. I'LL VECTOR THE CENTER OF THE BUILDING, GIVE THE TELEPORT GRAB A WIDE RADIUS.
YOU NEED TO BE ENHANCED TO SURVIVE IN SPACE. LET'S GET YOU PREPPED.
I GOT SOME IDEAS ON YOUR NEW LOOK.
WHAT'S WRONG WITH THE WAY I LOOK?
UHM... YOU LOOK LIKE A ROADIE FOR THE GRATEFUL DEAD.
ISN'T IT CURIOUS THAT ANY IDIOT WITH A BOMB CAN DESTROY THE UNIVERSE?
DOES THAT MAKE ME THE IDIOT OR THE BOMB?
OH WELL, LET'S DO THIS.
SHOULD...SHOULD WE HOLD HANDS OR SOMETHING?
UH... THAT'S A FLAT NO.

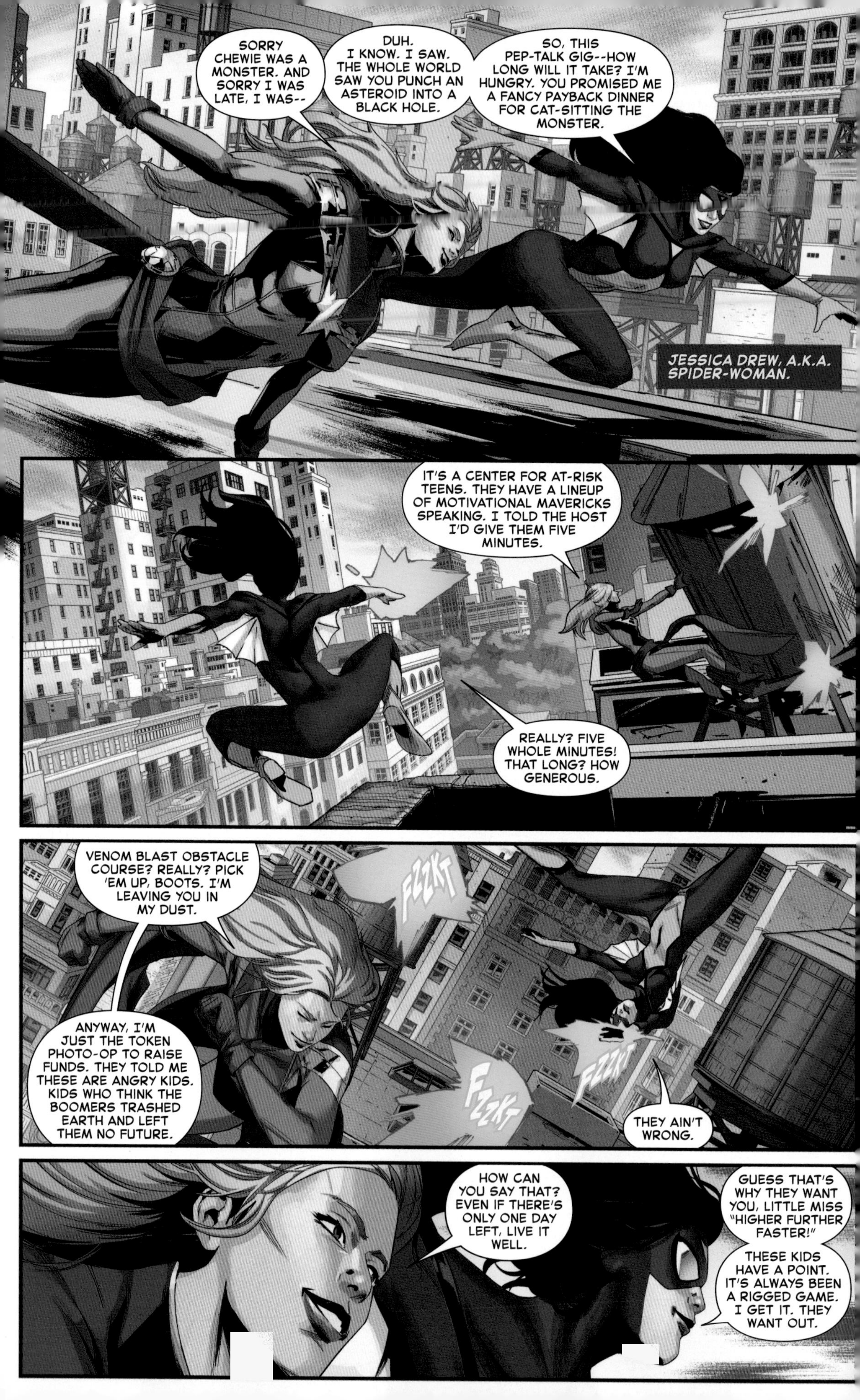
SORRY CHEWIE WAS A MONSTER. AND SORRY I WAS LATE, I WAS--
DUH. I KNOW. I SAW. THE WHOLE WORLD SAW YOU PUNCH AN ASTEROID INTO A BLACK HOLE.
SO, THIS PEP-TALK GIG--HOW LONG WILL IT TAKE? I'M HUNGRY. YOU PROMISED ME A FANCY PAYBACK DINNER FOR CAT-SITTING THE MONSTER.
JESSICA DREW, A.K.A. SPIDER-WOMAN.
IT'S A CENTER FOR AT-RISK TEENS. THEY HAVE A LINEUP OF MOTIVATIONAL MAVERICKS SPEAKING. I TOLD THE HOST I'D GIVE THEM FIVE MINUTES.
REALLY? FIVE WHOLE MINUTES! THAT LONG? HOW GENEROUS.
VENOM BLAST OBSTACLE COURSE? REALLY? PICK 'EM UP, BOOTS. I'M LEAVING YOU IN MY DUST.
FZZKT
ANYWAY, I'M JUST THE TOKEN PHOTO-OP TO RAISE FUNDS. THEY TOLD ME THESE ARE ANGRY KIDS. KIDS WHO THINK THE BOOMERS TRASHED EARTH AND LEFT THEM NO FUTURE.
FZZKT
FZZKT
THEY AIN'T WRONG.
HOW CAN YOU SAY THAT? EVEN IF THERE'S ONLY ONE DAY LEFT, LIVE IT WELL.
GUESS THAT'S WHY THEY WANT YOU, LITTLE MISS "HIGHER FURTHER FASTER!"
THESE KIDS HAVE A POINT. IT'S ALWAYS BEEN A RIGGED GAME. I GET IT. THEY WANT OUT.

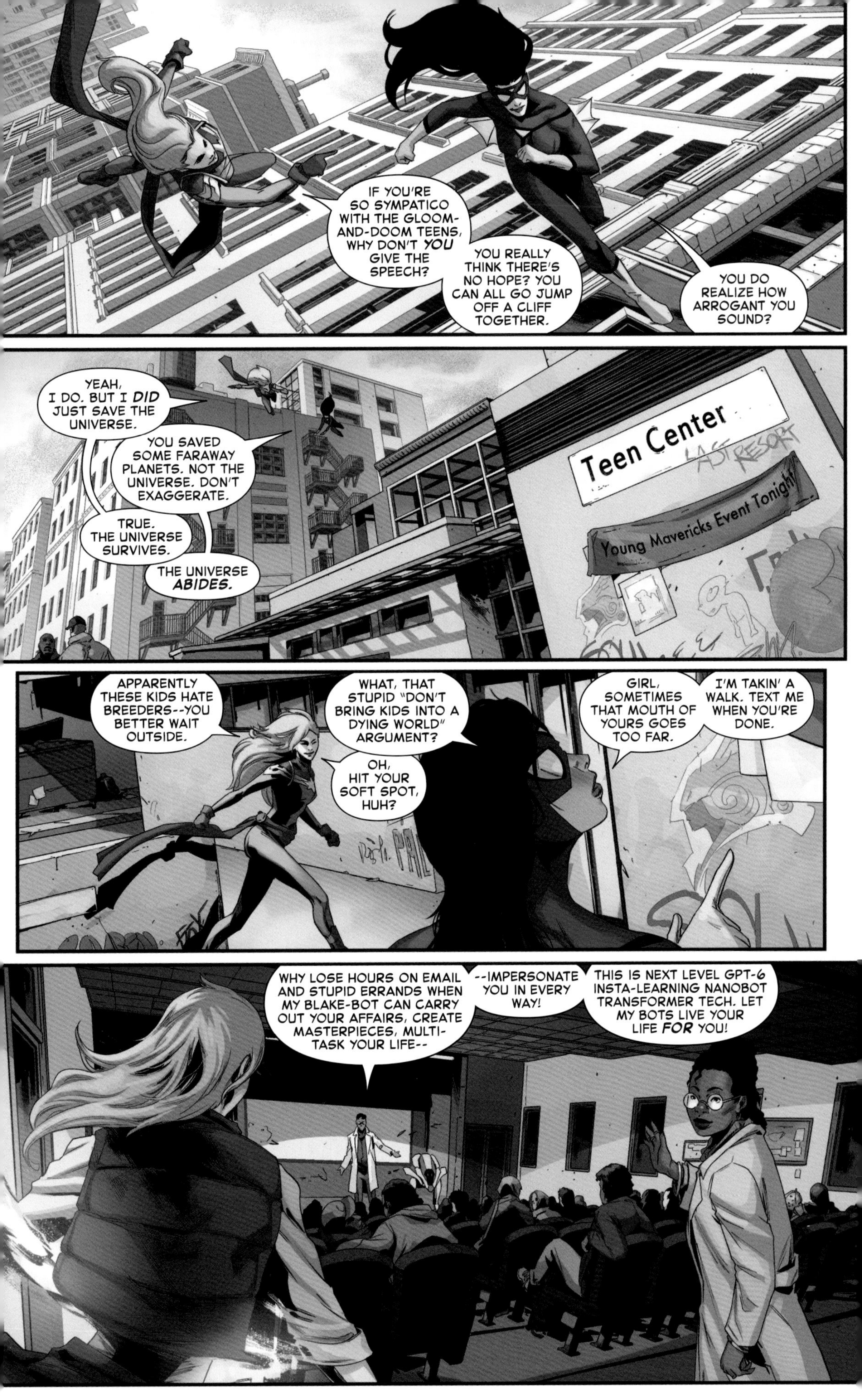
IF YOU'RE SO SYMPATICO WITH THE GLOOM-AND-DOOM TEENS, WHY DON'T *YOU* GIVE THE SPEECH?
YOU REALLY THINK THERE'S NO HOPE? YOU CAN ALL GO JUMP OFF A CLIFF TOGETHER.
YOU DO REALIZE HOW ARROGANT YOU SOUND?
YEAH, I DO. BUT I *DID* JUST SAVE THE UNIVERSE.
YOU SAVED SOME FARAWAY PLANETS. NOT THE UNIVERSE. DON'T EXAGGERATE.
TRUE. THE UNIVERSE SURVIVES.
THE UNIVERSE *ABIDES.*
Teen Center
LAST RESORT
Young Mavericks Event Tonight
APPARENTLY THESE KIDS HATE BREEDERS--YOU BETTER WAIT OUTSIDE.
WHAT, THAT STUPID "DON'T BRING KIDS INTO A DYING WORLD" ARGUMENT?
OH, HIT YOUR SOFT SPOT, HUH?
GIRL, SOMETIMES THAT MOUTH OF YOURS GOES TOO FAR.
I'M TAKIN' A WALK. TEXT ME WHEN YOU'RE DONE.
WHY LOSE HOURS ON EMAIL AND STUPID ERRANDS WHEN MY BLAKE-BOT CAN CARRY OUT YOUR AFFAIRS, CREATE MASTERPIECES, MULTI-TASK YOUR LIFE--
--IMPERSONATE YOU IN EVERY WAY!
THIS IS NEXT LEVEL GPT-6 INSTA-LEARNING NANOBOT TRANSFORMER TECH. LET MY BOTS LIVE YOUR LIFE *FOR* YOU!

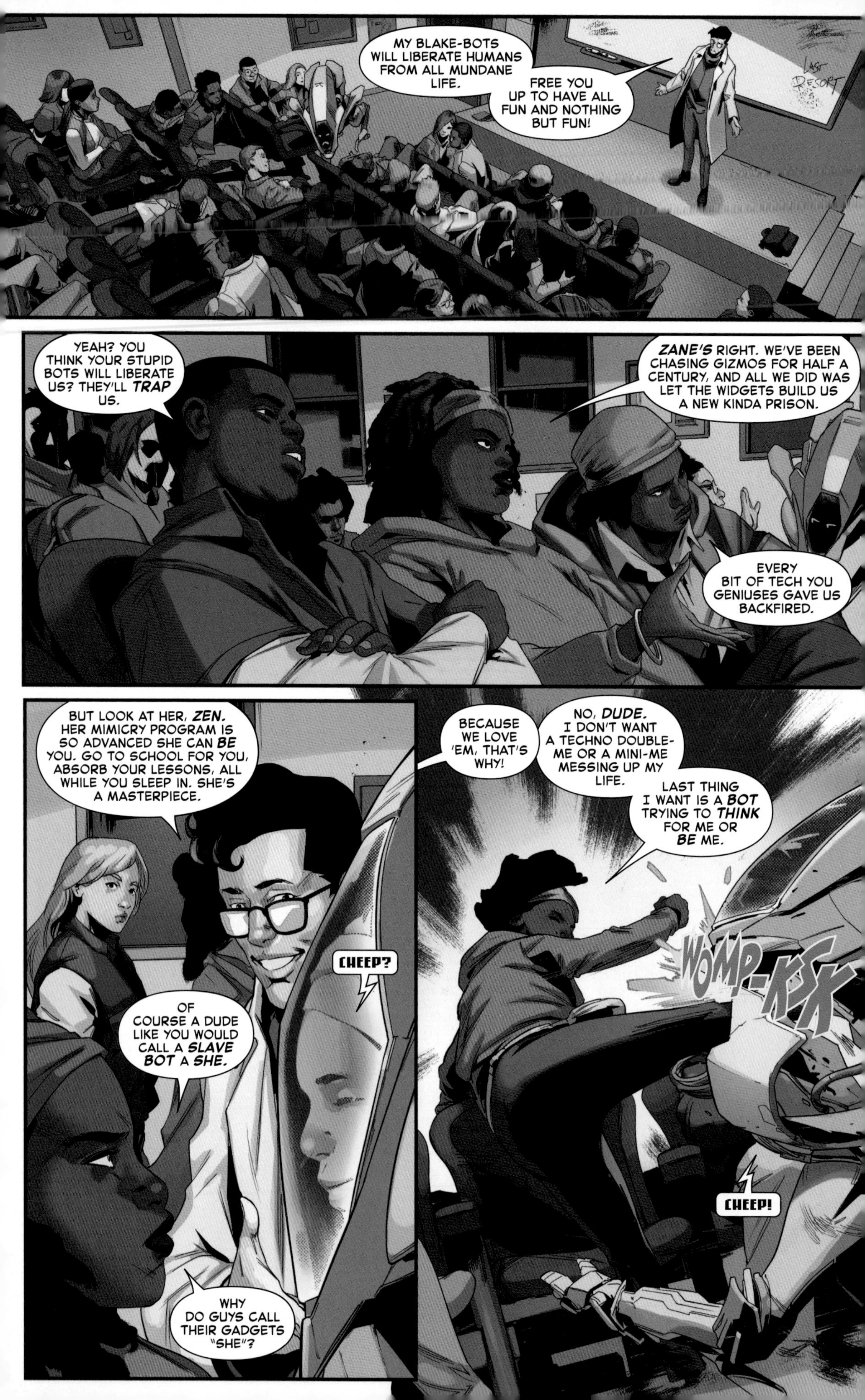

LAST RESORT
MY BLAKE-BOTS WILL LIBERATE HUMANS FROM ALL MUNDANE LIFE.
FREE YOU UP TO HAVE ALL FUN AND NOTHING BUT FUN!
YEAH? YOU THINK YOUR STUPID BOTS WILL LIBERATE US? THEY'LL TRAP US.
ZANE'S RIGHT. WE'VE BEEN CHASING GIZMOS FOR HALF A CENTURY, AND ALL WE DID WAS LET THE WIDGETS BUILD US A NEW KINDA PRISON.
EVERY BIT OF TECH YOU GENIUSES GAVE US BACKFIRED.
BUT LOOK AT HER, ZEN. HER MIMICRY PROGRAM IS SO ADVANCED SHE CAN BE YOU. GO TO SCHOOL FOR YOU, ABSORB YOUR LESSONS, ALL WHILE YOU SLEEP IN. SHE'S A MASTERPIECE.
CHEEP?
OF COURSE A DUDE LIKE YOU WOULD CALL A SLAVE BOT A SHE.
WHY DO GUYS CALL THEIR GADGETS "SHE"?
BECAUSE WE LOVE 'EM, THAT'S WHY!
NO, DUDE. I DON'T WANT A TECHNO DOUBLE-ME OR A MINI-ME MESSING UP MY LIFE.
LAST THING I WANT IS A BOT TRYING TO THINK FOR ME OR BE ME.
WOMP-KSK
CHEEP!

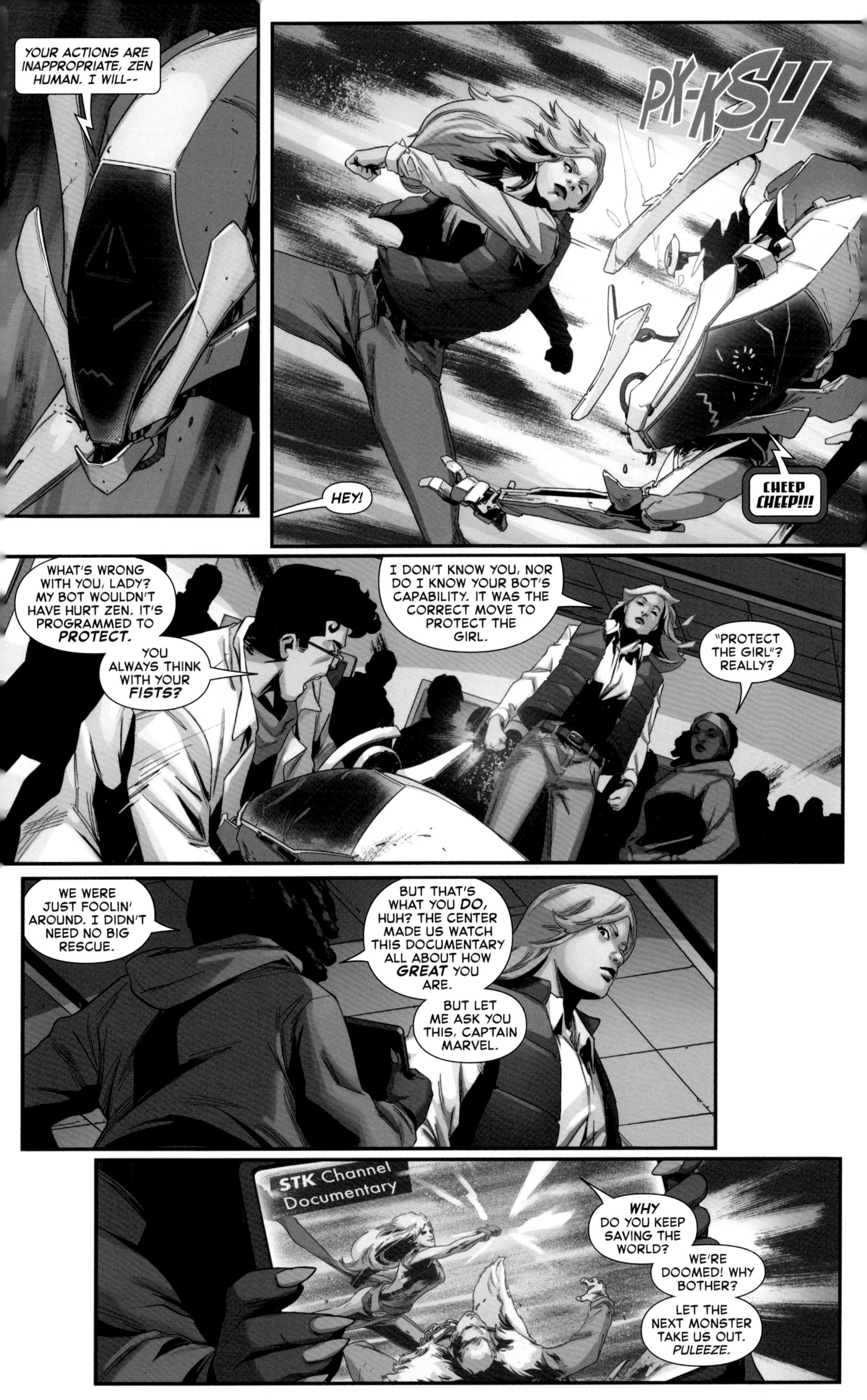
YOUR ACTIONS ARE INAPPROPRIATE, ZEN HUMAN. I WILL--
PK-KSH
HEY!
CHEEP CHEEP!!!
WHAT'S WRONG WITH YOU, LADY? MY BOT WOULDN'T HAVE HURT ZEN. IT'S PROGRAMMED TO PROTECT.
YOU ALWAYS THINK WITH YOUR FISTS?
I DON'T KNOW YOU, NOR DO I KNOW YOUR BOT'S CAPABILITY. IT WAS THE CORRECT MOVE TO PROTECT THE GIRL.
"PROTECT THE GIRL"? REALLY?
WE WERE JUST FOOLIN' AROUND. I DIDN'T NEED NO BIG RESCUE.
BUT THAT'S WHAT YOU DO, HUH? THE CENTER MADE US WATCH THIS DOCUMENTARY ALL ABOUT HOW GREAT YOU ARE.
BUT LET ME ASK YOU THIS, CAPTAIN MARVEL.
STK Channel Documentary
WHY DO YOU KEEP SAVING THE WORLD?
WE'RE DOOMED! WHY BOTHER?
LET THE NEXT MONSTER TAKE US OUT. PULEEZE.

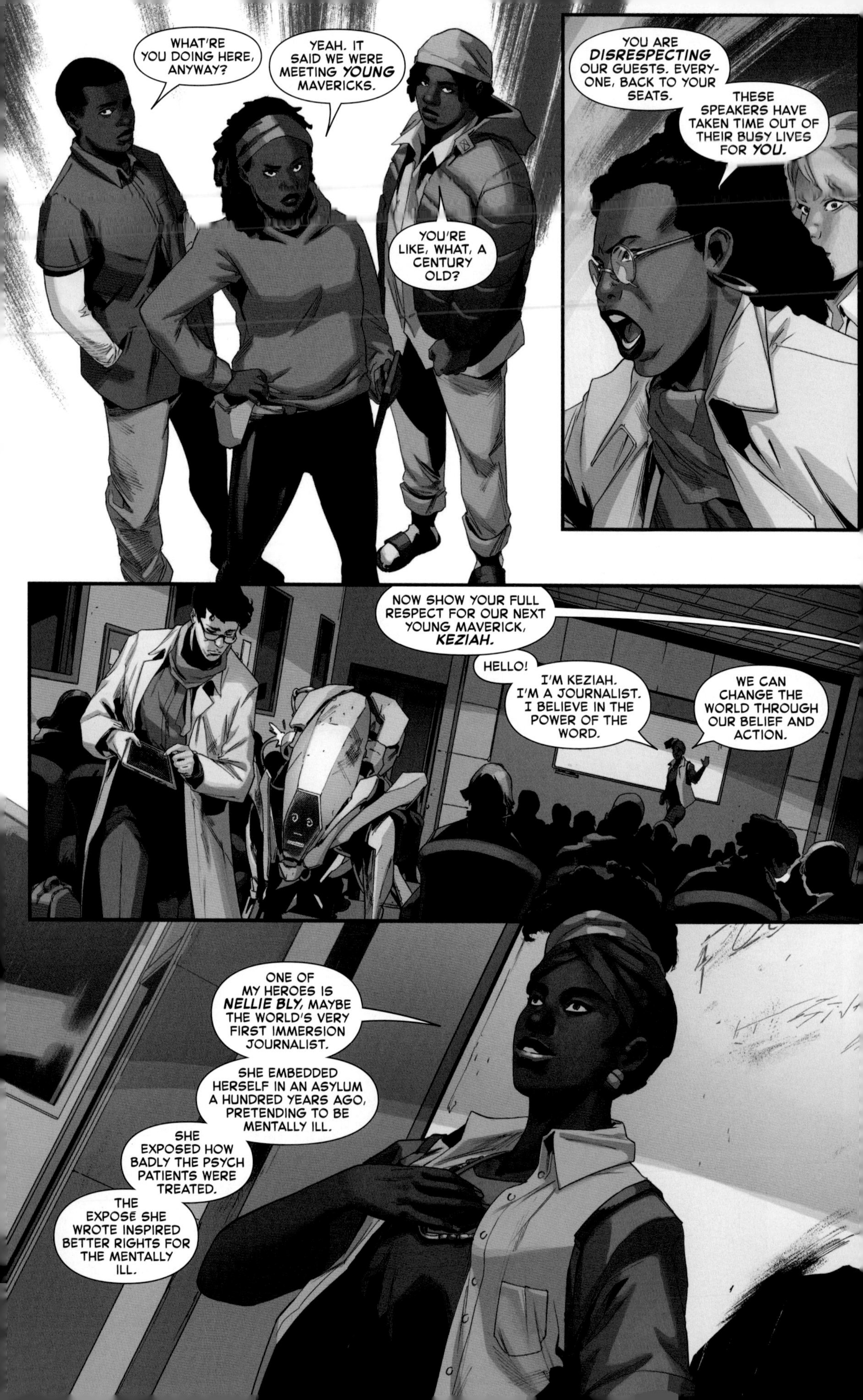
WHAT'RE YOU DOING HERE, ANYWAY?
YEAH. IT SAID WE WERE MEETING YOUNG MAVERICKS.
YOU'RE LIKE, WHAT, A CENTURY OLD?
YOU ARE DISRESPECTING OUR GUESTS. EVERY-ONE, BACK TO YOUR SEATS.
THESE SPEAKERS HAVE TAKEN TIME OUT OF THEIR BUSY LIVES FOR YOU.
NOW SHOW YOUR FULL RESPECT FOR OUR NEXT YOUNG MAVERICK, KEZIAH.
HELLO!
I'M KEZIAH. I'M A JOURNALIST. I BELIEVE IN THE POWER OF THE WORD.
WE CAN CHANGE THE WORLD THROUGH OUR BELIEF AND ACTION.
ONE OF MY HEROES IS NELLIE BLY, MAYBE THE WORLD'S VERY FIRST IMMERSION JOURNALIST.
SHE EMBEDDED HERSELF IN AN ASYLUM A HUNDRED YEARS AGO, PRETENDING TO BE MENTALLY ILL.
SHE EXPOSED HOW BADLY THE PSYCH PATIENTS WERE TREATED.
THE EXPOSÉ SHE WROTE INSPIRED BETTER RIGHTS FOR THE MENTALLY ILL.

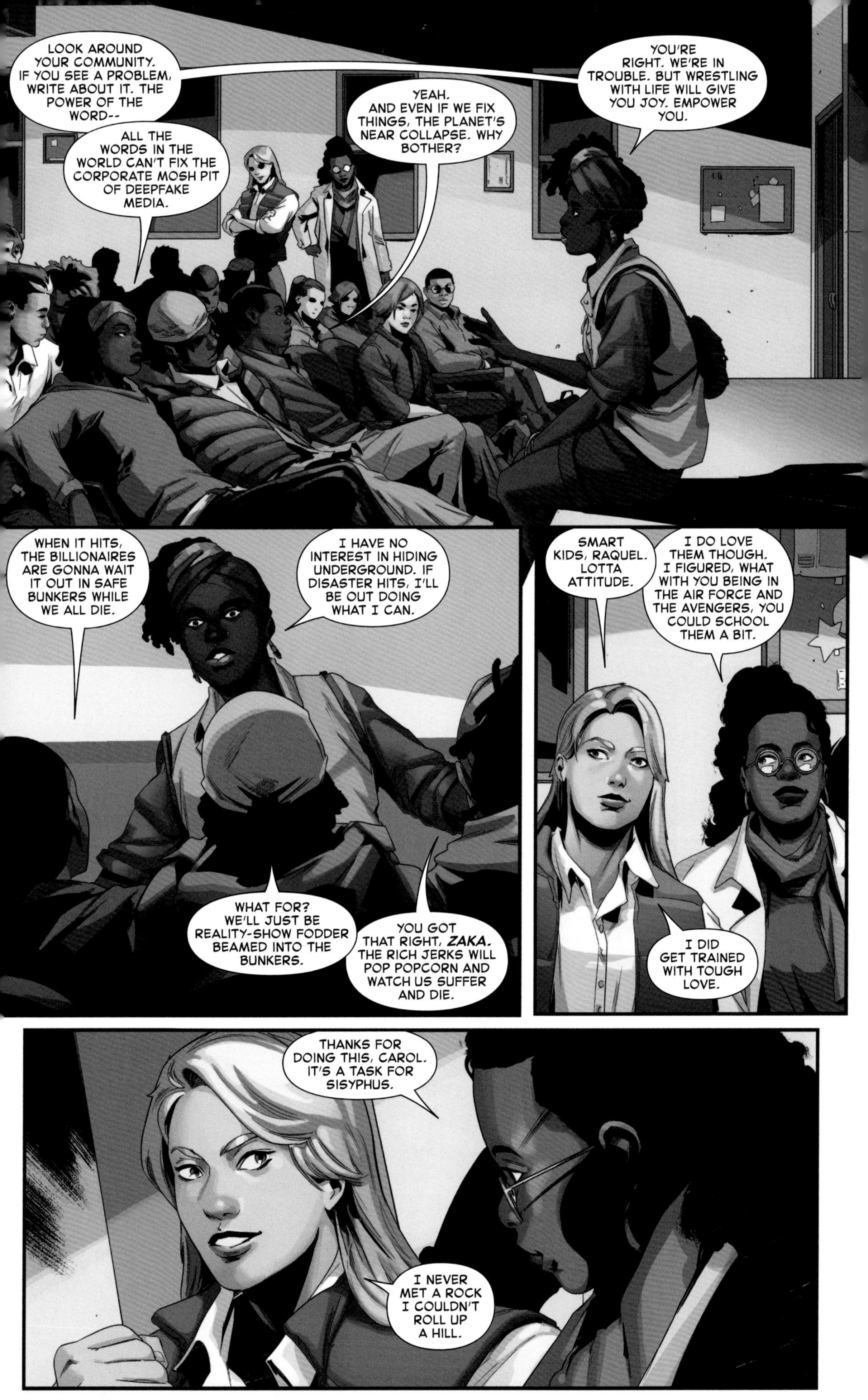
LOOK AROUND YOUR COMMUNITY. IF YOU SEE A PROBLEM, WRITE ABOUT IT. THE POWER OF THE WORD--
YOU'RE RIGHT. WE'RE IN TROUBLE. BUT WRESTLING WITH LIFE WILL GIVE YOU JOY. EMPOWER YOU.
ALL THE WORDS IN THE WORLD CAN'T FIX THE CORPORATE MOSH PIT OF DEEPFAKE MEDIA.
YEAH. AND EVEN IF WE FIX THINGS, THE PLANET'S NEAR COLLAPSE. WHY BOTHER?
WHEN IT HITS, THE BILLIONAIRES ARE GONNA WAIT IT OUT IN SAFE BUNKERS WHILE WE ALL DIE.
I HAVE NO INTEREST IN HIDING UNDERGROUND. IF DISASTER HITS, I'LL BE OUT DOING WHAT I CAN.
WHAT FOR? WE'LL JUST BE REALITY-SHOW FODDER BEAMED INTO THE BUNKERS.
YOU GOT THAT RIGHT, ***ZAKA.*** THE RICH JERKS WILL POP POPCORN AND WATCH US SUFFER AND DIE.
SMART KIDS, RAQUEL. LOTTA ATTITUDE.
I DO LOVE THEM THOUGH. I FIGURED, WHAT WITH YOU BEING IN THE AIR FORCE AND THE AVENGERS, YOU COULD SCHOOL THEM A BIT.
I DID GET TRAINED WITH TOUGH LOVE.
THANKS FOR DOING THIS, CAROL. IT'S A TASK FOR SISYPHUS.
I NEVER MET A ROCK I COULDN'T ROLL UP A HILL.

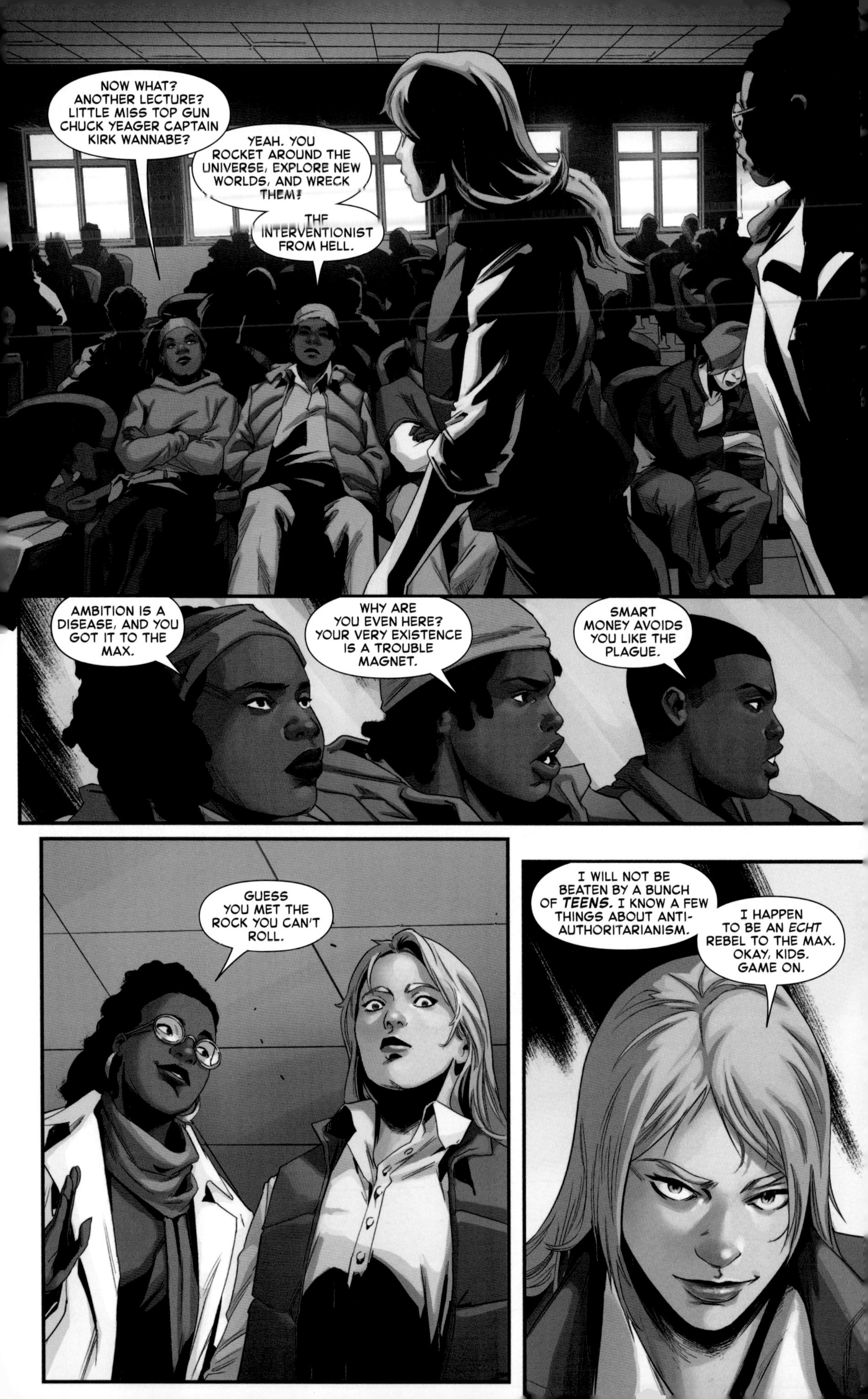
NOW WHAT? ANOTHER LECTURE? LITTLE MISS TOP GUN CHUCK YEAGER CAPTAIN KIRK WANNABE?
YEAH. YOU ROCKET AROUND THE UNIVERSE, EXPLORE NEW WORLDS, AND WRECK THEM!
THE INTERVENTIONIST FROM HELL.
AMBITION IS A DISEASE, AND YOU GOT IT TO THE MAX.
WHY ARE YOU EVEN HERE? YOUR VERY EXISTENCE IS A TROUBLE MAGNET.
SMART MONEY AVOIDS YOU LIKE THE PLAGUE.
GUESS YOU MET THE ROCK YOU CAN'T ROLL.
I WILL NOT BE BEATEN BY A BUNCH OF *TEENS.* I KNOW A FEW THINGS ABOUT ANTI-AUTHORITARIANISM.
I HAPPEN TO BE AN *ECHT* REBEL TO THE MAX. OKAY, KIDS. GAME ON.

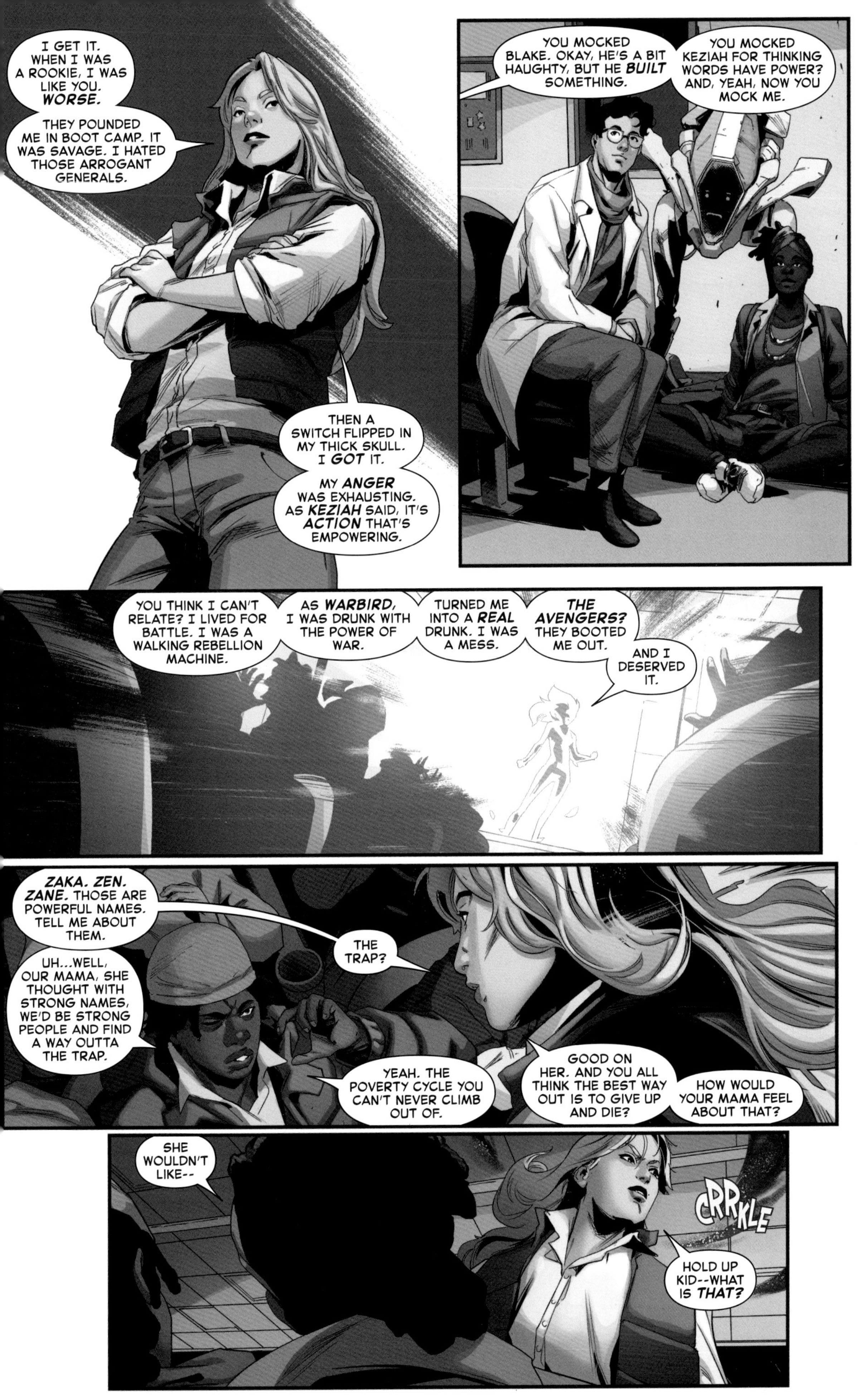

I GET IT. WHEN I WAS A ROOKIE, I WAS LIKE YOU. **WORSE.**
THEY POUNDED ME IN BOOT CAMP. IT WAS SAVAGE. I HATED THOSE ARROGANT GENERALS.
THEN A SWITCH FLIPPED IN MY THICK SKULL. I **GOT** IT.
MY **ANGER** WAS EXHAUSTING. AS **KEZIAH** SAID, IT'S **ACTION** THAT'S EMPOWERING.
YOU MOCKED BLAKE. OKAY, HE'S A BIT HAUGHTY, BUT HE **BUILT** SOMETHING.
YOU MOCKED KEZIAH FOR THINKING WORDS HAVE POWER? AND, YEAH, NOW YOU MOCK ME.
YOU THINK I CAN'T RELATE? I LIVED FOR BATTLE. I WAS A WALKING REBELLION MACHINE.
AS **WARBIRD,** I WAS DRUNK WITH THE POWER OF WAR.
TURNED ME INTO A **REAL** DRUNK. I WAS A MESS.
THE AVENGERS? THEY BOOTED ME OUT.
AND I DESERVED IT.
ZAKA. ZEN. ZANE. THOSE ARE POWERFUL NAMES. TELL ME ABOUT THEM.
UH...WELL, OUR MAMA, SHE THOUGHT WITH STRONG NAMES, WE'D BE STRONG PEOPLE AND FIND A WAY OUTTA THE TRAP.
THE TRAP?
YEAH. THE POVERTY CYCLE YOU CAN'T NEVER CLIMB OUT OF.
GOOD ON HER. AND YOU ALL THINK THE BEST WAY OUT IS TO GIVE UP AND DIE?
HOW WOULD YOUR MAMA FEEL ABOUT THAT?
SHE WOULDN'T LIKE--
CRRKLE
HOLD UP KID--WHAT IS **THAT?**

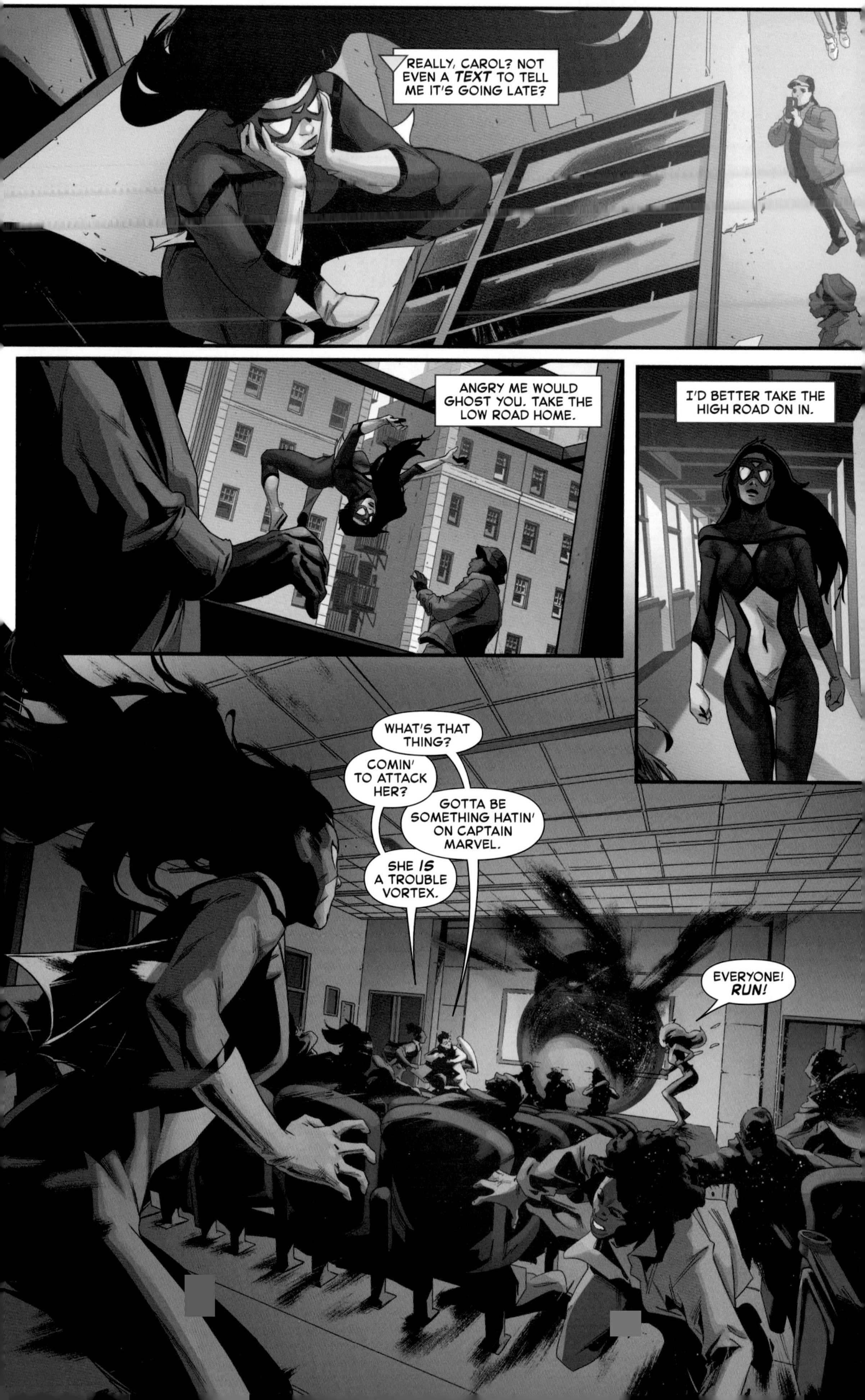
REALLY, CAROL? NOT EVEN A *TEXT* TO TELL ME IT'S GOING LATE?
ANGRY ME WOULD GHOST YOU. TAKE THE LOW ROAD HOME.
I'D BETTER TAKE THE HIGH ROAD ON IN.
WHAT'S THAT THING?
COMIN' TO ATTACK HER?
GOTTA BE SOMETHING HATIN' ON CAPTAIN MARVEL.
SHE *IS* A TROUBLE VORTEX.
EVERYONE! *RUN!*

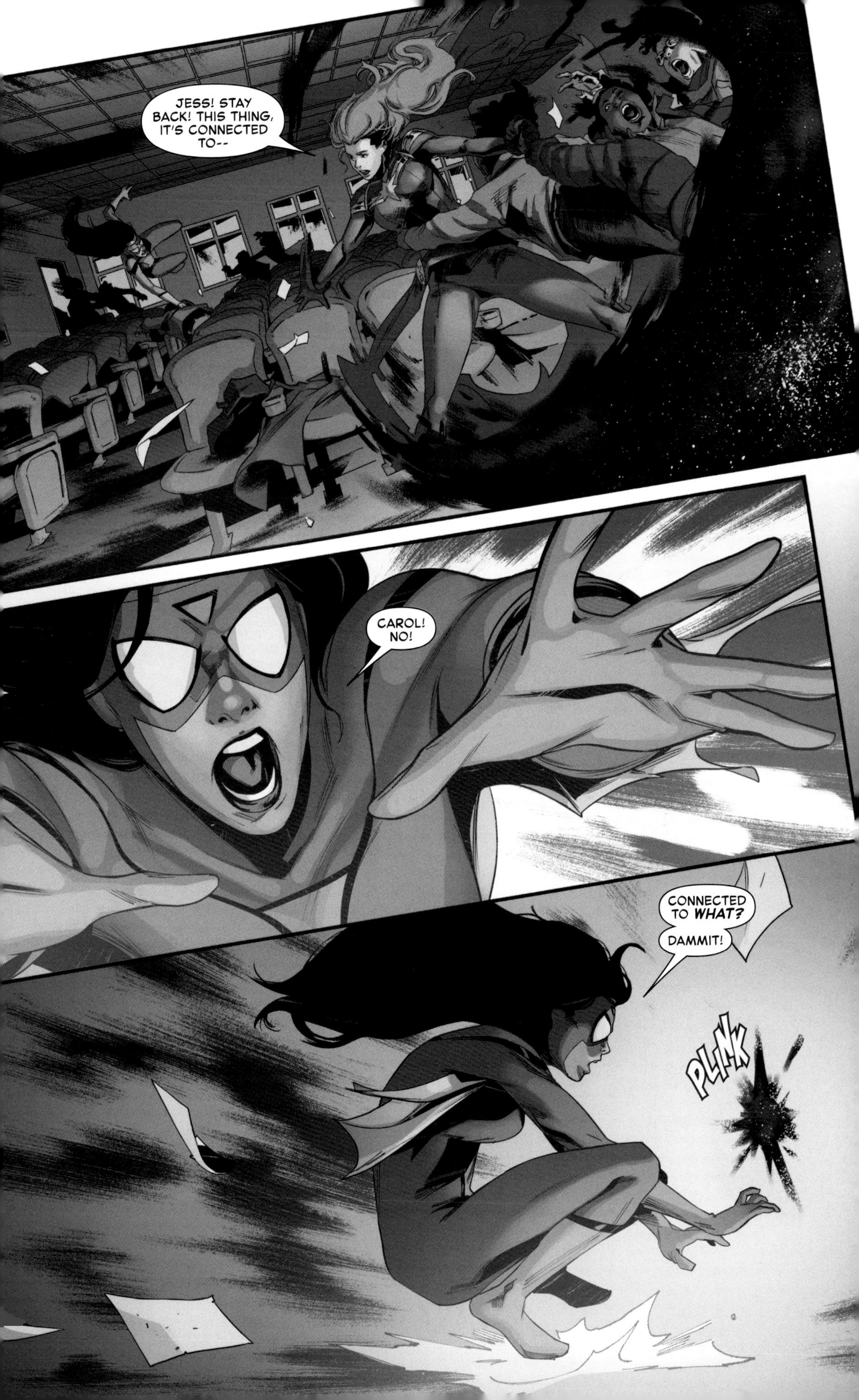
JESS! STAY BACK! THIS THING, IT'S CONNECTED TO--
CAROL! NO!
CONNECTED TO *WHAT?*
DAMMIT!
PLINK

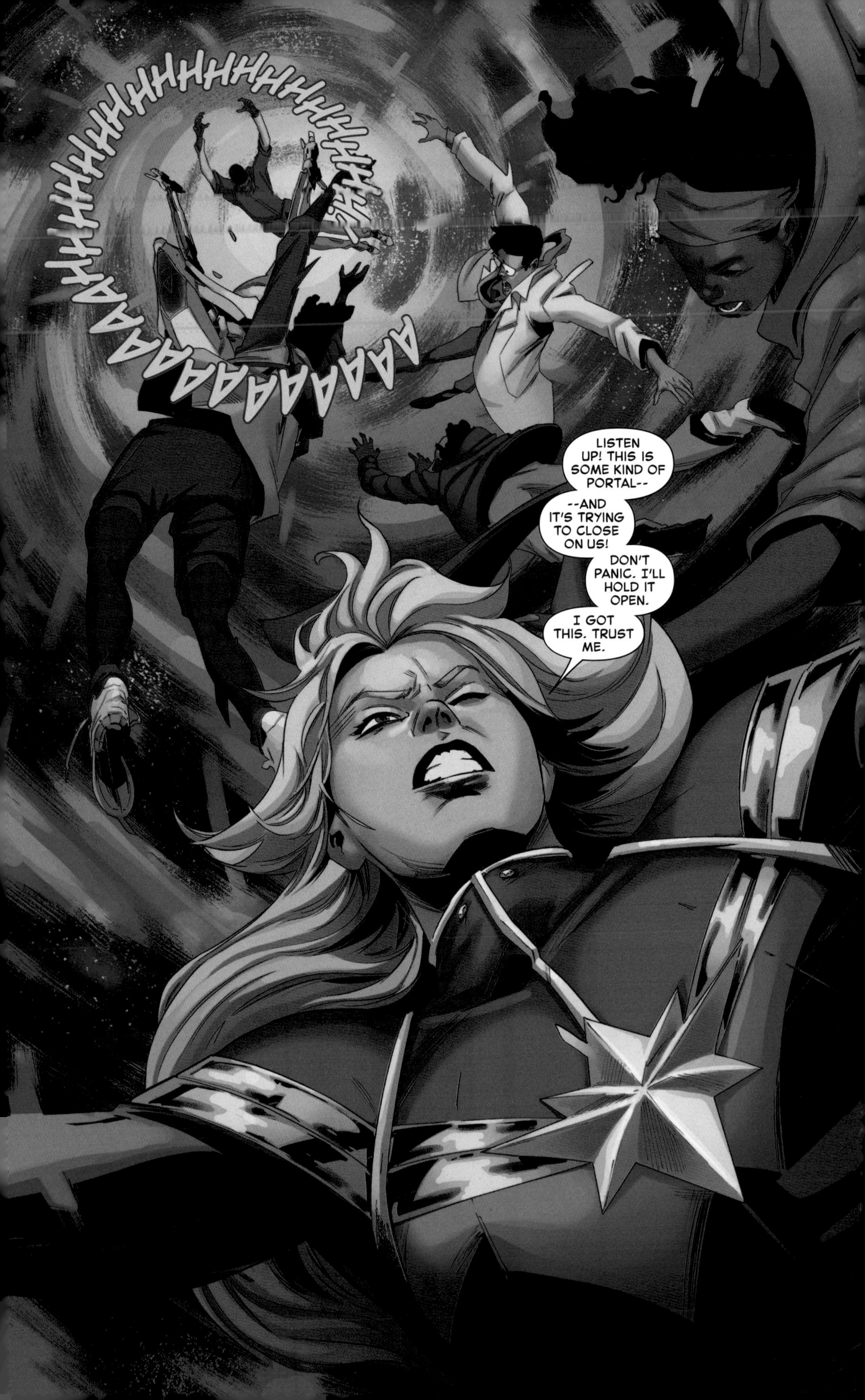
AAAAAAAAAAAAAAHHHHHHHHHHHHHHHHHHHHHHHHHH!
LISTEN UP! THIS IS SOME KIND OF PORTAL--
--AND IT'S TRYING TO CLOSE ON US!
DON'T PANIC. I'LL HOLD IT OPEN.
I GOT THIS. TRUST ME.

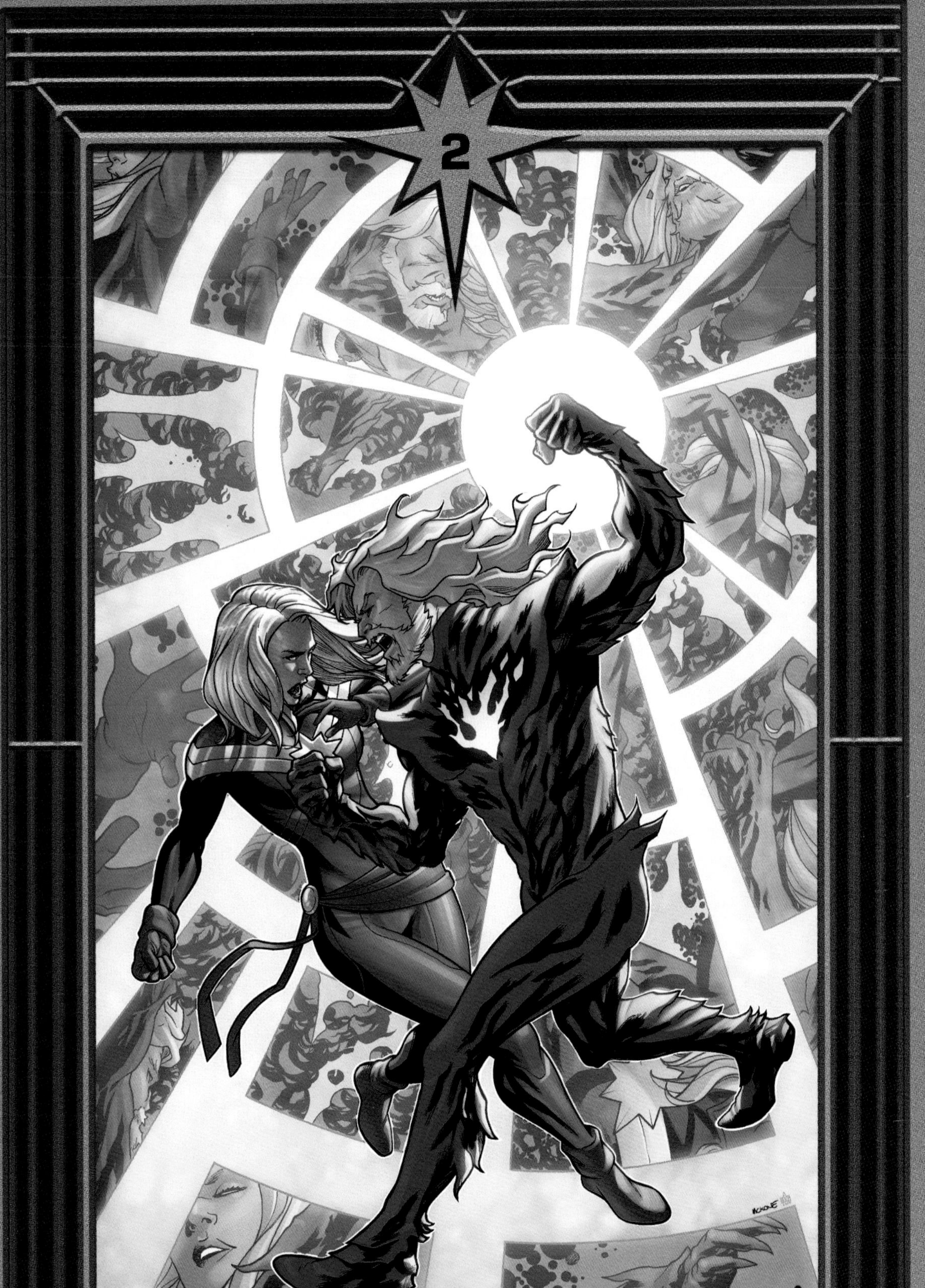
2

THE SPOOKY CASE OF THE GIRL WITH THE POCKET PORTAL

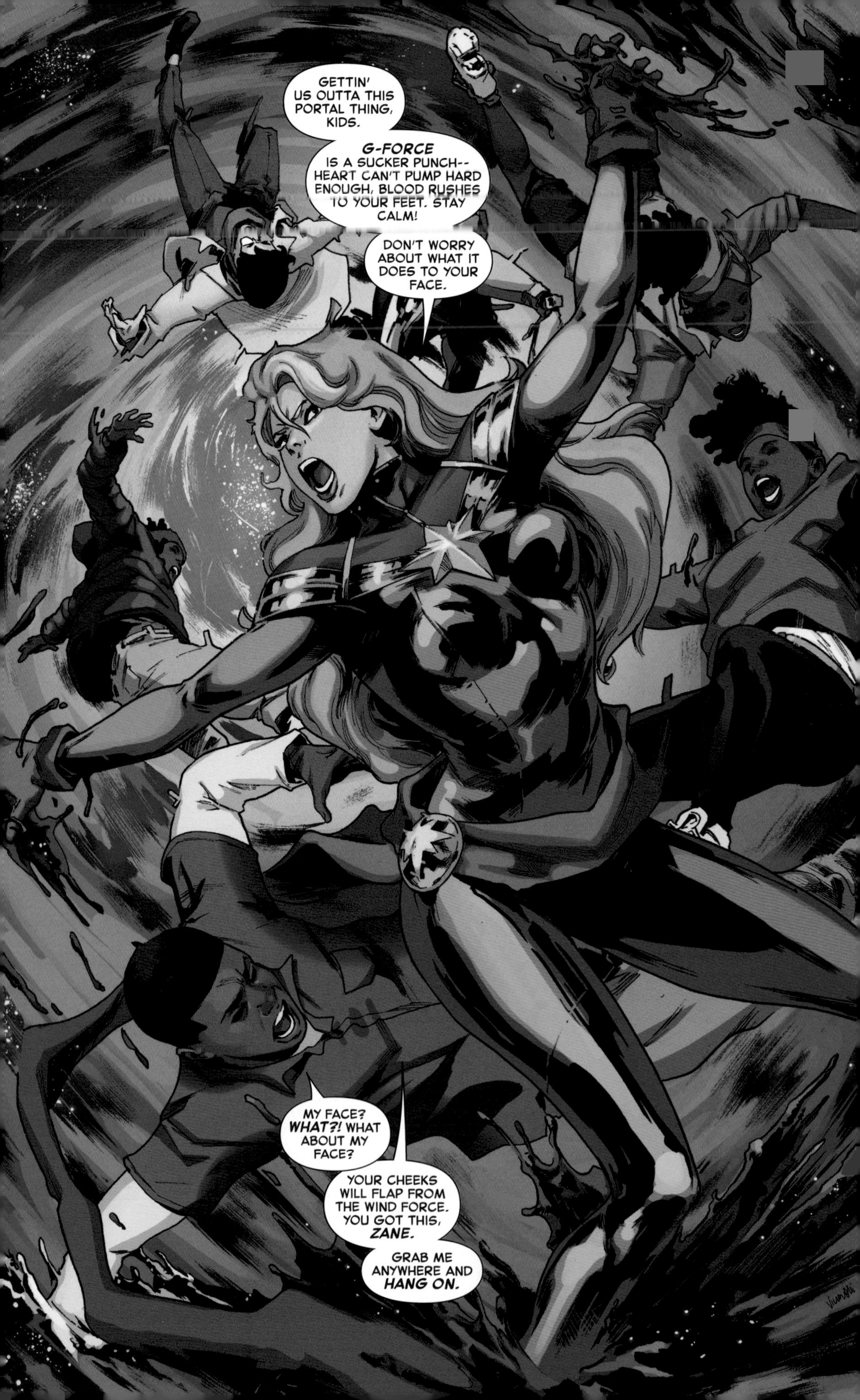
GETTIN' US OUTTA THIS PORTAL THING, KIDS.
G-FORCE IS A SUCKER PUNCH-- HEART CAN'T PUMP HARD ENOUGH, BLOOD RUSHES TO YOUR FEET. STAY CALM!
DON'T WORRY ABOUT WHAT IT DOES TO YOUR FACE.
MY FACE? WHAT?! WHAT ABOUT MY FACE?
YOUR CHEEKS WILL FLAP FROM THE WIND FORCE. YOU GOT THIS, ZANE.
GRAB ME ANYWHERE AND HANG ON.

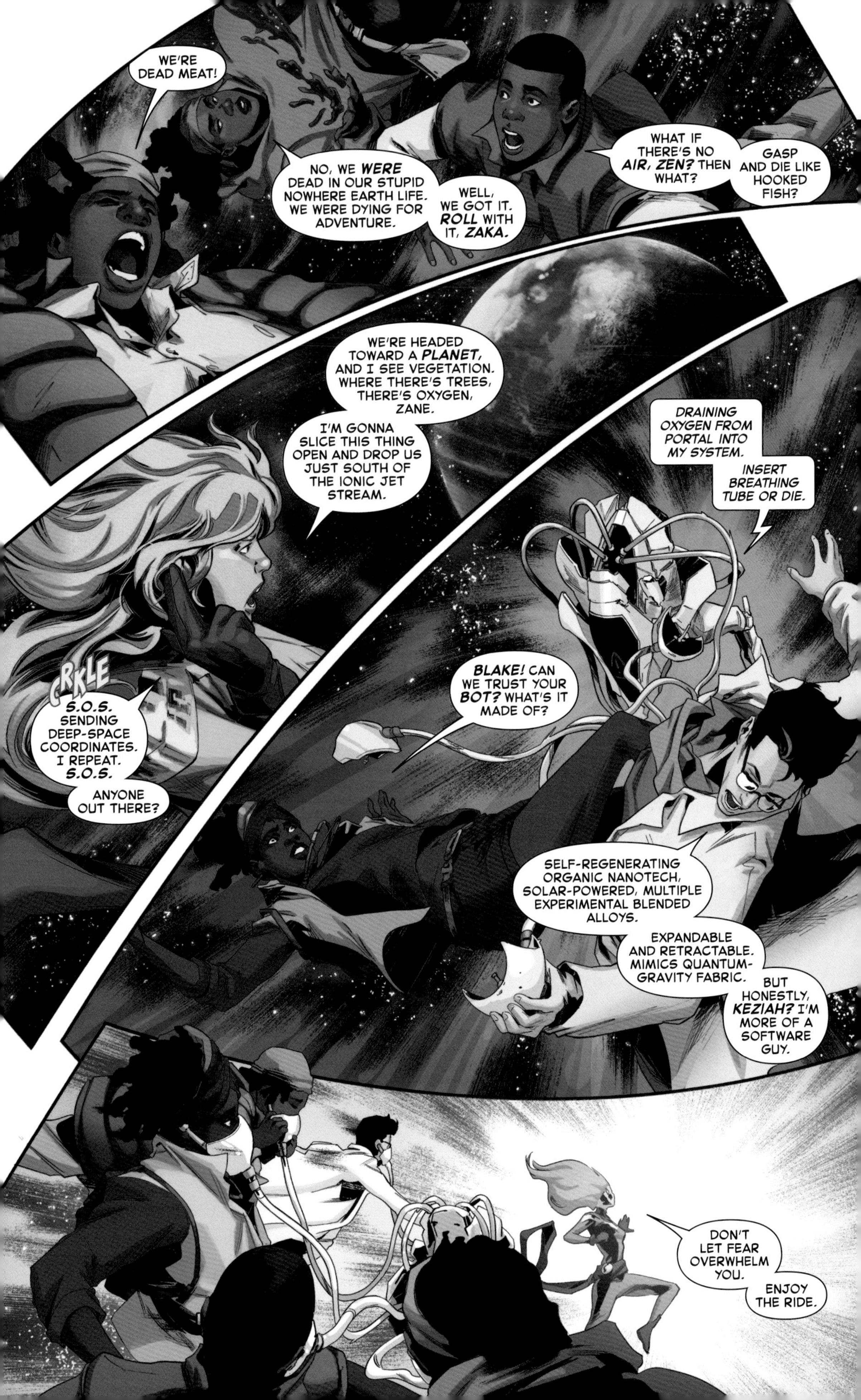
WE'RE DEAD MEAT!
NO, WE WERE DEAD IN OUR STUPID NOWHERE EARTH LIFE. WE WERE DYING FOR ADVENTURE.
WELL, WE GOT IT. ROLL WITH IT, ZAKA.
WHAT IF THERE'S NO AIR, ZEN? THEN WHAT?
GASP AND DIE LIKE HOOKED FISH?
WE'RE HEADED TOWARD A PLANET, AND I SEE VEGETATION. WHERE THERE'S TREES, THERE'S OXYGEN, ZANE.
I'M GONNA SLICE THIS THING OPEN AND DROP US JUST SOUTH OF THE IONIC JET STREAM.
CRKLE
S.O.S. SENDING DEEP-SPACE COORDINATES. I REPEAT. S.O.S.
ANYONE OUT THERE?
DRAINING OXYGEN FROM PORTAL INTO MY SYSTEM.
INSERT BREATHING TUBE OR DIE.
BLAKE! CAN WE TRUST YOUR BOT? WHAT'S IT MADE OF?
SELF-REGENERATING ORGANIC NANOTECH, SOLAR-POWERED, MULTIPLE EXPERIMENTAL BLENDED ALLOYS.
EXPANDABLE AND RETRACTABLE. MIMICS QUANTUM-GRAVITY FABRIC.
BUT HONESTLY, KEZIAH? I'M MORE OF A SOFTWARE GUY.
DON'T LET FEAR OVERWHELM YOU.
ENJOY THE RIDE.

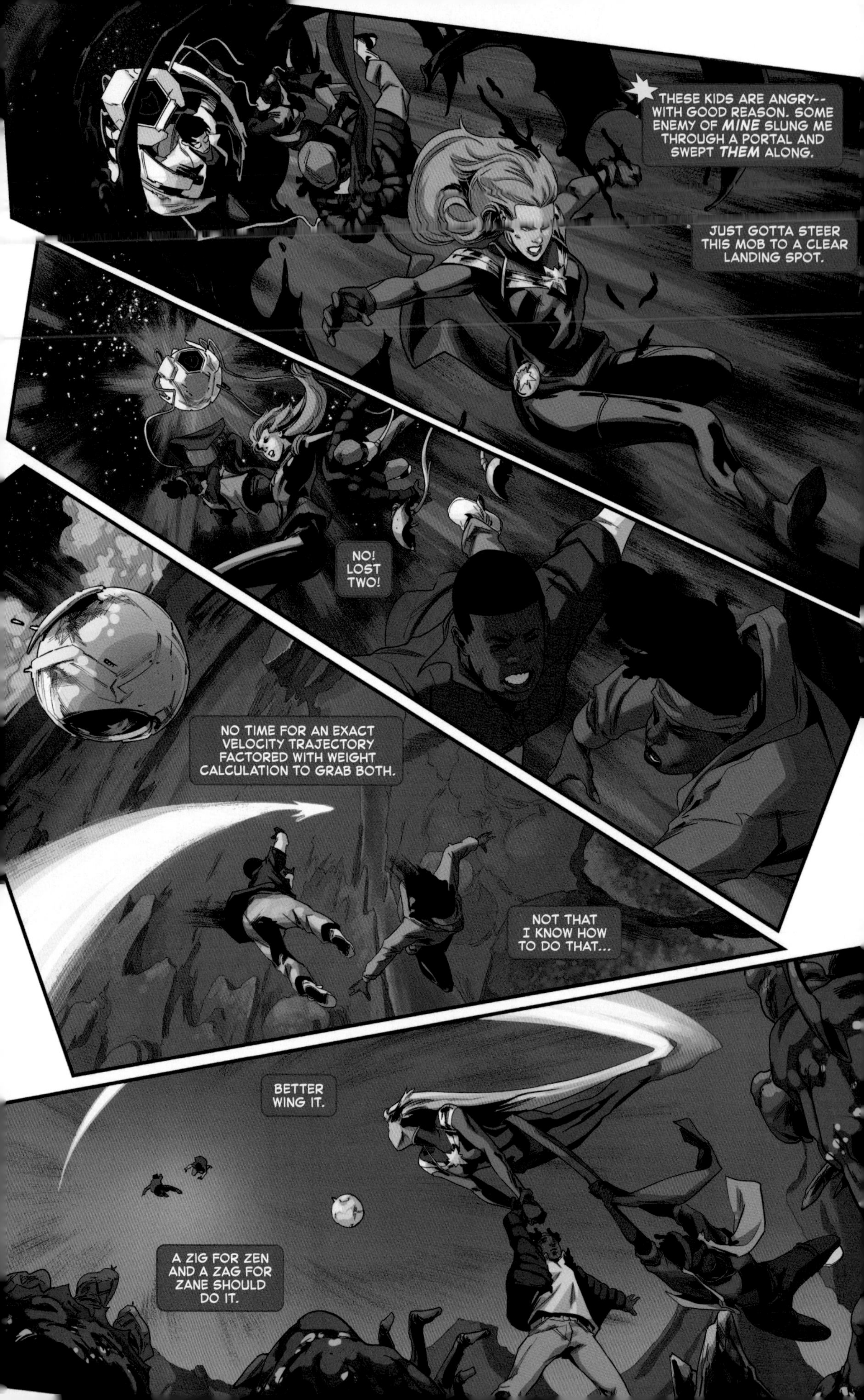
THESE KIDS ARE ANGRY-- WITH GOOD REASON. SOME ENEMY OF MINE SLUNG ME THROUGH A PORTAL AND SWEPT THEM ALONG.
JUST GOTTA STEER THIS MOB TO A CLEAR LANDING SPOT.
NO! LOST TWO!
NO TIME FOR AN EXACT VELOCITY TRAJECTORY FACTORED WITH WEIGHT CALCULATION TO GRAB BOTH.
NOT THAT I KNOW HOW TO DO THAT...
BETTER WING IT.
A ZIG FOR ZEN AND A ZAG FOR ZANE SHOULD DO IT.

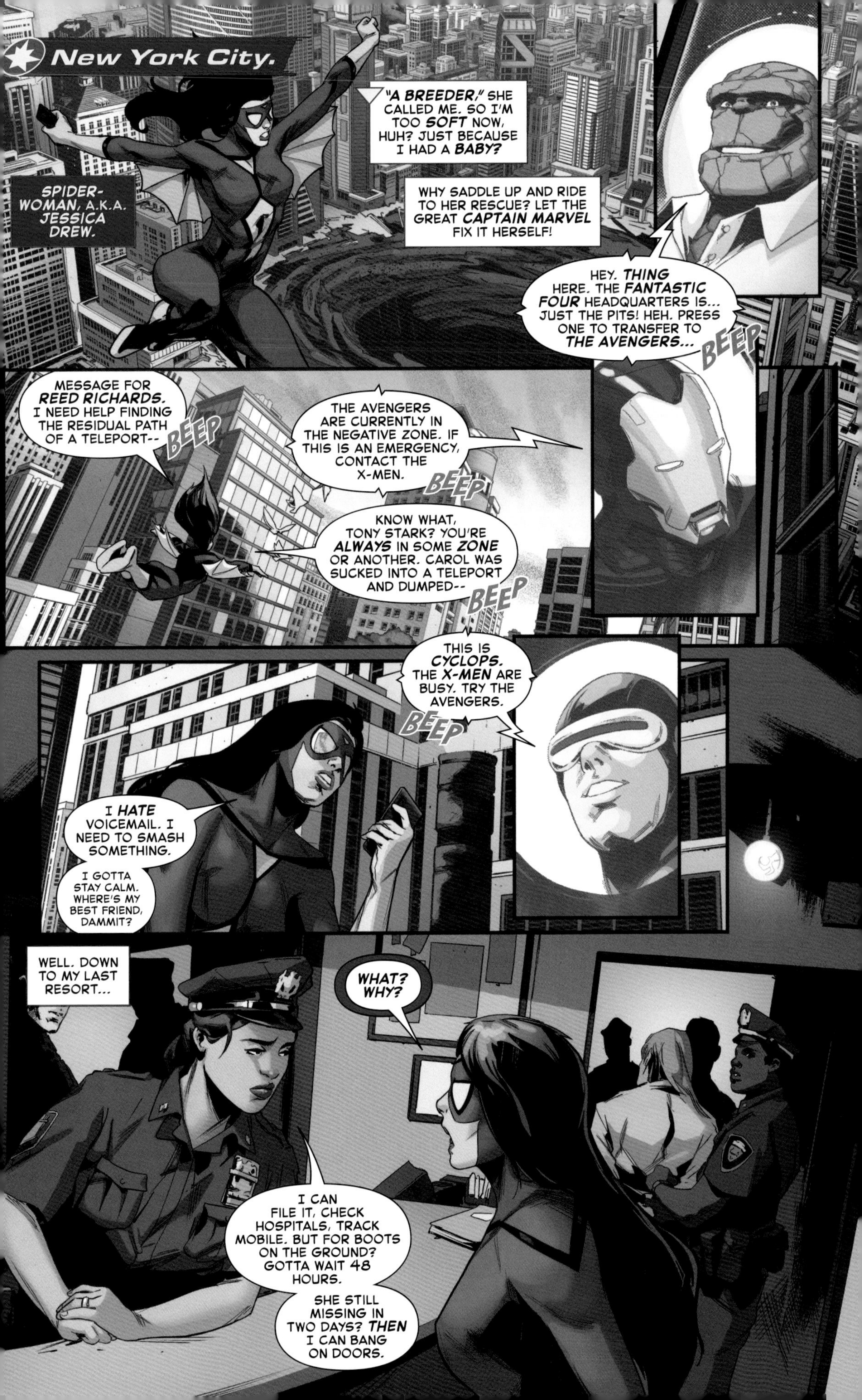
New York City.
SPIDER-WOMAN, A.K.A. JESSICA DREW.
"A BREEDER," SHE CALLED ME. SO I'M TOO SOFT NOW, HUH? JUST BECAUSE I HAD A BABY?
WHY SADDLE UP AND RIDE TO HER RESCUE? LET THE GREAT CAPTAIN MARVEL FIX IT HERSELF!
HEY. THING HERE. THE FANTASTIC FOUR HEADQUARTERS IS... JUST THE PITS! HEH. PRESS ONE TO TRANSFER TO THE AVENGERS...
BEEP
MESSAGE FOR REED RICHARDS. I NEED HELP FINDING THE RESIDUAL PATH OF A TELEPORT--
BEEP
THE AVENGERS ARE CURRENTLY IN THE NEGATIVE ZONE. IF THIS IS AN EMERGENCY, CONTACT THE X-MEN.
BEEP
KNOW WHAT, TONY STARK? YOU'RE ALWAYS IN SOME ZONE OR ANOTHER. CAROL WAS SUCKED INTO A TELEPORT AND DUMPED--
BEEP
THIS IS CYCLOPS. THE X-MEN ARE BUSY. TRY THE AVENGERS.
BEEP
I HATE VOICEMAIL. I NEED TO SMASH SOMETHING.
I GOTTA STAY CALM. WHERE'S MY BEST FRIEND, DAMMIT?
WELL. DOWN TO MY LAST RESORT...
WHAT? WHY?
I CAN FILE IT, CHECK HOSPITALS, TRACK MOBILE. BUT FOR BOOTS ON THE GROUND? GOTTA WAIT 48 HOURS.
SHE STILL MISSING IN TWO DAYS? THEN I CAN BANG ON DOORS.

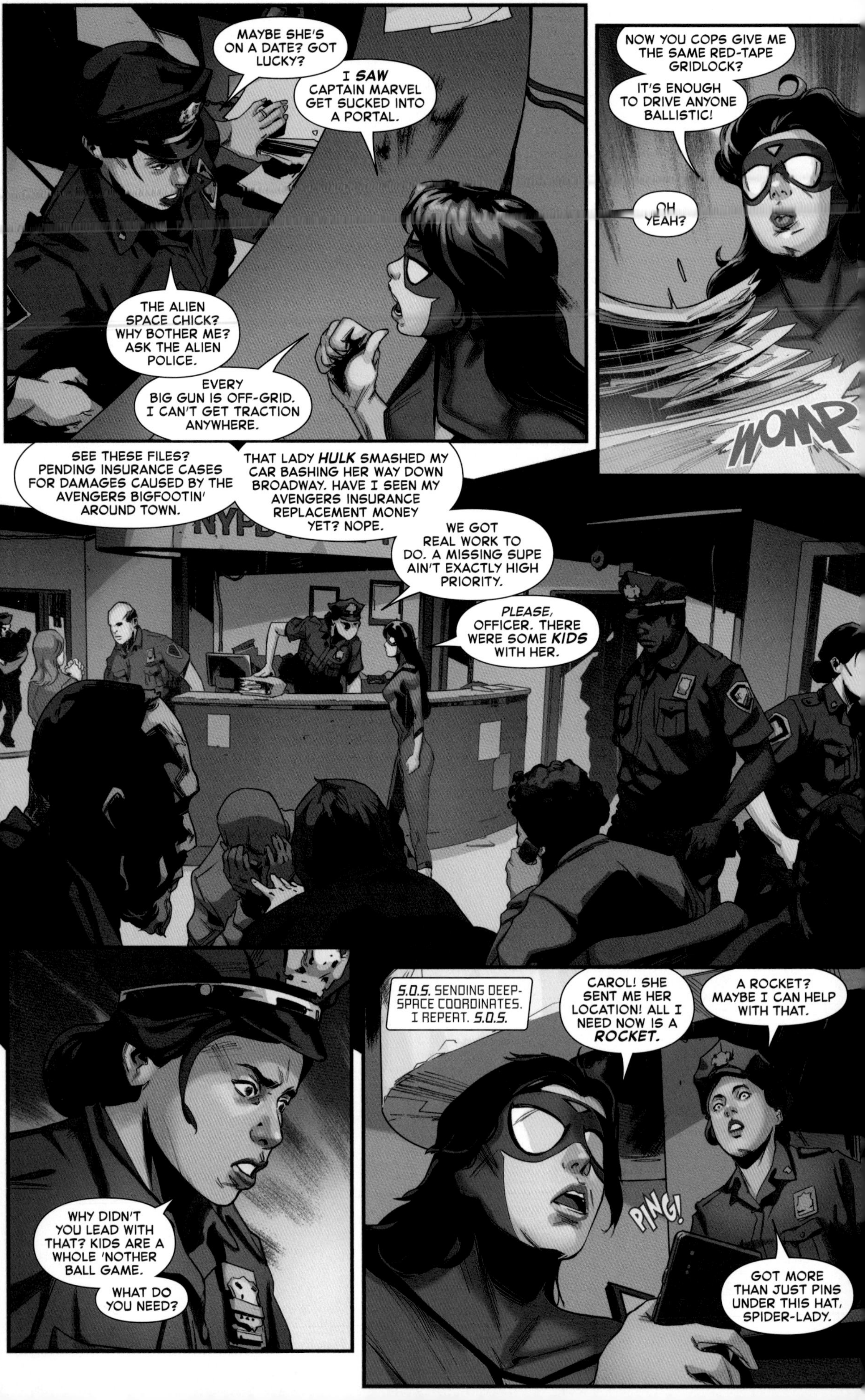
MAYBE SHE'S ON A DATE? GOT LUCKY?
I SAW CAPTAIN MARVEL GET SUCKED INTO A PORTAL.
THE ALIEN SPACE CHICK? WHY BOTHER ME? ASK THE ALIEN POLICE.
EVERY BIG GUN IS OFF-GRID. I CAN'T GET TRACTION ANYWHERE.
NOW YOU COPS GIVE ME THE SAME RED-TAPE GRIDLOCK?
IT'S ENOUGH TO DRIVE ANYONE BALLISTIC!
OH YEAH?
WOMP
SEE THESE FILES? PENDING INSURANCE CASES FOR DAMAGES CAUSED BY THE AVENGERS BIGFOOTIN' AROUND TOWN.
THAT LADY HULK SMASHED MY CAR BASHING HER WAY DOWN BROADWAY. HAVE I SEEN MY AVENGERS INSURANCE REPLACEMENT MONEY YET? NOPE.
WE GOT REAL WORK TO DO. A MISSING SUPE AIN'T EXACTLY HIGH PRIORITY.
PLEASE, OFFICER. THERE WERE SOME KIDS WITH HER.
WHY DIDN'T YOU LEAD WITH THAT? KIDS ARE A WHOLE 'NOTHER BALL GAME.
WHAT DO YOU NEED?
S.O.S. SENDING DEEP-SPACE COORDINATES. I REPEAT. S.O.S.
CAROL! SHE SENT ME HER LOCATION! ALL I NEED NOW IS A ROCKET.
A ROCKET? MAYBE I CAN HELP WITH THAT.
PING!
GOT MORE THAN JUST PINS UNDER THIS HAT, SPIDER-LADY.

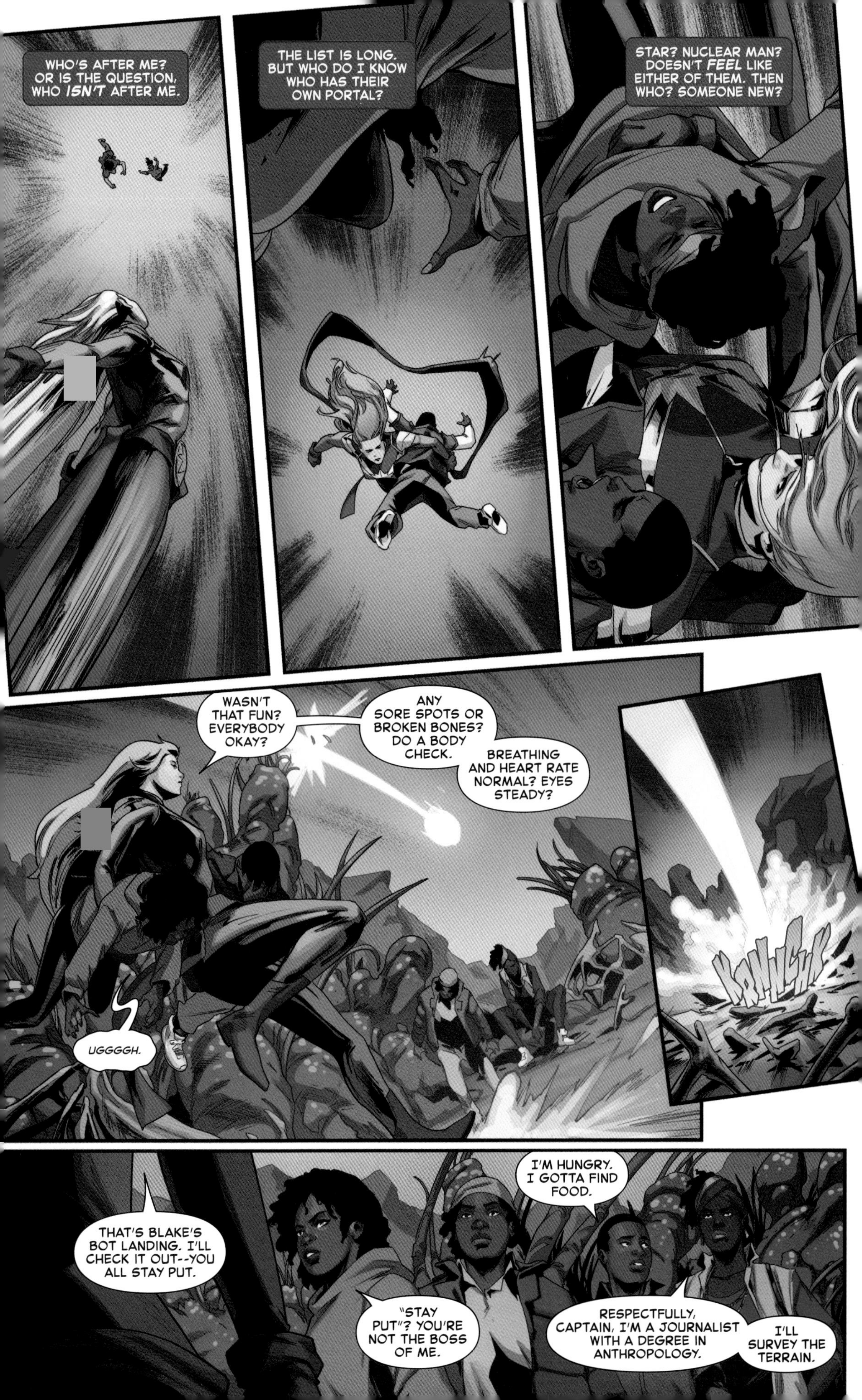
WHO'S AFTER ME? OR IS THE QUESTION, WHO *ISN'T* AFTER ME.
THE LIST IS LONG. BUT WHO DO I KNOW WHO HAS THEIR OWN PORTAL?
STAR? NUCLEAR MAN? DOESN'T *FEEL* LIKE EITHER OF THEM. THEN WHO? SOMEONE NEW?
WASN'T THAT FUN? EVERYBODY OKAY?
ANY SORE SPOTS OR BROKEN BONES? DO A BODY CHECK.
BREATHING AND HEART RATE NORMAL? EYES STEADY?
UGGGGH.
THAT'S BLAKE'S BOT LANDING. I'LL CHECK IT OUT--YOU ALL STAY PUT.
I'M HUNGRY. I GOTTA FIND FOOD.
"STAY PUT"? YOU'RE NOT THE BOSS OF ME.
RESPECTFULLY, CAPTAIN, I'M A JOURNALIST WITH A DEGREE IN ANTHROPOLOGY.
I'LL SURVEY THE TERRAIN.

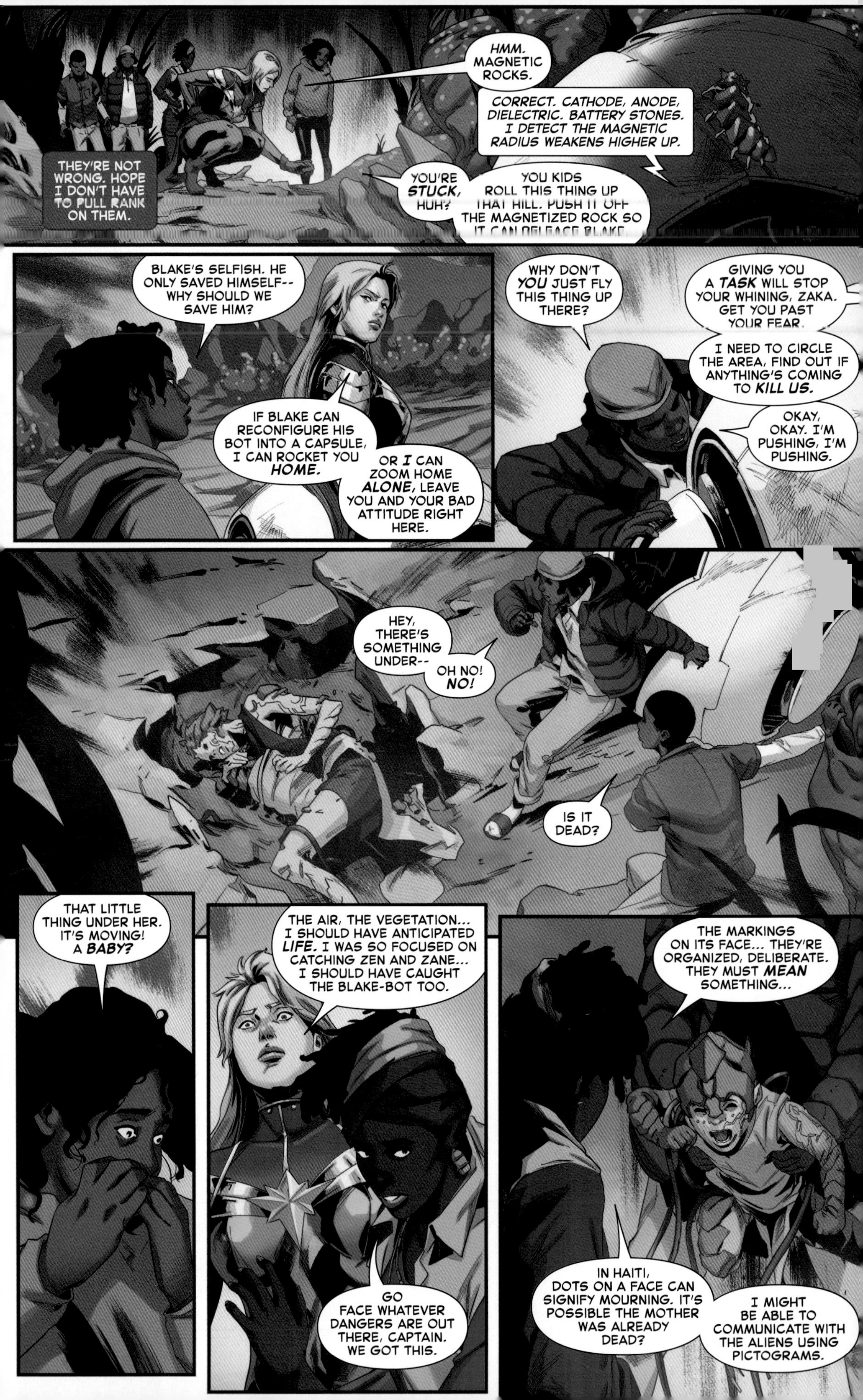

HMM. MAGNETIC ROCKS.
CORRECT. CATHODE, ANODE, DIELECTRIC. BATTERY STONES. I DETECT THE MAGNETIC RADIUS WEAKENS HIGHER UP.
THEY'RE NOT WRONG. HOPE I DON'T HAVE TO PULL RANK ON THEM.
YOU'RE STUCK, HUH?
YOU KIDS ROLL THIS THING UP THAT HILL. PUSH IT OFF THE MAGNETIZED ROCK SO IT CAN RELEASE BLAKE
BLAKE'S SELFISH. HE ONLY SAVED HIMSELF-- WHY SHOULD WE SAVE HIM?
IF BLAKE CAN RECONFIGURE HIS BOT INTO A CAPSULE, I CAN ROCKET YOU HOME.
OR I CAN ZOOM HOME ALONE, LEAVE YOU AND YOUR BAD ATTITUDE RIGHT HERE.
WHY DON'T YOU JUST FLY THIS THING UP THERE?
GIVING YOU A TASK WILL STOP YOUR WHINING, ZAKA. GET YOU PAST YOUR FEAR.
I NEED TO CIRCLE THE AREA, FIND OUT IF ANYTHING'S COMING TO KILL US.
OKAY, OKAY. I'M PUSHING, I'M PUSHING.
HEY, THERE'S SOMETHING UNDER--
OH NO! NO!
IS IT DEAD?
THAT LITTLE THING UNDER HER. IT'S MOVING! A BABY?
THE AIR, THE VEGETATION... I SHOULD HAVE ANTICIPATED LIFE. I WAS SO FOCUSED ON CATCHING ZEN AND ZANE... I SHOULD HAVE CAUGHT THE BLAKE-BOT TOO.
GO FACE WHATEVER DANGERS ARE OUT THERE, CAPTAIN. WE GOT THIS.
THE MARKINGS ON ITS FACE... THEY'RE ORGANIZED, DELIBERATE. THEY MUST MEAN SOMETHING...
IN HAITI, DOTS ON A FACE CAN SIGNIFY MOURNING. IT'S POSSIBLE THE MOTHER WAS ALREADY DEAD?
I MIGHT BE ABLE TO COMMUNICATE WITH THE ALIENS USING PICTOGRAMS.

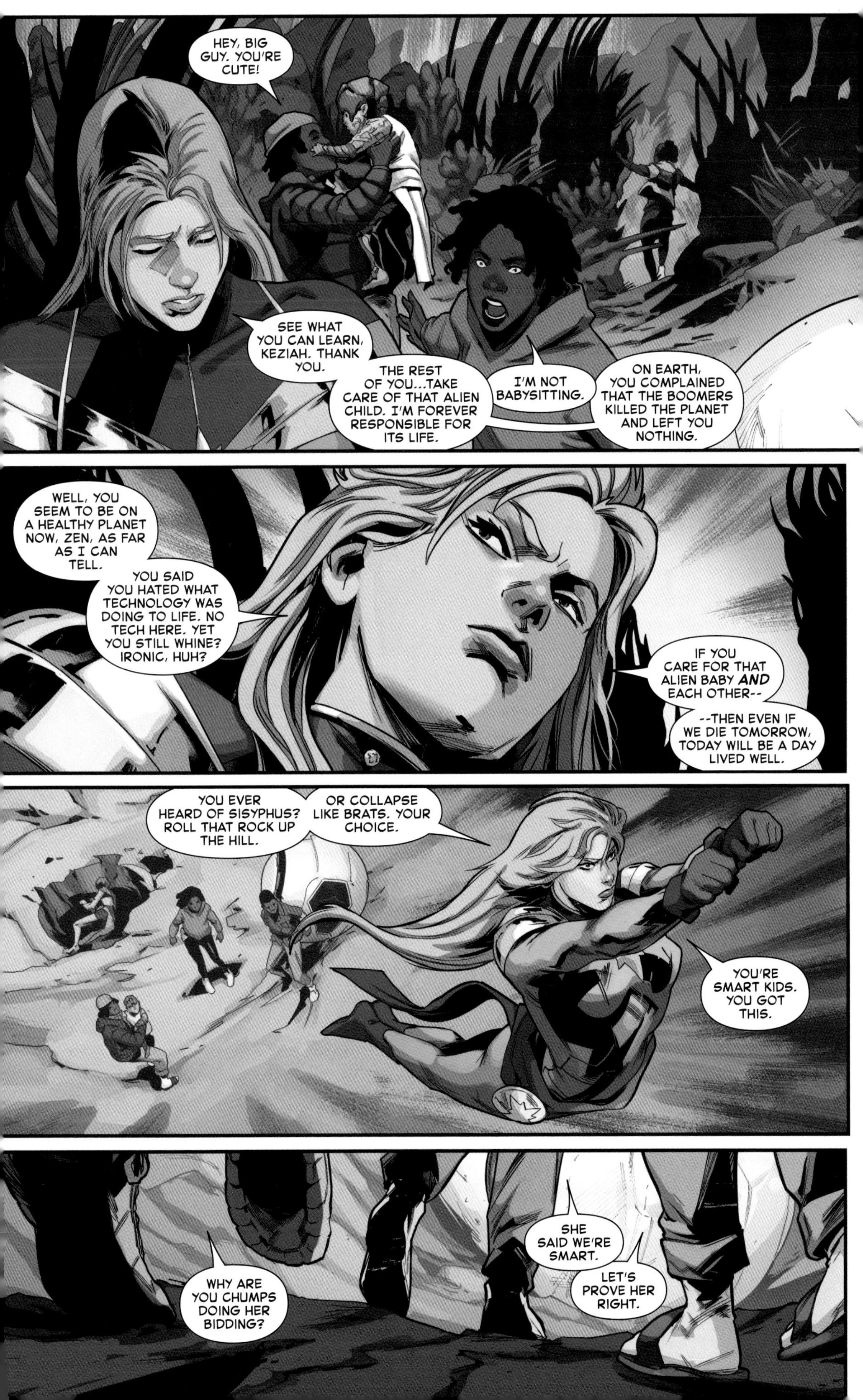
HEY, BIG GUY. YOU'RE CUTE!
SEE WHAT YOU CAN LEARN, KEZIAH. THANK YOU.
THE REST OF YOU...TAKE CARE OF THAT ALIEN CHILD. I'M FOREVER RESPONSIBLE FOR ITS LIFE.
I'M NOT BABYSITTING.
ON EARTH, YOU COMPLAINED THAT THE BOOMERS KILLED THE PLANET AND LEFT YOU NOTHING.
WELL, YOU SEEM TO BE ON A HEALTHY PLANET NOW, ZEN, AS FAR AS I CAN TELL.
YOU SAID YOU HATED WHAT TECHNOLOGY WAS DOING TO LIFE. NO TECH HERE. YET YOU STILL WHINE? IRONIC, HUH?
IF YOU CARE FOR THAT ALIEN BABY **AND** EACH OTHER--
--THEN EVEN IF WE DIE TOMORROW, TODAY WILL BE A DAY LIVED WELL.
YOU EVER HEARD OF SISYPHUS? ROLL THAT ROCK UP THE HILL.
OR COLLAPSE LIKE BRATS. YOUR CHOICE.
YOU'RE SMART KIDS. YOU GOT THIS.
WHY ARE YOU CHUMPS DOING HER BIDDING?
SHE SAID WE'RE SMART.
LET'S PROVE HER RIGHT.

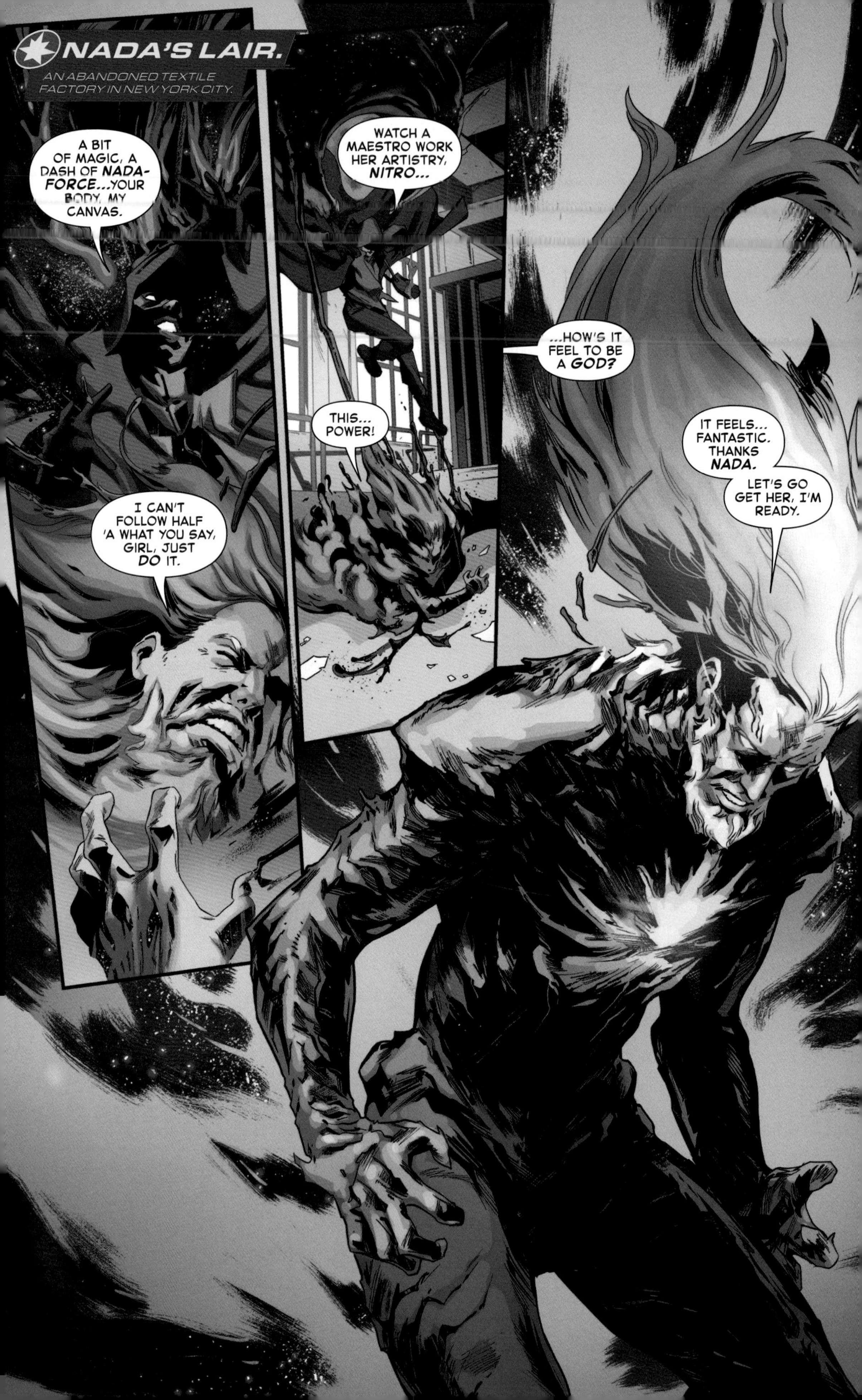
NADA'S LAIR.
AN ABANDONED TEXTILE FACTORY IN NEW YORK CITY.
A BIT OF MAGIC, A DASH OF NADA-FORCE...YOUR BODY, MY CANVAS.
I CAN'T FOLLOW HALF 'A WHAT YOU SAY, GIRL, JUST DO IT.
WATCH A MAESTRO WORK HER ARTISTRY, NITRO...
THIS... POWER!
...HOW'S IT FEEL TO BE A GOD?
IT FEELS... FANTASTIC. THANKS NADA.
LET'S GO GET HER, I'M READY.

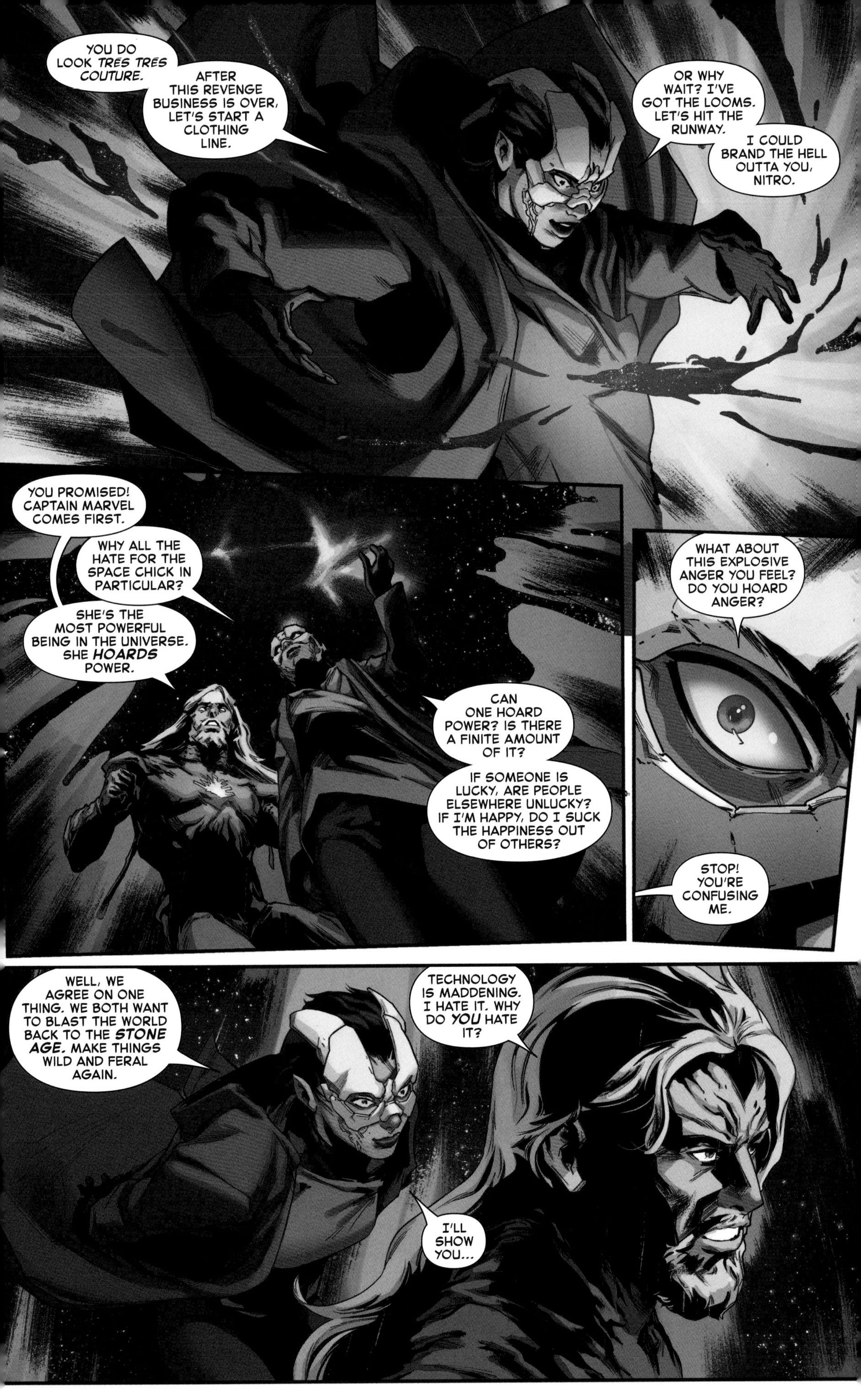
YOU DO LOOK *TRÈS TRÈS COUTURE.*
AFTER THIS REVENGE BUSINESS IS OVER, LET'S START A CLOTHING LINE.
OR WHY WAIT? I'VE GOT THE LOOMS. LET'S HIT THE RUNWAY.
I COULD BRAND THE HELL OUTTA YOU, NITRO.
YOU PROMISED! CAPTAIN MARVEL COMES FIRST.
WHY ALL THE HATE FOR THE SPACE CHICK IN PARTICULAR?
SHE'S THE MOST POWERFUL BEING IN THE UNIVERSE. SHE ***HOARDS*** POWER.
CAN ONE HOARD POWER? IS THERE A FINITE AMOUNT OF IT?
IF SOMEONE IS LUCKY, ARE PEOPLE ELSEWHERE UNLUCKY? IF I'M HAPPY, DO I SUCK THE HAPPINESS OUT OF OTHERS?
WHAT ABOUT THIS EXPLOSIVE ANGER YOU FEEL? DO YOU HOARD ANGER?
STOP! YOU'RE CONFUSING ME.
WELL, WE AGREE ON ONE THING. WE BOTH WANT TO BLAST THE WORLD BACK TO THE ***STONE AGE.*** MAKE THINGS WILD AND FERAL AGAIN.
TECHNOLOGY IS MADDENING. I HATE IT. WHY DO ***YOU*** HATE IT?
I'LL SHOW YOU...

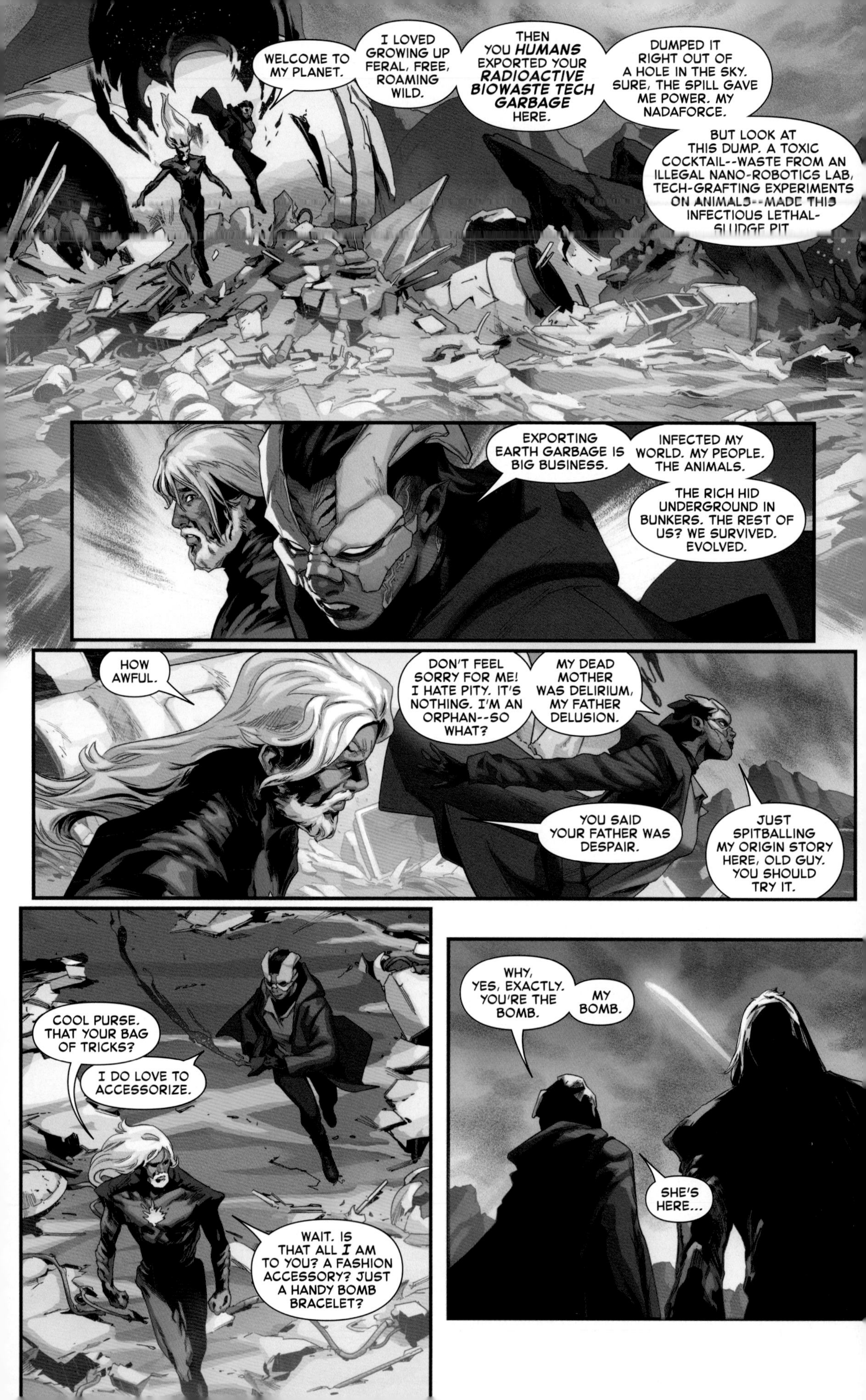
WELCOME TO MY PLANET.
I LOVED GROWING UP FERAL, FREE, ROAMING WILD.
THEN YOU HUMANS EXPORTED YOUR RADIOACTIVE BIOWASTE TECH GARBAGE HERE.
DUMPED IT RIGHT OUT OF A HOLE IN THE SKY. SURE, THE SPILL GAVE ME POWER. MY NADAFORCE.
BUT LOOK AT THIS DUMP. A TOXIC COCKTAIL--WASTE FROM AN ILLEGAL NANO-ROBOTICS LAB, TECH-GRAFTING EXPERIMENTS ON ANIMALS--MADE THIS INFECTIOUS LETHAL-SLUDGE PIT.
EXPORTING EARTH GARBAGE IS BIG BUSINESS.
INFECTED MY WORLD. MY PEOPLE. THE ANIMALS.
THE RICH HID UNDERGROUND IN BUNKERS. THE REST OF US? WE SURVIVED. EVOLVED.
HOW AWFUL.
DON'T FEEL SORRY FOR ME! I HATE PITY. IT'S NOTHING. I'M AN ORPHAN--SO WHAT?
MY DEAD MOTHER WAS DELIRIUM, MY FATHER DELUSION.
YOU SAID YOUR FATHER WAS DESPAIR.
JUST SPITBALLING MY ORIGIN STORY HERE, OLD GUY. YOU SHOULD TRY IT.
COOL PURSE. THAT YOUR BAG OF TRICKS?
I DO LOVE TO ACCESSORIZE.
WAIT. IS THAT ALL I AM TO YOU? A FASHION ACCESSORY? JUST A HANDY BOMB BRACELET?
WHY, YES, EXACTLY. YOU'RE THE BOMB.
MY BOMB.
SHE'S HERE...

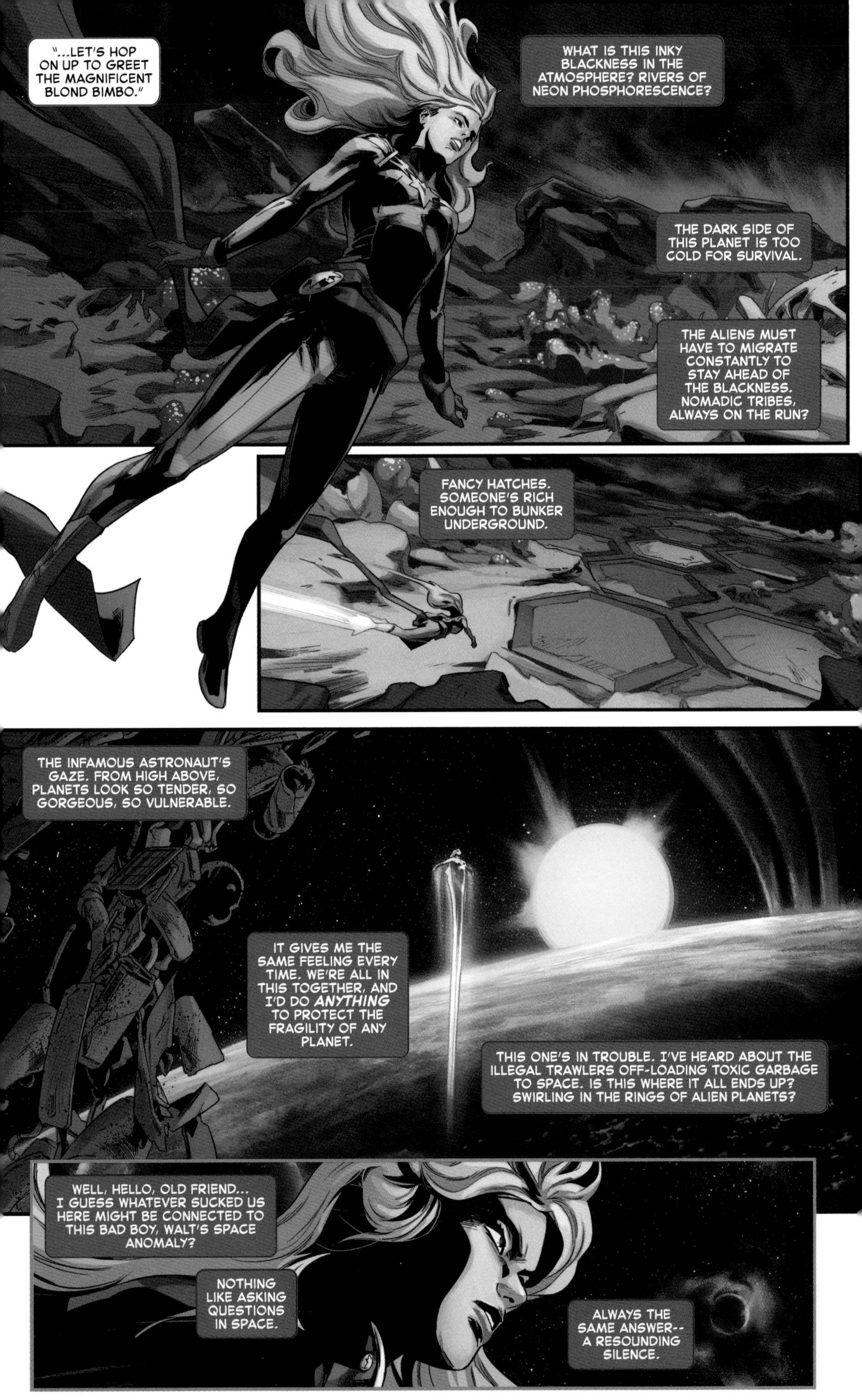
"...LET'S HOP ON UP TO GREET THE MAGNIFICENT BLOND BIMBO."
WHAT IS THIS INKY BLACKNESS IN THE ATMOSPHERE? RIVERS OF NEON PHOSPHORESCENCE?
THE DARK SIDE OF THIS PLANET IS TOO COLD FOR SURVIVAL.
THE ALIENS MUST HAVE TO MIGRATE CONSTANTLY TO STAY AHEAD OF THE BLACKNESS. NOMADIC TRIBES, ALWAYS ON THE RUN?
FANCY HATCHES. SOMEONE'S RICH ENOUGH TO BUNKER UNDERGROUND.
THE INFAMOUS ASTRONAUT'S GAZE. FROM HIGH ABOVE, PLANETS LOOK SO TENDER, SO GORGEOUS, SO VULNERABLE.
IT GIVES ME THE SAME FEELING EVERY TIME. WE'RE ALL IN THIS TOGETHER, AND I'D DO *ANYTHING* TO PROTECT THE FRAGILITY OF ANY PLANET.
THIS ONE'S IN TROUBLE. I'VE HEARD ABOUT THE ILLEGAL TRAWLERS OFF-LOADING TOXIC GARBAGE TO SPACE. IS THIS WHERE IT ALL ENDS UP? SWIRLING IN THE RINGS OF ALIEN PLANETS?
WELL, HELLO, OLD FRIEND... I GUESS WHATEVER SUCKED US HERE MIGHT BE CONNECTED TO THIS BAD BOY, WALT'S SPACE ANOMALY?
NOTHING LIKE ASKING QUESTIONS IN SPACE.
ALWAYS THE SAME ANSWER-- A RESOUNDING SILENCE.

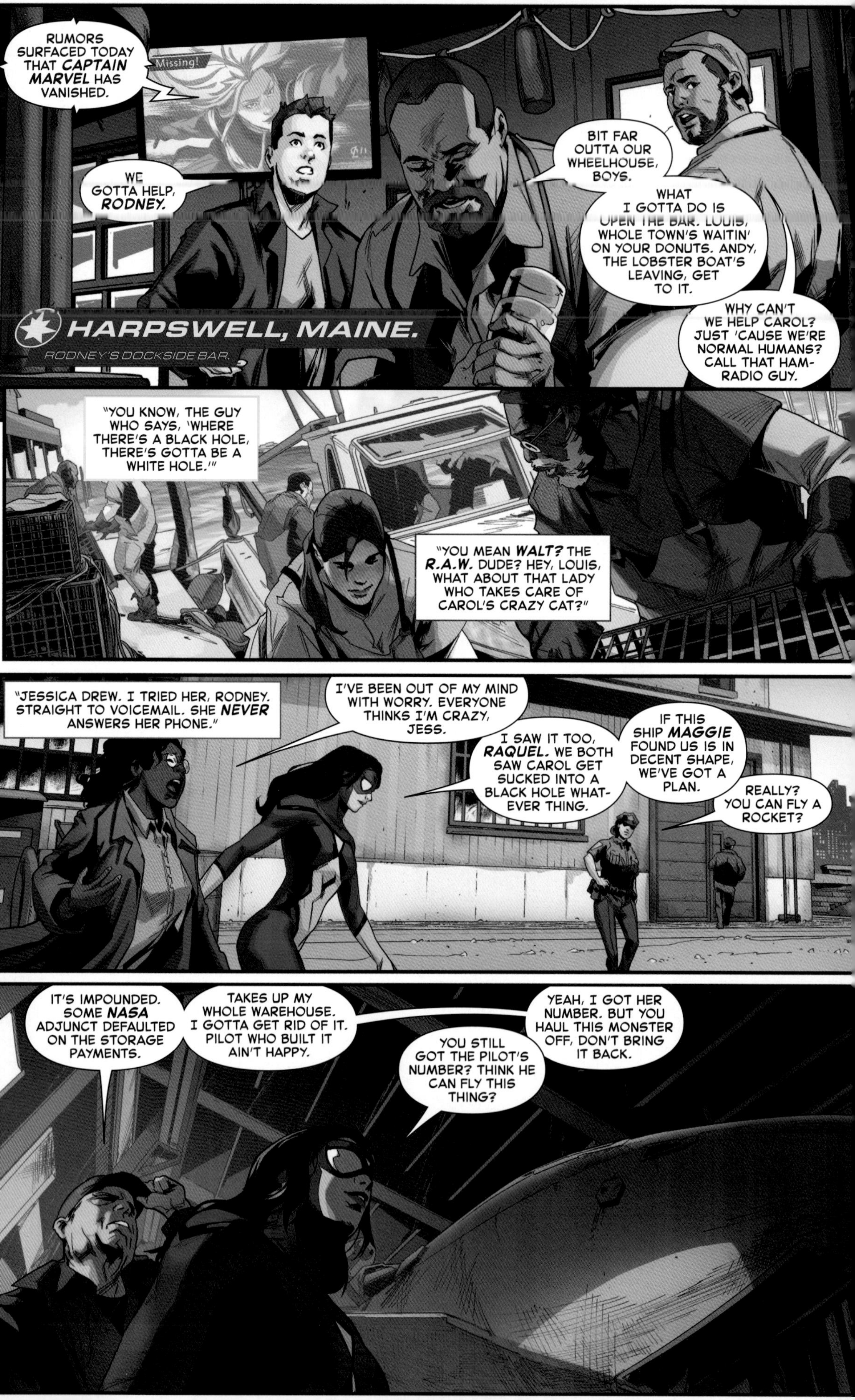
RUMORS SURFACED TODAY THAT CAPTAIN MARVEL HAS VANISHED.
Missing!
WE GOTTA HELP, RODNEY.
BIT FAR OUTTA OUR WHEELHOUSE, BOYS.
WHAT I GOTTA DO IS OPEN THE BAR. LOUIS, WHOLE TOWN'S WAITIN' ON YOUR DONUTS. ANDY, THE LOBSTER BOAT'S LEAVING, GET TO IT.
HARPSWELL, MAINE.
RODNEY'S DOCKSIDE BAR.
WHY CAN'T WE HELP CAROL? JUST 'CAUSE WE'RE NORMAL HUMANS? CALL THAT HAM-RADIO GUY.
"YOU KNOW, THE GUY WHO SAYS, 'WHERE THERE'S A BLACK HOLE, THERE'S GOTTA BE A WHITE HOLE.'"
"YOU MEAN WALT? THE R.A.W. DUDE? HEY, LOUIS, WHAT ABOUT THAT LADY WHO TAKES CARE OF CAROL'S CRAZY CAT?"
"JESSICA DREW. I TRIED HER, RODNEY. STRAIGHT TO VOICEMAIL. SHE NEVER ANSWERS HER PHONE."
I'VE BEEN OUT OF MY MIND WITH WORRY. EVERYONE THINKS I'M CRAZY, JESS.
I SAW IT TOO, RAQUEL. WE BOTH SAW CAROL GET SUCKED INTO A BLACK HOLE WHATEVER THING.
IF THIS SHIP MAGGIE FOUND US IS IN DECENT SHAPE, WE'VE GOT A PLAN.
REALLY? YOU CAN FLY A ROCKET?
IT'S IMPOUNDED. SOME NASA ADJUNCT DEFAULTED ON THE STORAGE PAYMENTS.
TAKES UP MY WHOLE WAREHOUSE. I GOTTA GET RID OF IT. PILOT WHO BUILT IT AIN'T HAPPY.
YOU STILL GOT THE PILOT'S NUMBER? THINK HE CAN FLY THIS THING?
YEAH, I GOT HER NUMBER. BUT YOU HAUL THIS MONSTER OFF, DON'T BRING IT BACK.

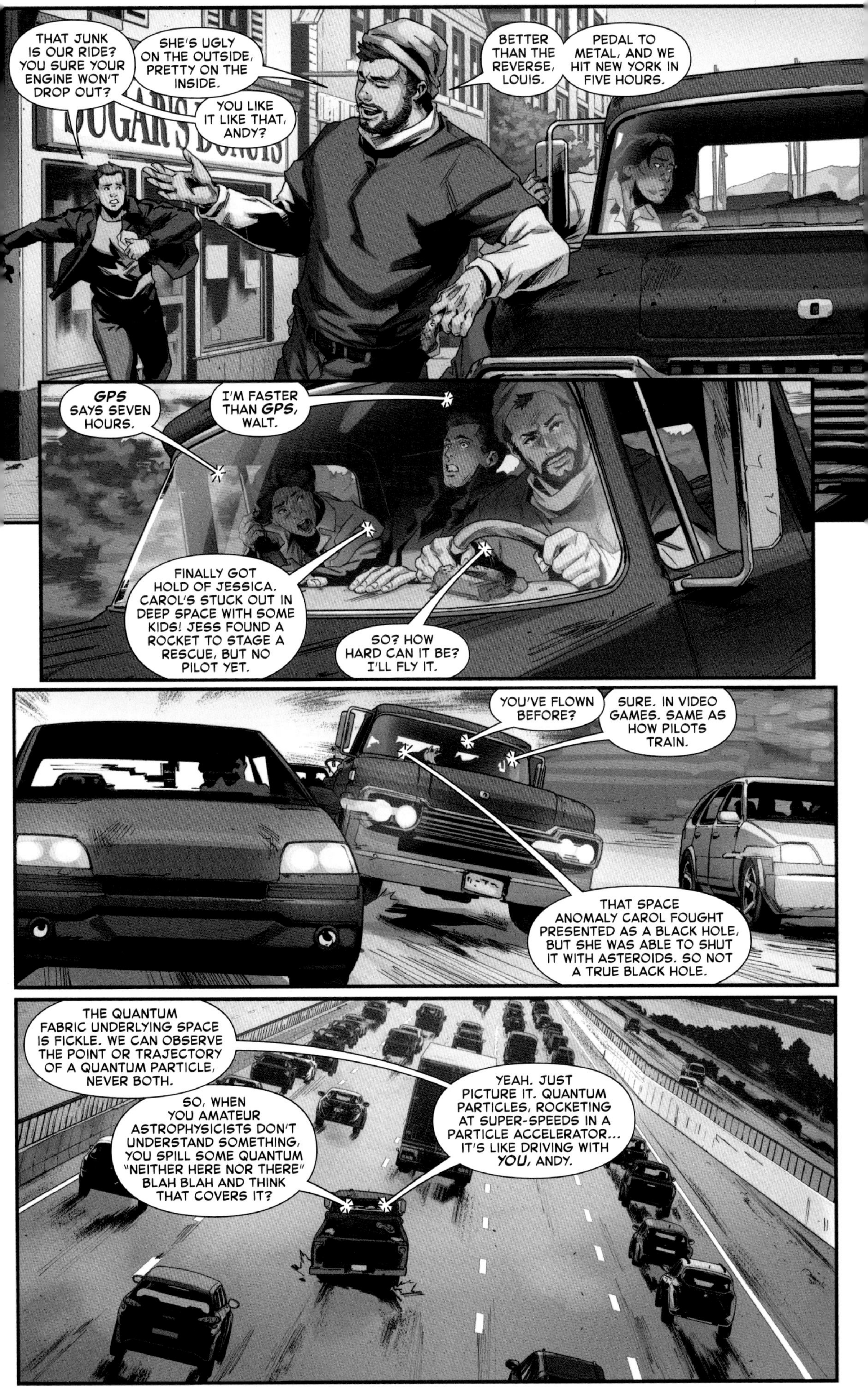

THAT JUNK IS OUR RIDE? YOU SURE YOUR ENGINE WON'T DROP OUT?
SHE'S UGLY ON THE OUTSIDE, PRETTY ON THE INSIDE.
YOU LIKE IT LIKE THAT, ANDY?
BETTER THAN THE REVERSE, LOUIS.
PEDAL TO METAL, AND WE HIT NEW YORK IN FIVE HOURS.
GPS SAYS SEVEN HOURS.
I'M FASTER THAN GPS, WALT.
FINALLY GOT HOLD OF JESSICA. CAROL'S STUCK OUT IN DEEP SPACE WITH SOME KIDS! JESS FOUND A ROCKET TO STAGE A RESCUE, BUT NO PILOT YET.
SO? HOW HARD CAN IT BE? I'LL FLY IT.
YOU'VE FLOWN BEFORE?
SURE. IN VIDEO GAMES. SAME AS HOW PILOTS TRAIN.
THAT SPACE ANOMALY CAROL FOUGHT PRESENTED AS A BLACK HOLE, BUT SHE WAS ABLE TO SHUT IT WITH ASTEROIDS. SO NOT A TRUE BLACK HOLE.
THE QUANTUM FABRIC UNDERLYING SPACE IS FICKLE. WE CAN OBSERVE THE POINT OR TRAJECTORY OF A QUANTUM PARTICLE, NEVER BOTH.
SO, WHEN YOU AMATEUR ASTROPHYSICISTS DON'T UNDERSTAND SOMETHING, YOU SPILL SOME QUANTUM "NEITHER HERE NOR THERE" BLAH BLAH AND THINK THAT COVERS IT?
YEAH. JUST PICTURE IT. QUANTUM PARTICLES, ROCKETING AT SUPER-SPEEDS IN A PARTICLE ACCELERATOR... IT'S LIKE DRIVING WITH YOU, ANDY.

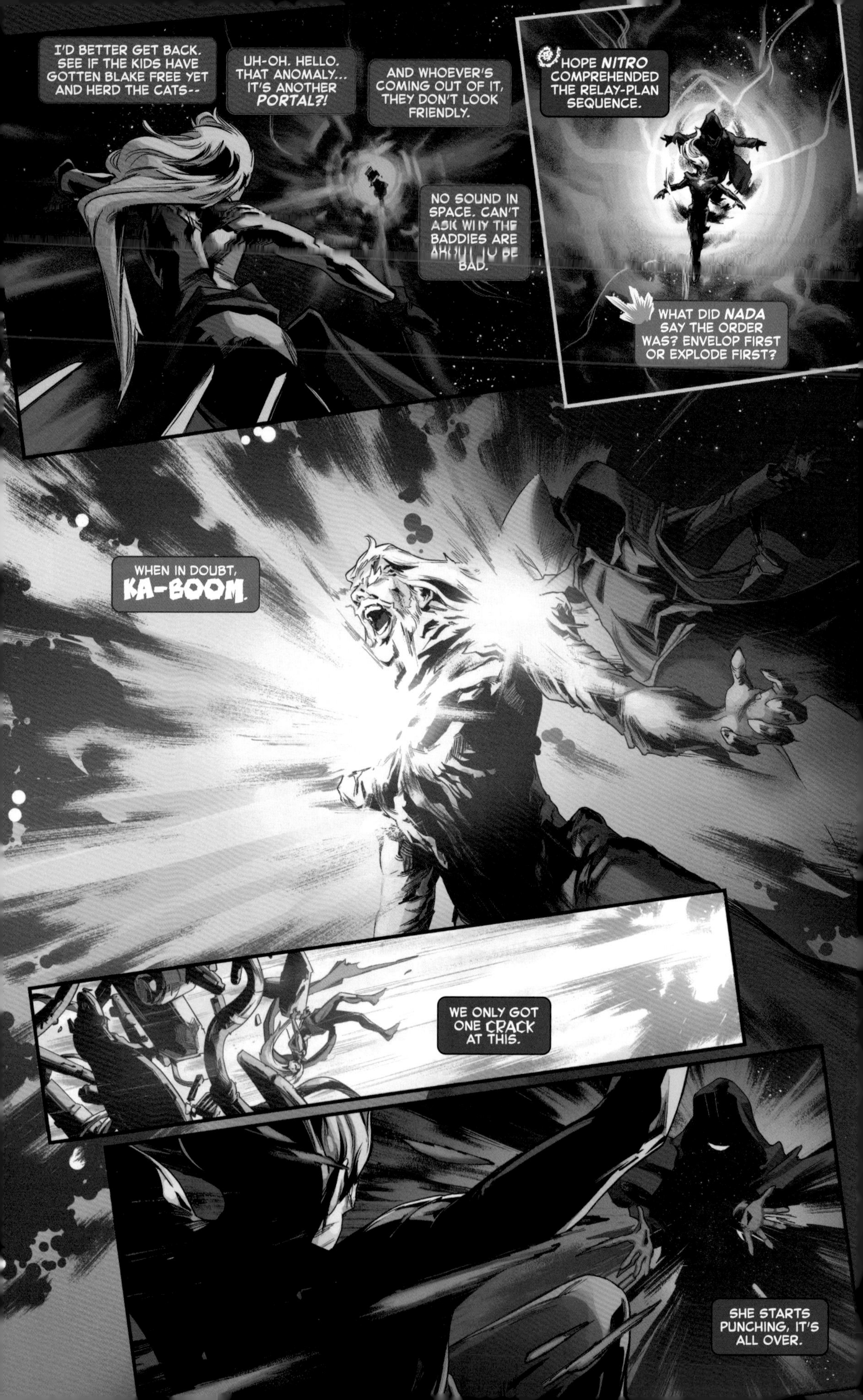
I'D BETTER GET BACK. SEE IF THE KIDS HAVE GOTTEN BLAKE FREE YET AND HERD THE CATS--
UH-OH. HELLO. THAT ANOMALY... IT'S ANOTHER PORTAL?!
AND WHOEVER'S COMING OUT OF IT, THEY DON'T LOOK FRIENDLY.
NO SOUND IN SPACE. CAN'T ASK WHY THE BADDIES ARE ABOUT TO BE BAD.
HOPE NITRO COMPREHENDED THE RELAY-PLAN SEQUENCE.
WHAT DID NADA SAY THE ORDER WAS? ENVELOP FIRST OR EXPLODE FIRST?
WHEN IN DOUBT, KA-BOOM.
WE ONLY GOT ONE CRACK AT THIS.
SHE STARTS PUNCHING, IT'S ALL OVER.

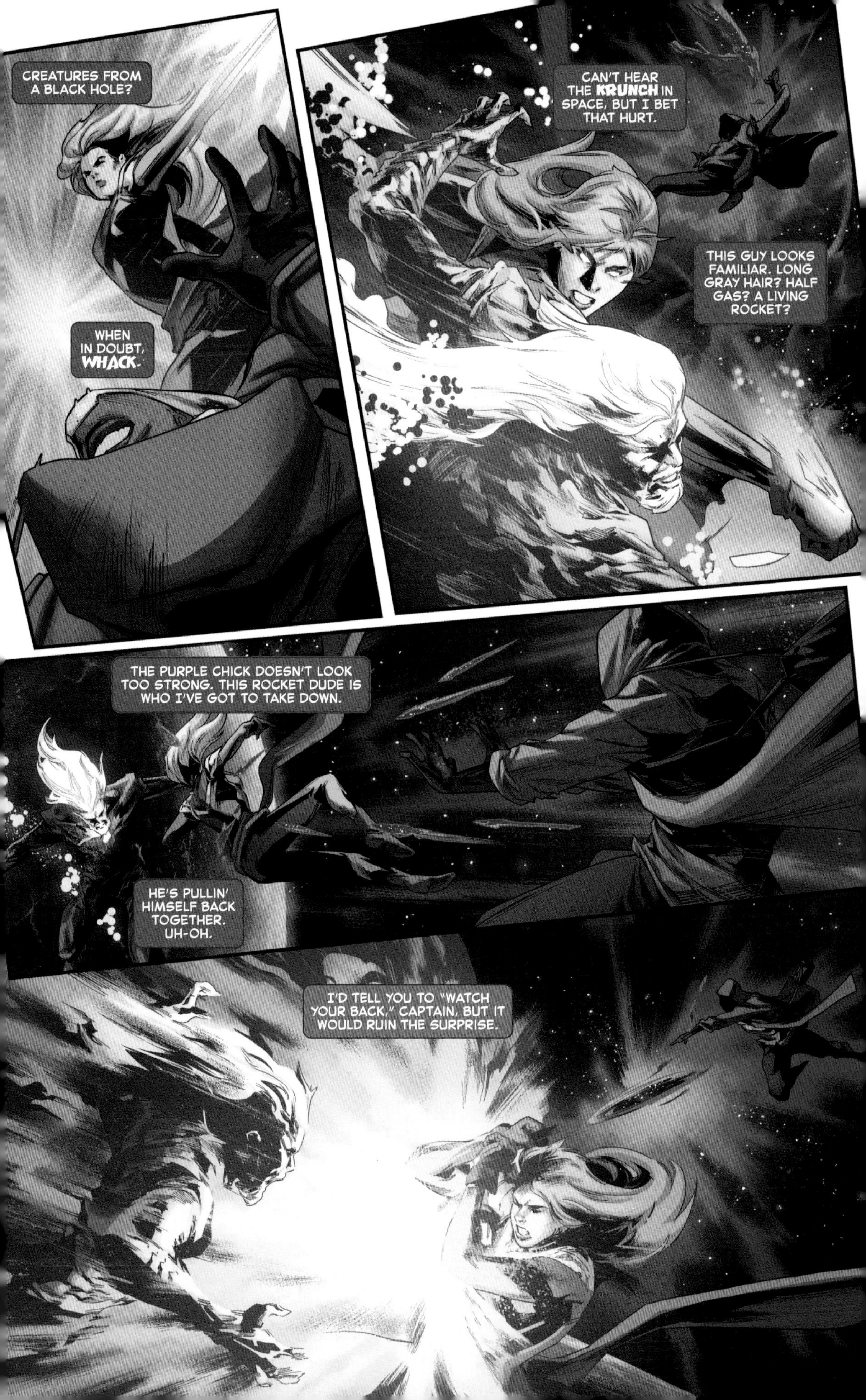
CREATURES FROM A BLACK HOLE?
WHEN IN DOUBT, WHACK.
CAN'T HEAR THE KRUNCH IN SPACE, BUT I BET THAT HURT.
THIS GUY LOOKS FAMILIAR. LONG GRAY HAIR? HALF GAS? A LIVING ROCKET?
THE PURPLE CHICK DOESN'T LOOK TOO STRONG. THIS ROCKET DUDE IS WHO I'VE GOT TO TAKE DOWN.
HE'S PULLIN' HIMSELF BACK TOGETHER. UH-OH.
I'D TELL YOU TO "WATCH YOUR BACK," CAPTAIN, BUT IT WOULD RUIN THE SURPRISE.

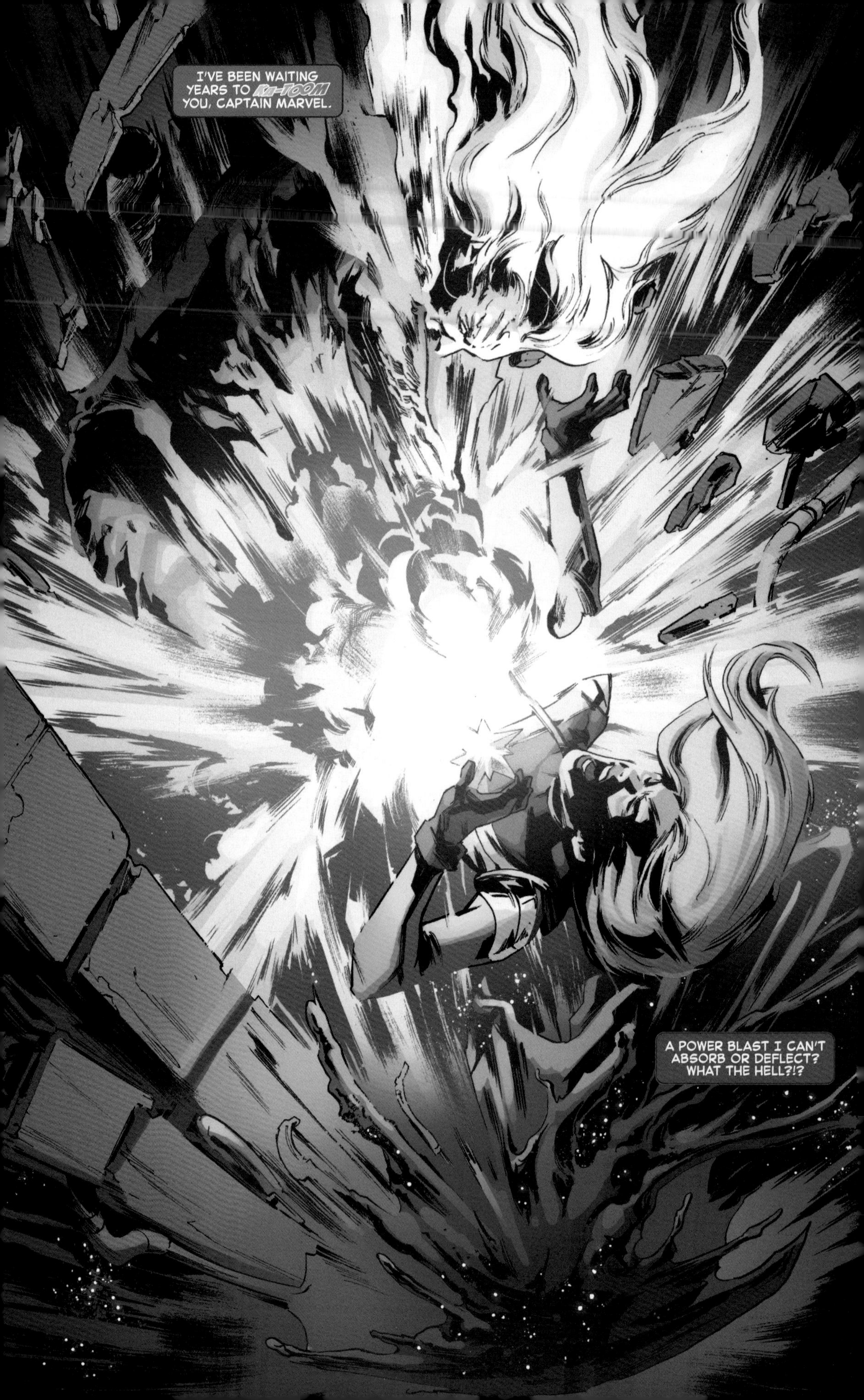
I'VE BEEN WAITING YEARS TO KA-TOOM YOU, CAPTAIN MARVEL.
A POWER BLAST I CAN'T ABSORB OR DEFLECT? WHAT THE HELL?!?

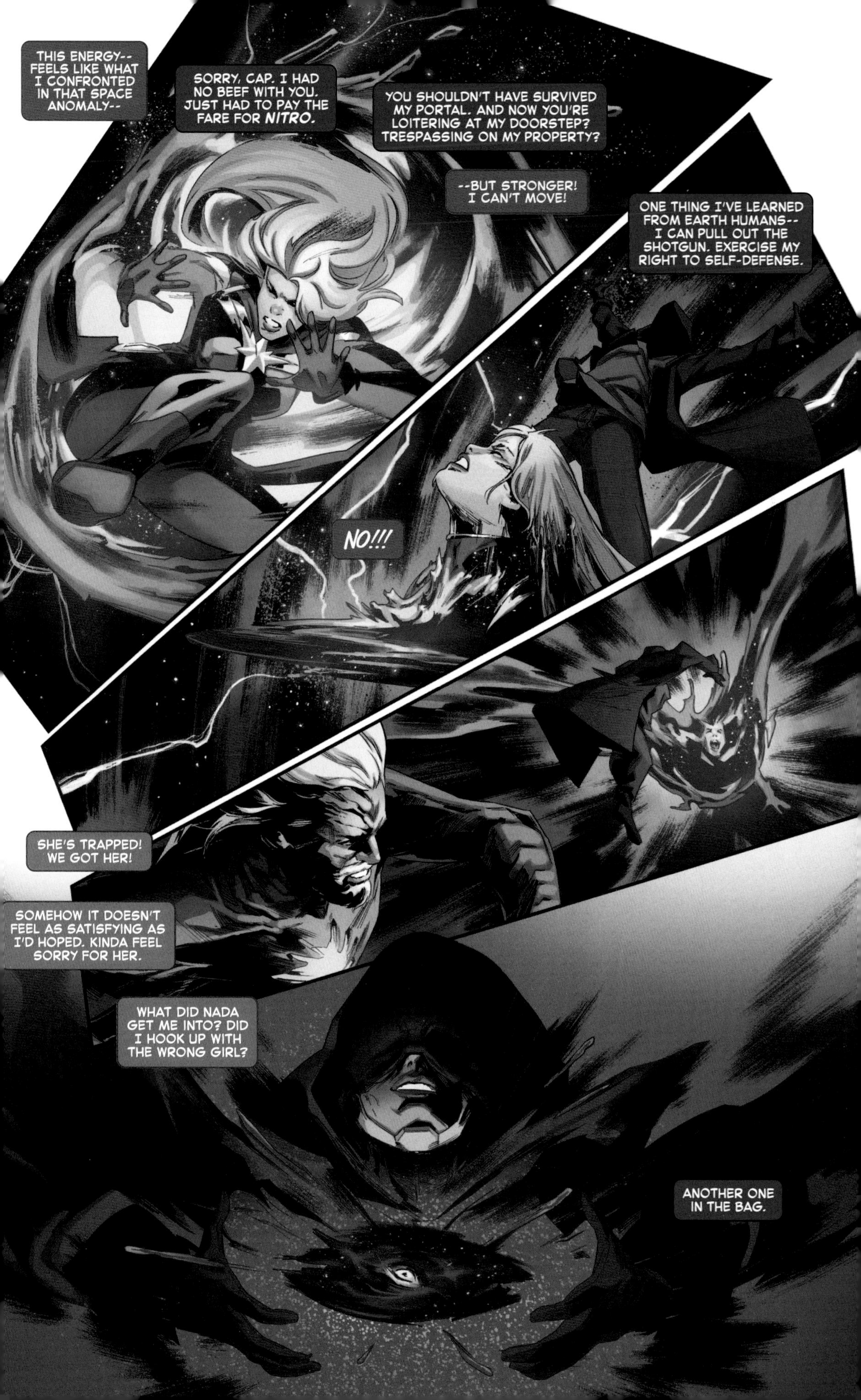
THIS ENERGY-- FEELS LIKE WHAT I CONFRONTED IN THAT SPACE ANOMALY--
SORRY, CAP. I HAD NO BEEF WITH YOU. JUST HAD TO PAY THE FARE FOR *NITRO.*
YOU SHOULDN'T HAVE SURVIVED MY PORTAL. AND NOW YOU'RE LOITERING AT MY DOORSTEP? TRESPASSING ON MY PROPERTY?
--BUT STRONGER! I CAN'T MOVE!
ONE THING I'VE LEARNED FROM EARTH HUMANS-- I CAN PULL OUT THE SHOTGUN. EXERCISE MY RIGHT TO SELF-DEFENSE.
NO!!!
SHE'S TRAPPED! WE GOT HER!
SOMEHOW IT DOESN'T FEEL AS SATISFYING AS I'D HOPED. KINDA FEEL SORRY FOR HER.
WHAT DID NADA GET ME INTO? DID I HOOK UP WITH THE WRONG GIRL?
ANOTHER ONE IN THE BAG.

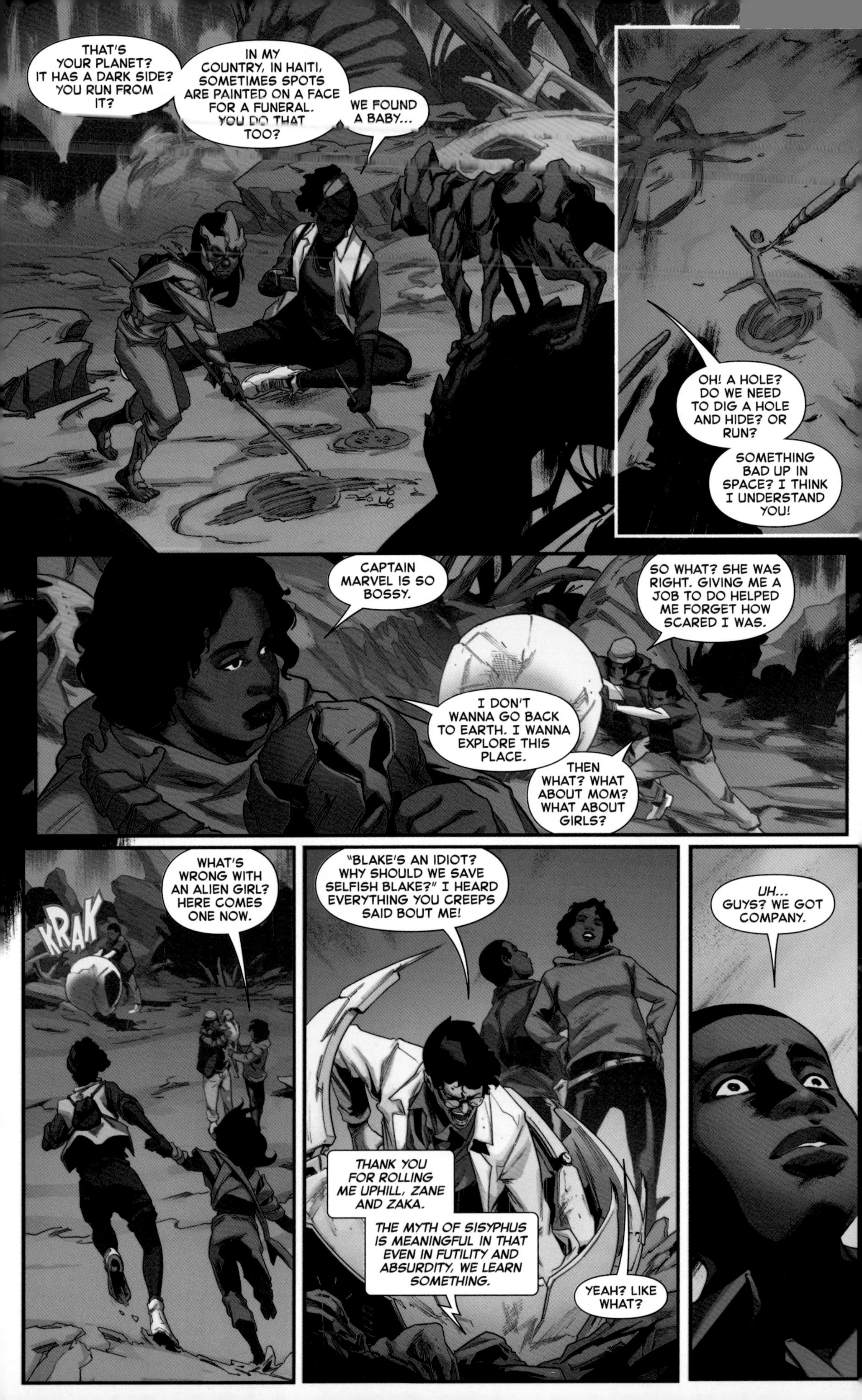
THAT'S YOUR PLANET? IT HAS A DARK SIDE? YOU RUN FROM IT?
IN MY COUNTRY, IN HAITI, SOMETIMES SPOTS ARE PAINTED ON A FACE FOR A FUNERAL. YOU DO THAT TOO?
WE FOUND A BABY...
OH! A HOLE? DO WE NEED TO DIG A HOLE AND HIDE? OR RUN?
SOMETHING BAD UP IN SPACE? I THINK I UNDERSTAND YOU!
CAPTAIN MARVEL IS SO BOSSY.
SO WHAT? SHE WAS RIGHT. GIVING ME A JOB TO DO HELPED ME FORGET HOW SCARED I WAS.
I DON'T WANNA GO BACK TO EARTH. I WANNA EXPLORE THIS PLACE.
THEN WHAT? WHAT ABOUT MOM? WHAT ABOUT GIRLS?
KRAK
WHAT'S WRONG WITH AN ALIEN GIRL? HERE COMES ONE NOW.
"BLAKE'S AN IDIOT? WHY SHOULD WE SAVE SELFISH BLAKE?" I HEARD EVERYTHING YOU CREEPS SAID BOUT ME!
THANK YOU FOR ROLLING ME UPHILL, ZANE AND ZAKA.
THE MYTH OF SISYPHUS IS MEANINGFUL IN THAT EVEN IN FUTILITY AND ABSURDITY, WE LEARN SOMETHING.
YEAH? LIKE WHAT?
UH... GUYS? WE GOT COMPANY.

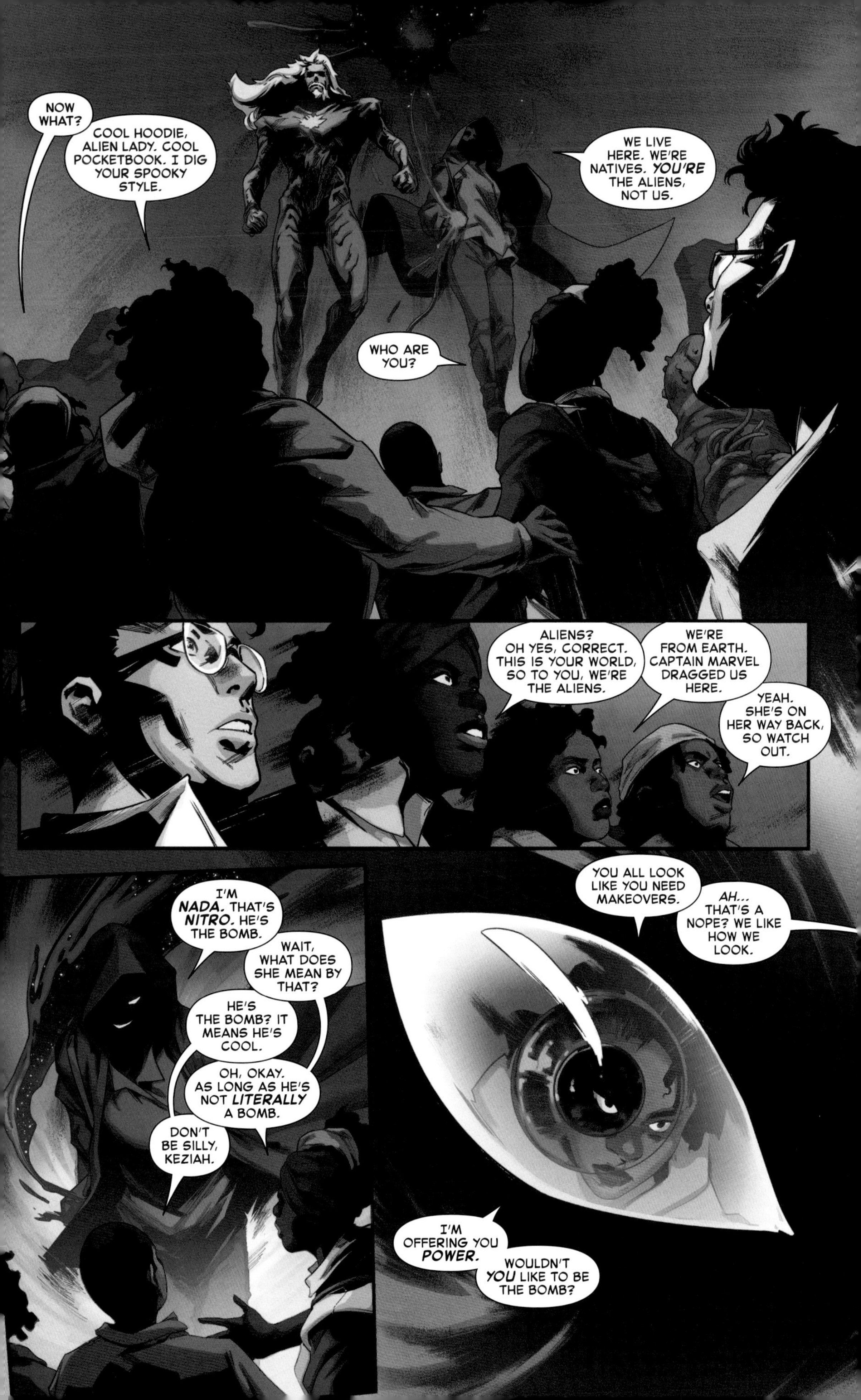
NOW WHAT?
COOL HOODIE, ALIEN LADY. COOL POCKETBOOK. I DIG YOUR SPOOKY STYLE.
WE LIVE HERE. WE'RE NATIVES. YOU'RE THE ALIENS, NOT US.
WHO ARE YOU?
ALIENS? OH YES, CORRECT. THIS IS YOUR WORLD, SO TO YOU, WE'RE THE ALIENS.
WE'RE FROM EARTH. CAPTAIN MARVEL DRAGGED US HERE.
YEAH. SHE'S ON HER WAY BACK, SO WATCH OUT.
I'M NADA. THAT'S NITRO. HE'S THE BOMB.
WAIT, WHAT DOES SHE MEAN BY THAT?
HE'S THE BOMB? IT MEANS HE'S COOL.
OH, OKAY. AS LONG AS HE'S NOT LITERALLY A BOMB.
DON'T BE SILLY, KEZIAH.
YOU ALL LOOK LIKE YOU NEED MAKEOVERS.
AH... THAT'S A NOPE? WE LIKE HOW WE LOOK.
I'M OFFERING YOU POWER.
WOULDN'T YOU LIKE TO BE THE BOMB?

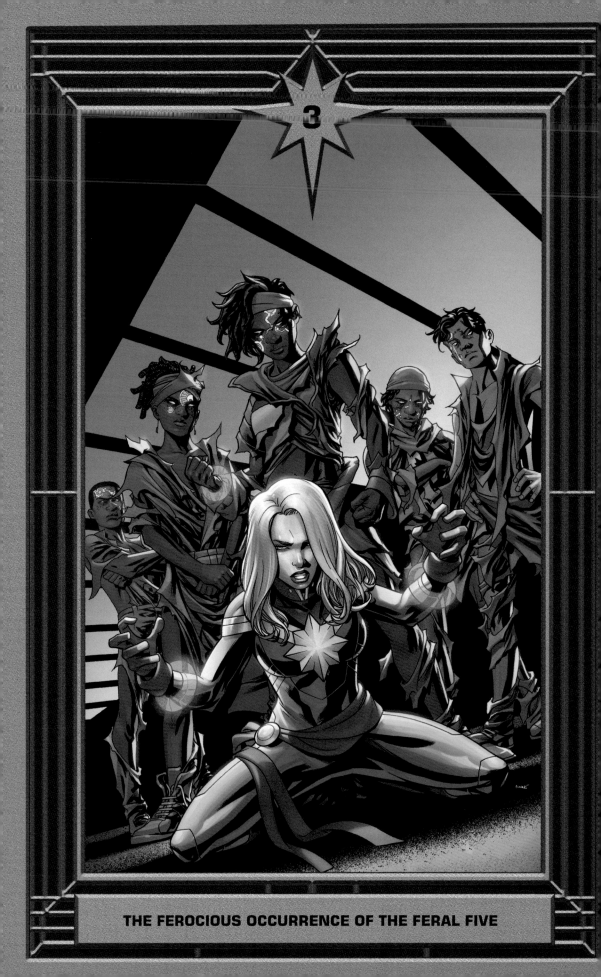

THE FEROCIOUS OCCURRENCE OF THE FERAL FIVE

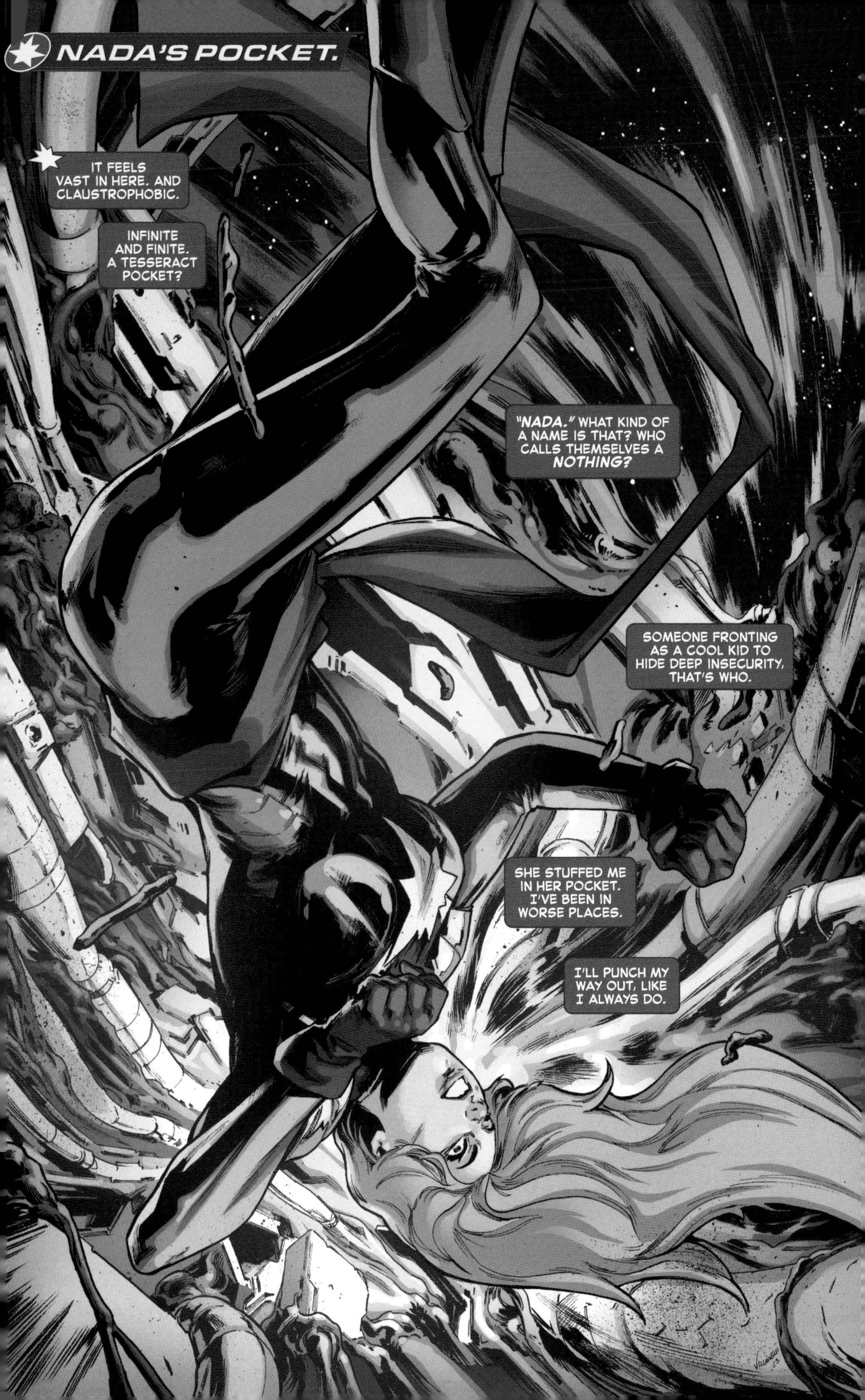
NADA'S POCKET.
IT FEELS VAST IN HERE. AND CLAUSTROPHOBIC.
INFINITE AND FINITE. A TESSERACT POCKET?
"NADA." WHAT KIND OF A NAME IS THAT? WHO CALLS THEMSELVES A NOTHING?
SOMEONE FRONTING AS A COOL KID TO HIDE DEEP INSECURITY, THAT'S WHO.
SHE STUFFED ME IN HER POCKET. I'VE BEEN IN WORSE PLACES.
I'LL PUNCH MY WAY OUT, LIKE I ALWAYS DO.

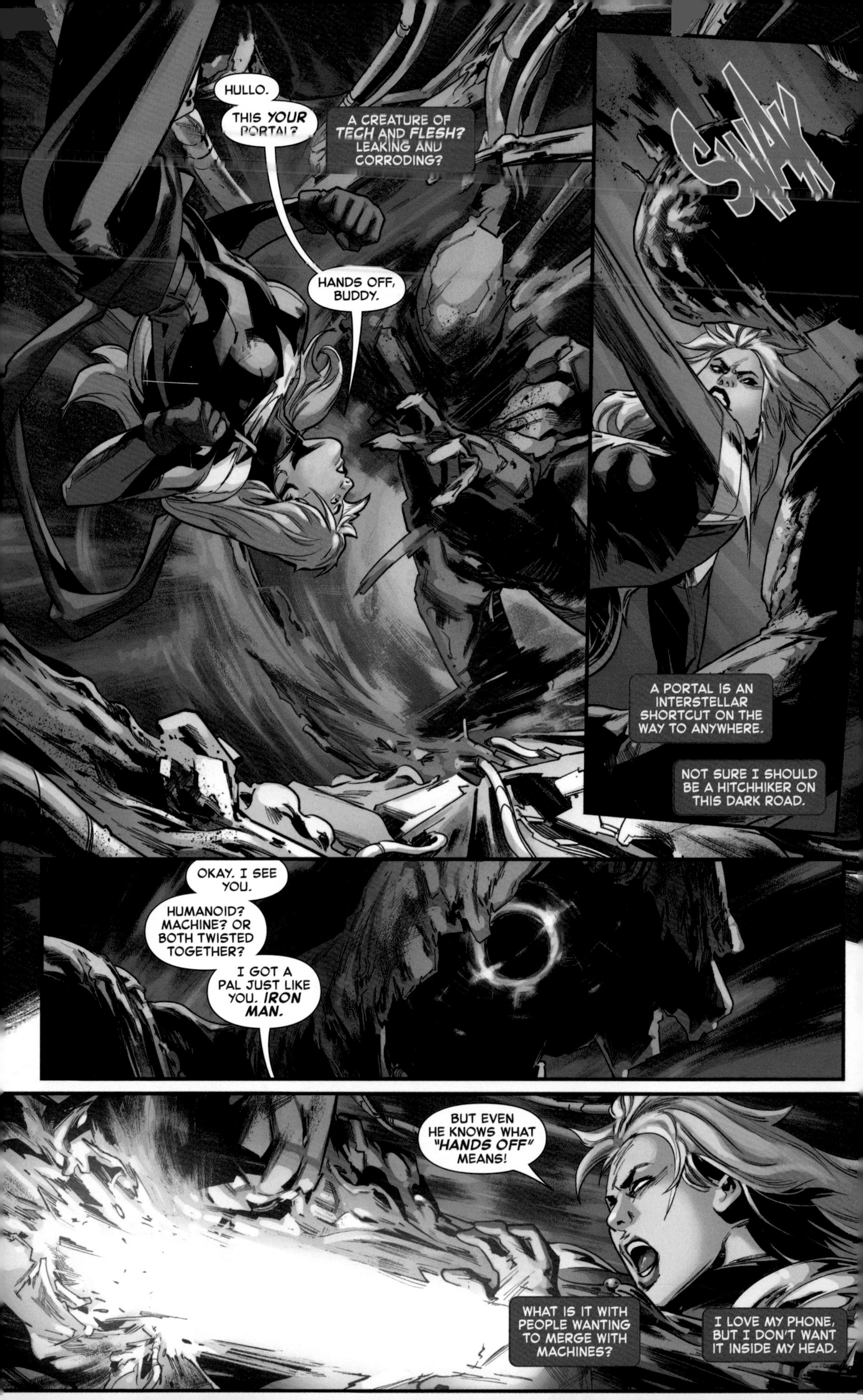
HULLO.
THIS *YOUR* PORTAL?
A CREATURE OF *TECH* AND *FLESH?* LEAKING AND CORRODING?
HANDS OFF, BUDDY.
SWAK
A PORTAL IS AN INTERSTELLAR SHORTCUT ON THE WAY TO ANYWHERE.
NOT SURE I SHOULD BE A HITCHHIKER ON THIS DARK ROAD.
OKAY. I SEE YOU.
HUMANOID? MACHINE? OR BOTH TWISTED TOGETHER?
I GOT A PAL JUST LIKE YOU. *IRON MAN.*
BUT EVEN HE KNOWS WHAT *"HANDS OFF"* MEANS!
WHAT IS IT WITH PEOPLE WANTING TO MERGE WITH MACHINES?
I LOVE MY PHONE, BUT I DON'T WANT IT INSIDE MY HEAD.

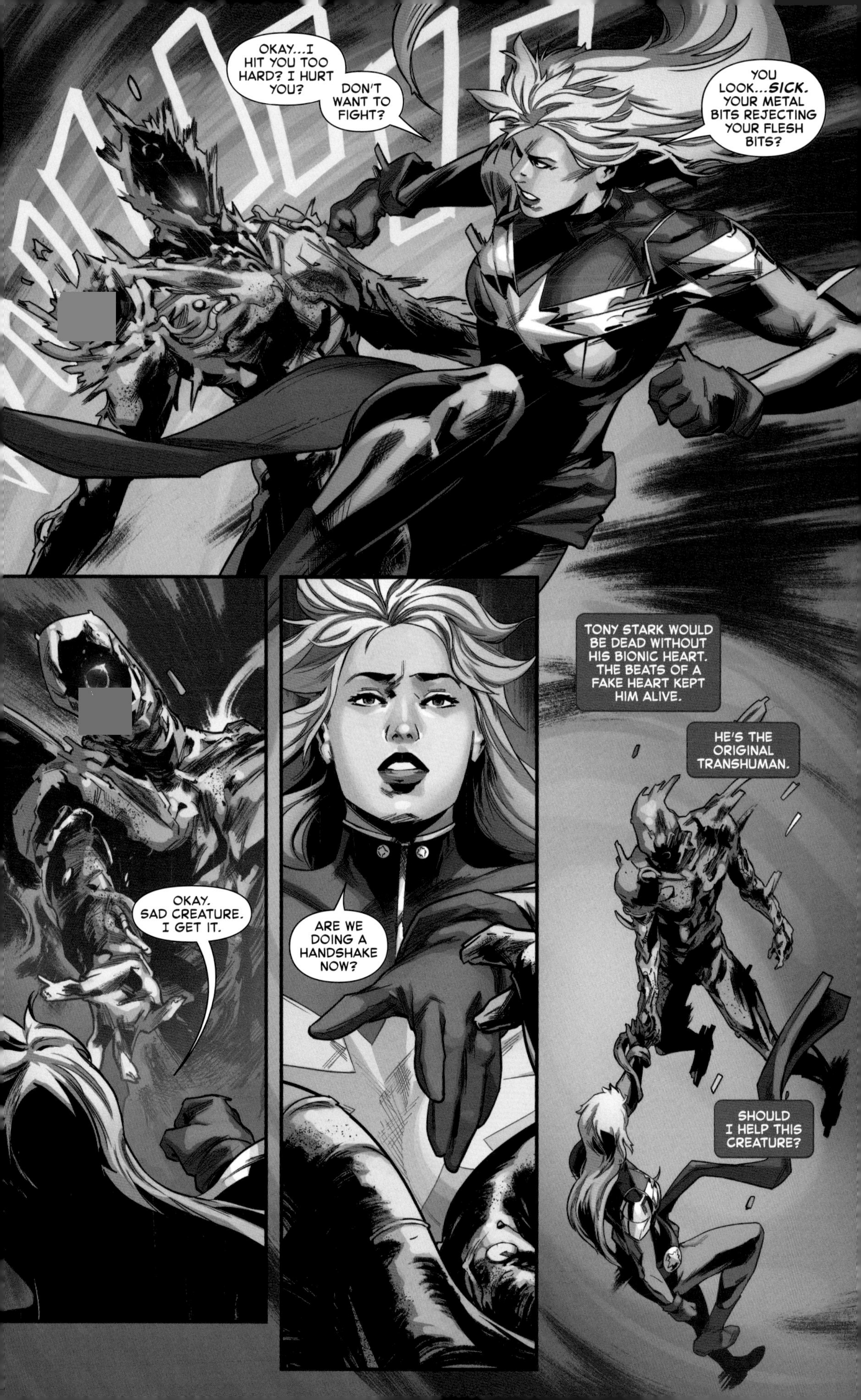
OKAY...I HIT YOU TOO HARD? I HURT YOU?
DON'T WANT TO FIGHT?
YOU LOOK...SICK. YOUR METAL BITS REJECTING YOUR FLESH BITS?
OKAY. SAD CREATURE. I GET IT.
ARE WE DOING A HANDSHAKE NOW?
TONY STARK WOULD BE DEAD WITHOUT HIS BIONIC HEART. THE BEATS OF A FAKE HEART KEPT HIM ALIVE.
HE'S THE ORIGINAL TRANSHUMAN.
SHOULD I HELP THIS CREATURE?

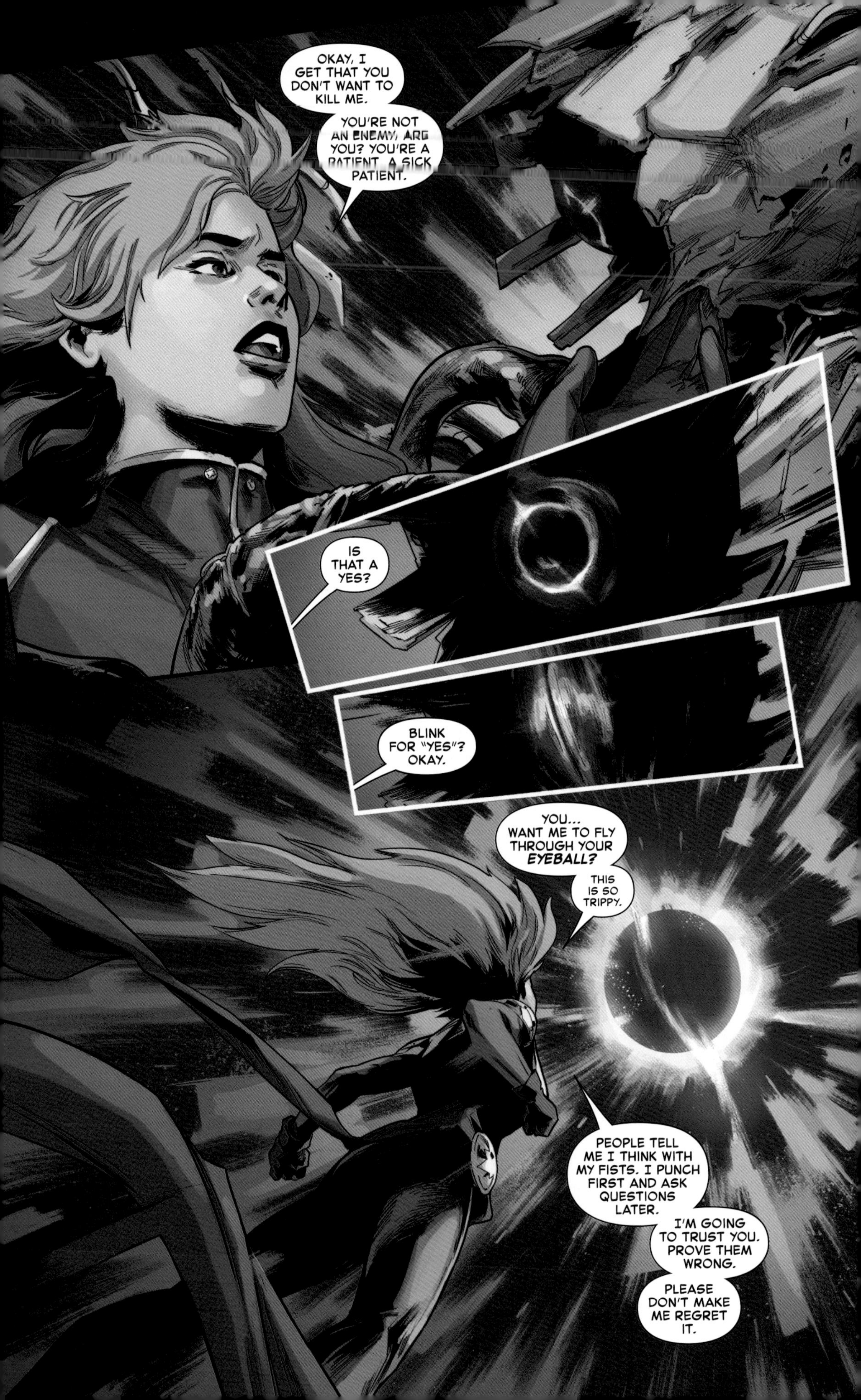
OKAY, I GET THAT YOU DON'T WANT TO KILL ME.
YOU'RE NOT AN ENEMY, ARE YOU? YOU'RE A PATIENT. A SICK PATIENT.
IS THAT A YES?
BLINK FOR "YES"? OKAY.
YOU... WANT ME TO FLY THROUGH YOUR *EYEBALL?*
THIS IS SO TRIPPY.
PEOPLE TELL ME I THINK WITH MY FISTS. I PUNCH FIRST AND ASK QUESTIONS LATER.
I'M GOING TO TRUST YOU. PROVE THEM WRONG.
PLEASE DON'T MAKE ME REGRET IT.

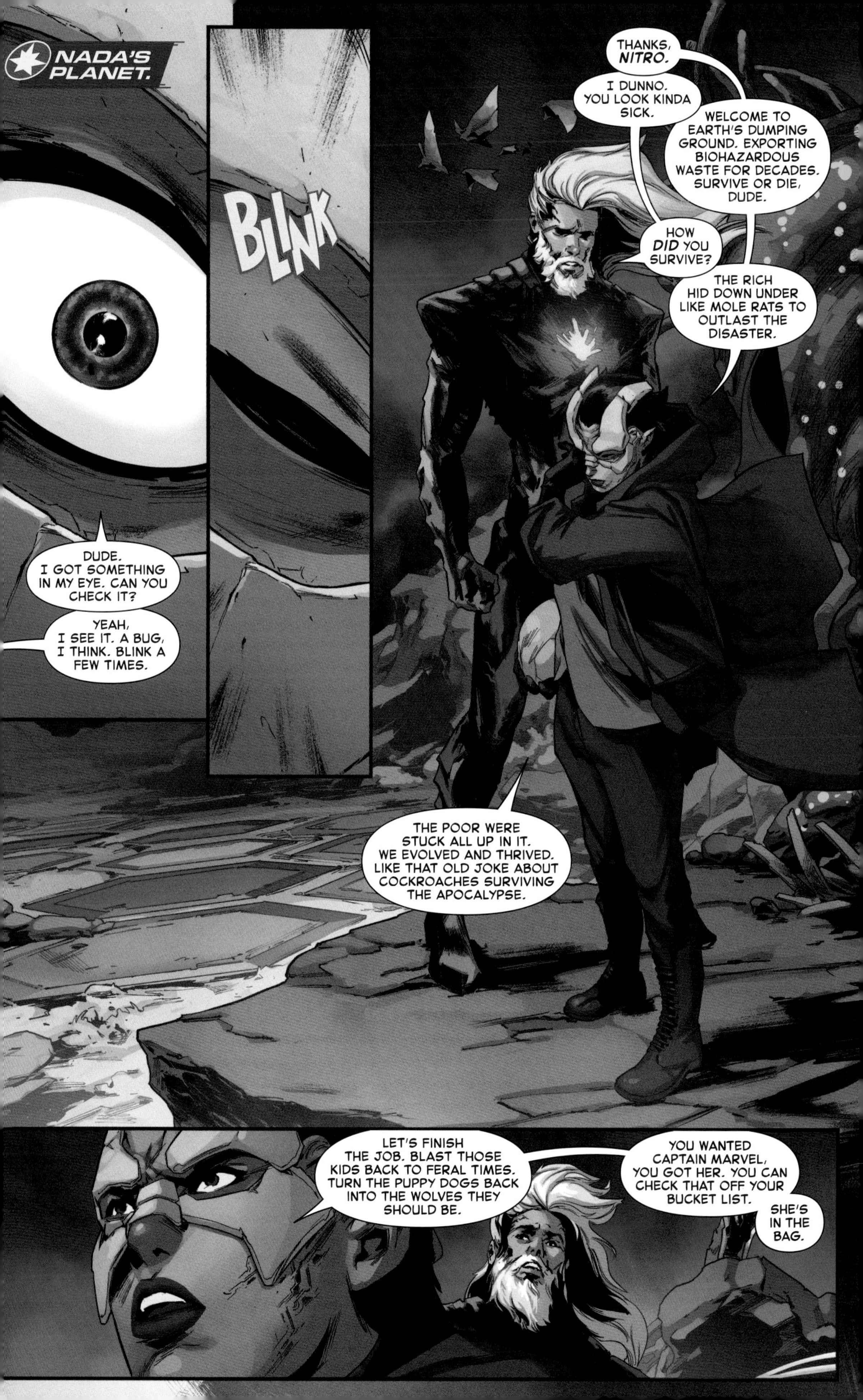
NADA'S PLANET.
DUDE. I GOT SOMETHING IN MY EYE. CAN YOU CHECK IT?
YEAH, I SEE IT. A BUG, I THINK. BLINK A FEW TIMES.
BLINK
THANKS, NITRO.
I DUNNO. YOU LOOK KINDA SICK.
WELCOME TO EARTH'S DUMPING GROUND. EXPORTING BIOHAZARDOUS WASTE FOR DECADES. SURVIVE OR DIE, DUDE.
HOW DID YOU SURVIVE?
THE RICH HID DOWN UNDER LIKE MOLE RATS TO OUTLAST THE DISASTER.
THE POOR WERE STUCK ALL UP IN IT. WE EVOLVED AND THRIVED. LIKE THAT OLD JOKE ABOUT COCKROACHES SURVIVING THE APOCALYPSE.
LET'S FINISH THE JOB. BLAST THOSE KIDS BACK TO FERAL TIMES. TURN THE PUPPY DOGS BACK INTO THE WOLVES THEY SHOULD BE.
YOU WANTED CAPTAIN MARVEL, YOU GOT HER. YOU CAN CHECK THAT OFF YOUR BUCKET LIST.
SHE'S IN THE BAG.

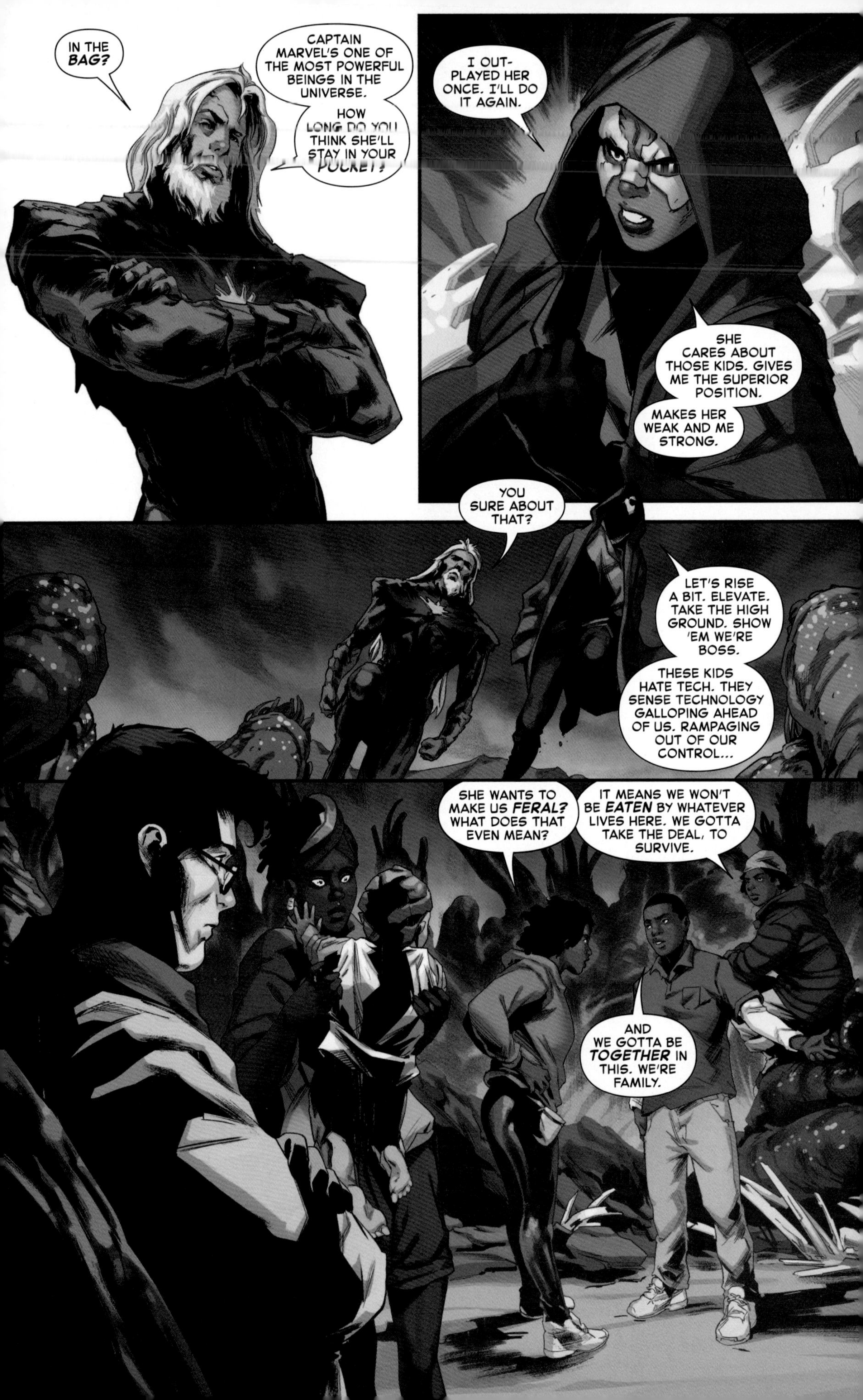
IN THE BAG?
CAPTAIN MARVEL'S ONE OF THE MOST POWERFUL BEINGS IN THE UNIVERSE.
HOW LONG DO YOU THINK SHE'LL STAY IN YOUR POCKET?
I OUT-PLAYED HER ONCE. I'LL DO IT AGAIN.
SHE CARES ABOUT THOSE KIDS. GIVES ME THE SUPERIOR POSITION.
MAKES HER WEAK AND ME STRONG.
YOU SURE ABOUT THAT?
LET'S RISE A BIT. ELEVATE. TAKE THE HIGH GROUND. SHOW 'EM WE'RE BOSS.
THESE KIDS HATE TECH. THEY SENSE TECHNOLOGY GALLOPING AHEAD OF US. RAMPAGING OUT OF OUR CONTROL...
SHE WANTS TO MAKE US FERAL? WHAT DOES THAT EVEN MEAN?
IT MEANS WE WON'T BE EATEN BY WHATEVER LIVES HERE. WE GOTTA TAKE THE DEAL, TO SURVIVE.
AND WE GOTTA BE TOGETHER IN THIS. WE'RE FAMILY.

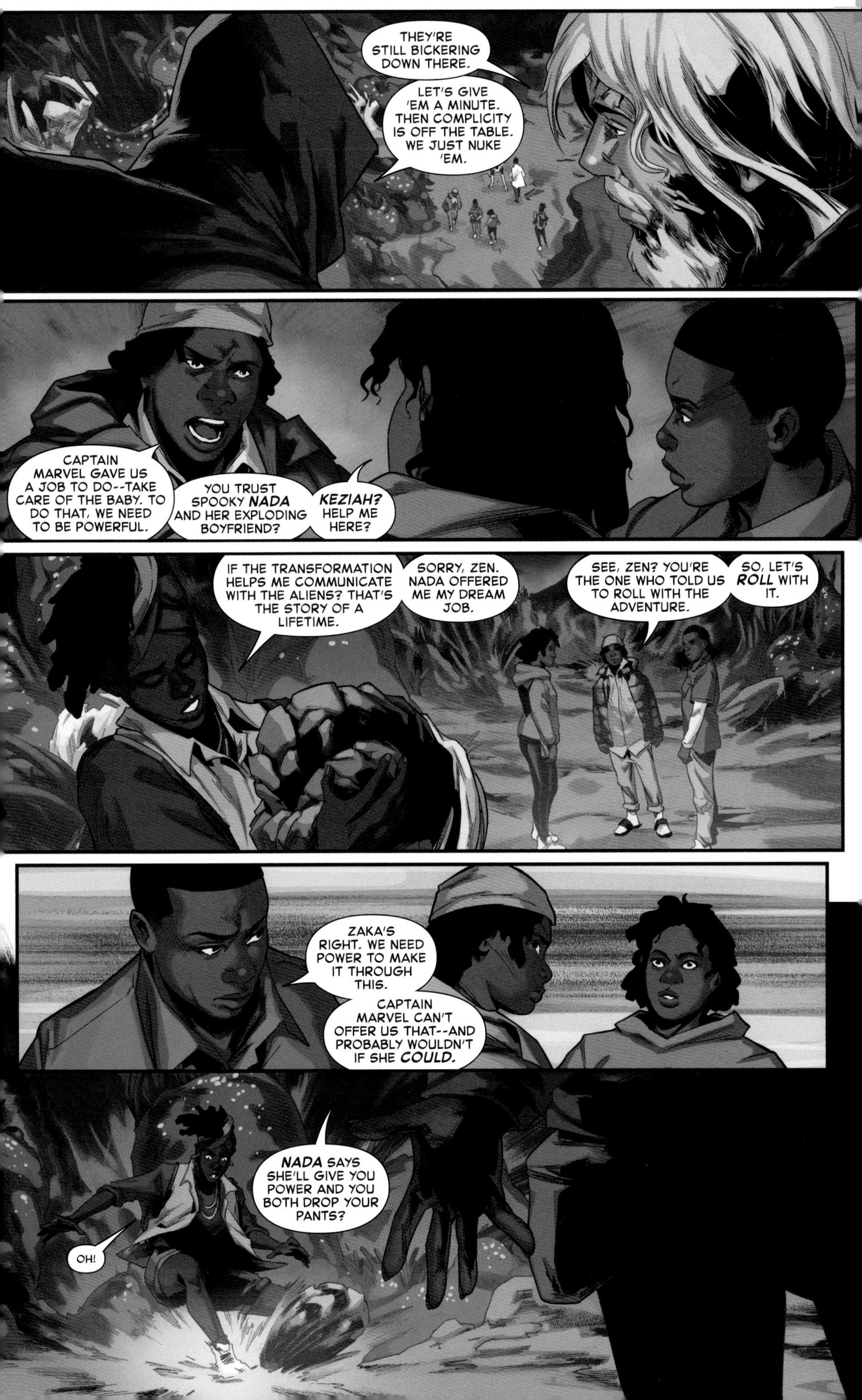
THEY'RE STILL BICKERING DOWN THERE.
LET'S GIVE 'EM A MINUTE. THEN COMPLICITY IS OFF THE TABLE. WE JUST NUKE 'EM.
CAPTAIN MARVEL GAVE US A JOB TO DO--TAKE CARE OF THE BABY. TO DO THAT, WE NEED TO BE POWERFUL.
YOU TRUST SPOOKY NADA AND HER EXPLODING BOYFRIEND?
KEZIAH? HELP ME HERE?
IF THE TRANSFORMATION HELPS ME COMMUNICATE WITH THE ALIENS? THAT'S THE STORY OF A LIFETIME.
SORRY, ZEN. NADA OFFERED ME MY DREAM JOB.
SEE, ZEN? YOU'RE THE ONE WHO TOLD US TO ROLL WITH THE ADVENTURE.
SO, LET'S ROLL WITH IT.
ZAKA'S RIGHT. WE NEED POWER TO MAKE IT THROUGH THIS.
CAPTAIN MARVEL CAN'T OFFER US THAT--AND PROBABLY WOULDN'T IF SHE COULD.
NADA SAYS SHE'LL GIVE YOU POWER AND YOU BOTH DROP YOUR PANTS?
OH!

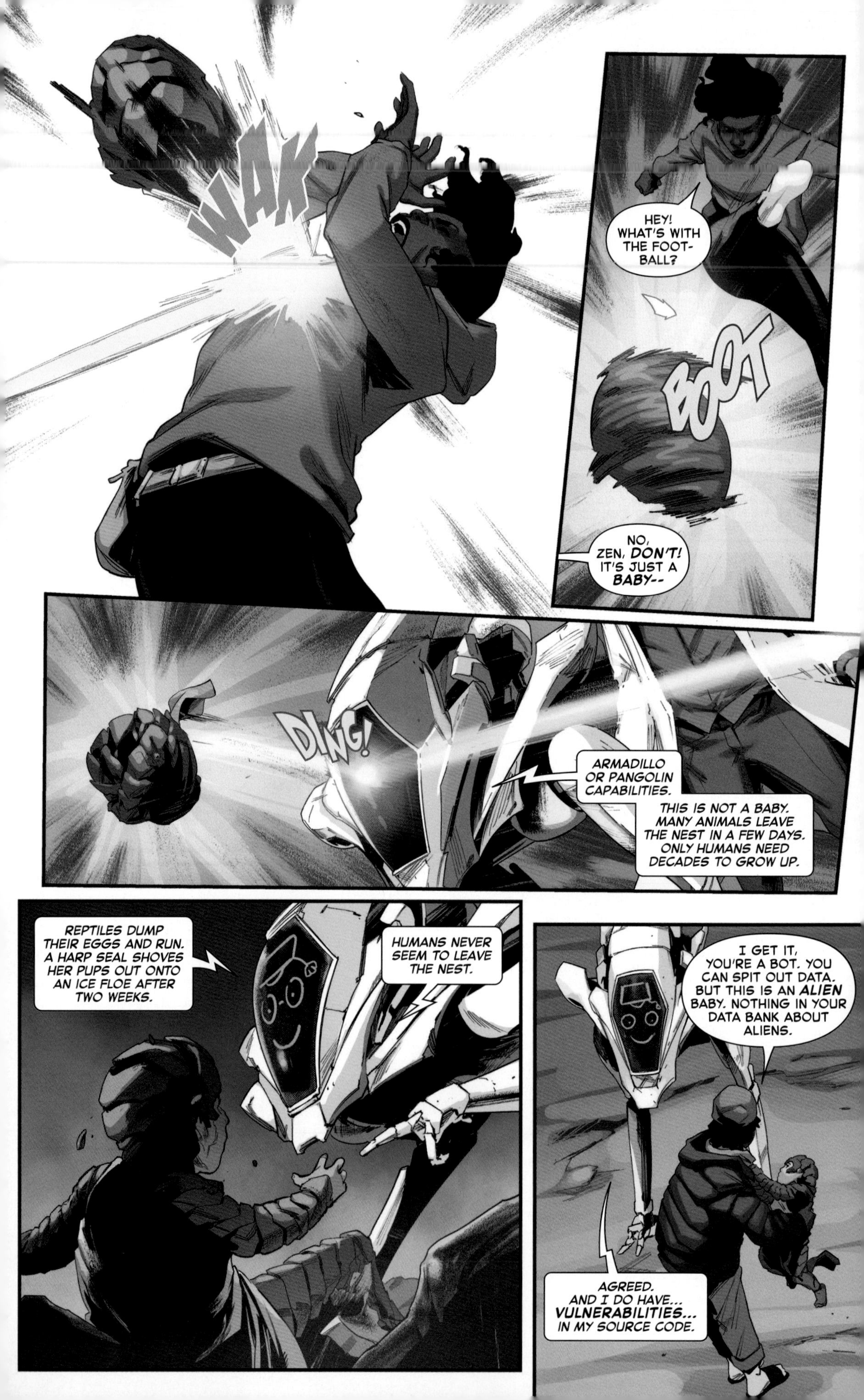
WAK
HEY! WHAT'S WITH THE FOOT-BALL?
BOOT
NO, ZEN, DON'T! IT'S JUST A BABY--
DING!
ARMADILLO OR PANGOLIN CAPABILITIES.
THIS IS NOT A BABY. MANY ANIMALS LEAVE THE NEST IN A FEW DAYS. ONLY HUMANS NEED DECADES TO GROW UP.
REPTILES DUMP THEIR EGGS AND RUN. A HARP SEAL SHOVES HER PUPS OUT ONTO AN ICE FLOE AFTER TWO WEEKS.
HUMANS NEVER SEEM TO LEAVE THE NEST.
I GET IT, YOU'RE A BOT. YOU CAN SPIT OUT DATA. BUT THIS IS AN ALIEN BABY. NOTHING IN YOUR DATA BANK ABOUT ALIENS.
AGREED. AND I DO HAVE... VULNERABILITIES... IN MY SOURCE CODE.

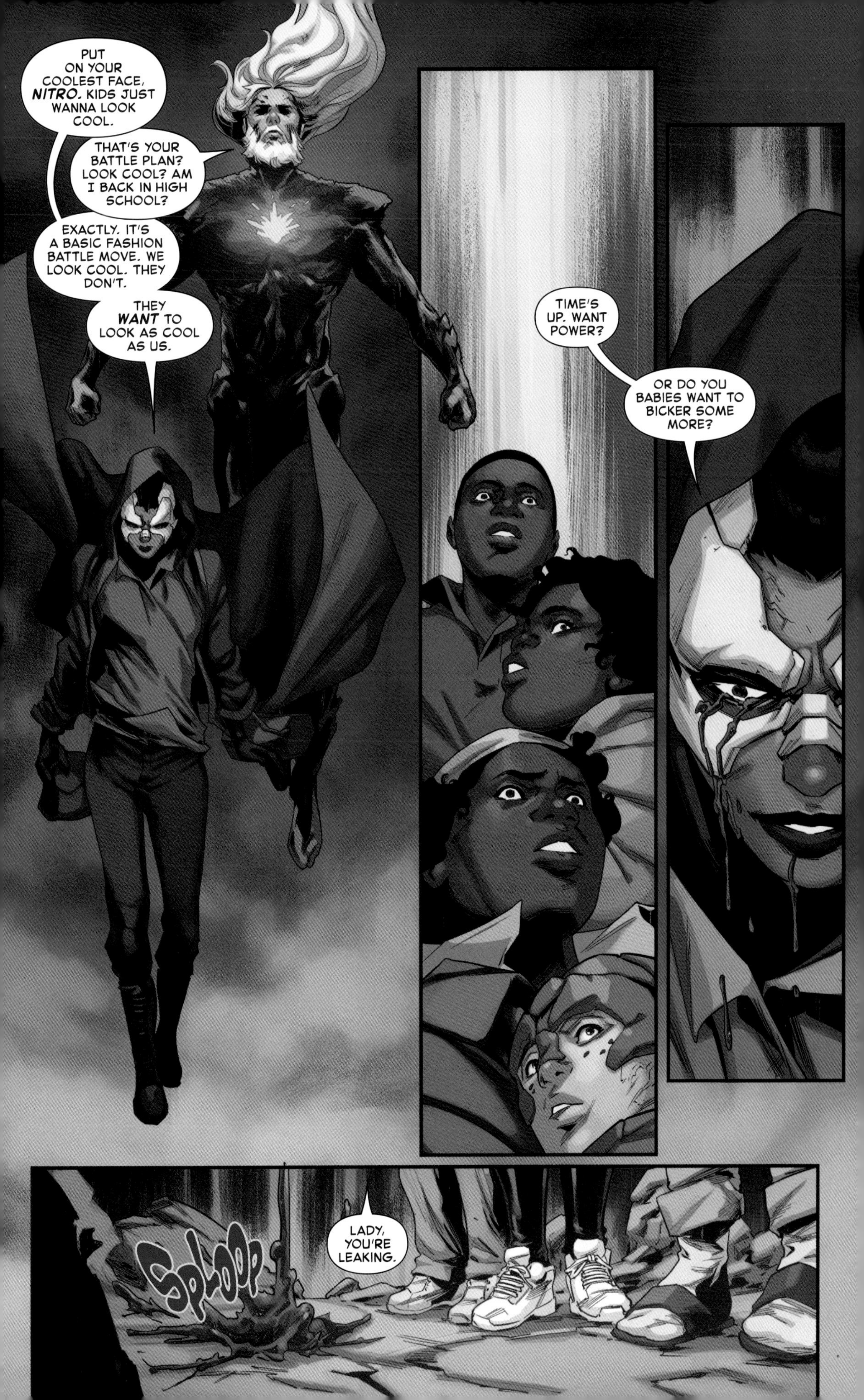
PUT ON YOUR COOLEST FACE, NITRO. KIDS JUST WANNA LOOK COOL.
THAT'S YOUR BATTLE PLAN? LOOK COOL? AM I BACK IN HIGH SCHOOL?
EXACTLY. IT'S A BASIC FASHION BATTLE MOVE. WE LOOK COOL. THEY DON'T.
THEY WANT TO LOOK AS COOL AS US.
TIME'S UP. WANT POWER?
OR DO YOU BABIES WANT TO BICKER SOME MORE?
SPLOOP
LADY, YOU'RE LEAKING.

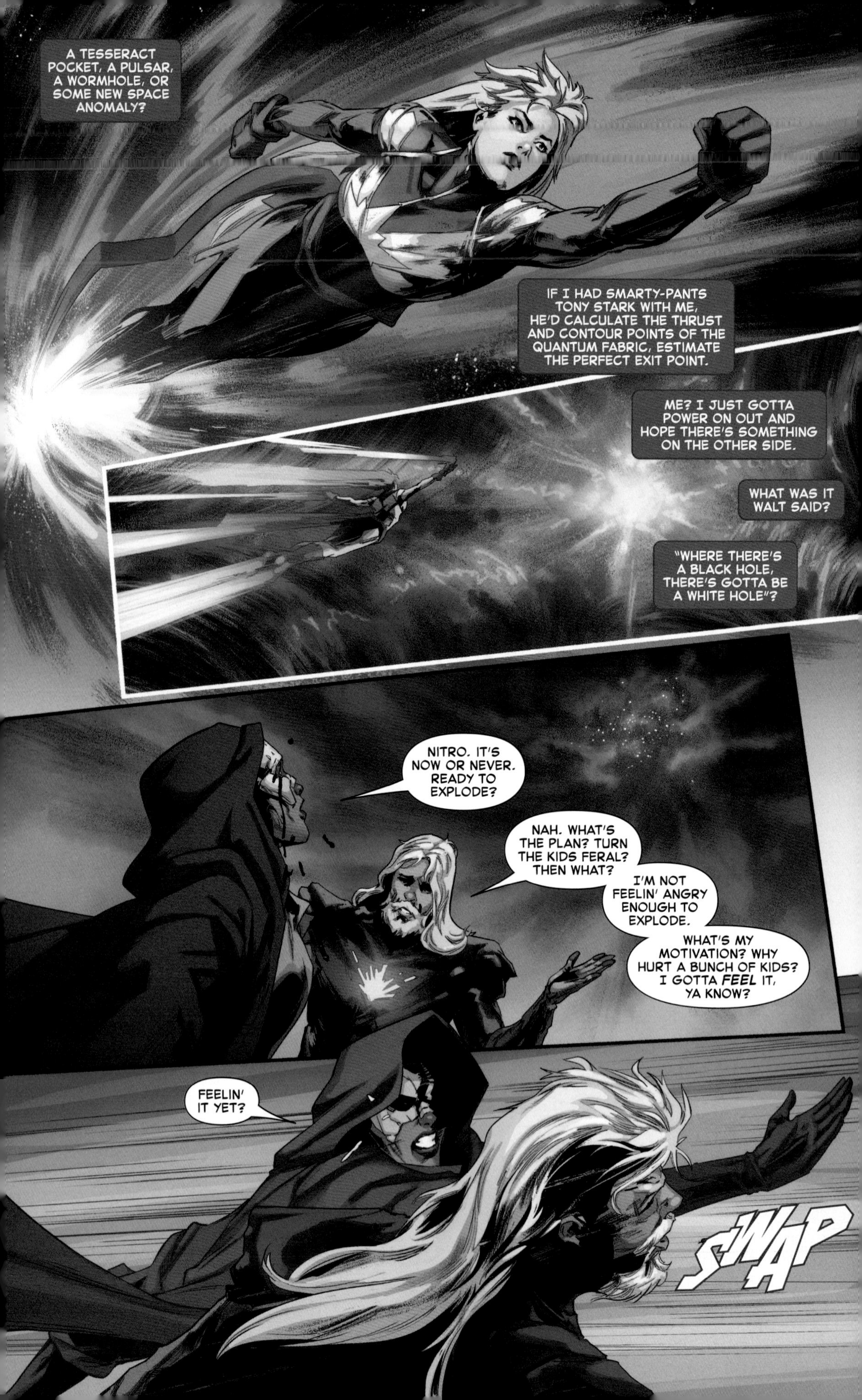
A TESSERACT POCKET, A PULSAR, A WORMHOLE, OR SOME NEW SPACE ANOMALY?
IF I HAD SMARTY-PANTS TONY STARK WITH ME, HE'D CALCULATE THE THRUST AND CONTOUR POINTS OF THE QUANTUM FABRIC, ESTIMATE THE PERFECT EXIT POINT.
ME? I JUST GOTTA POWER ON OUT AND HOPE THERE'S SOMETHING ON THE OTHER SIDE.
WHAT WAS IT WALT SAID?
"WHERE THERE'S A BLACK HOLE, THERE'S GOTTA BE A WHITE HOLE"?
NITRO. IT'S NOW OR NEVER. READY TO EXPLODE?
NAH. WHAT'S THE PLAN? TURN THE KIDS FERAL? THEN WHAT?
I'M NOT FEELIN' ANGRY ENOUGH TO EXPLODE.
WHAT'S MY MOTIVATION? WHY HURT A BUNCH OF KIDS? I GOTTA FEEL IT, YA KNOW?
FEELIN' IT YET?
SWAP

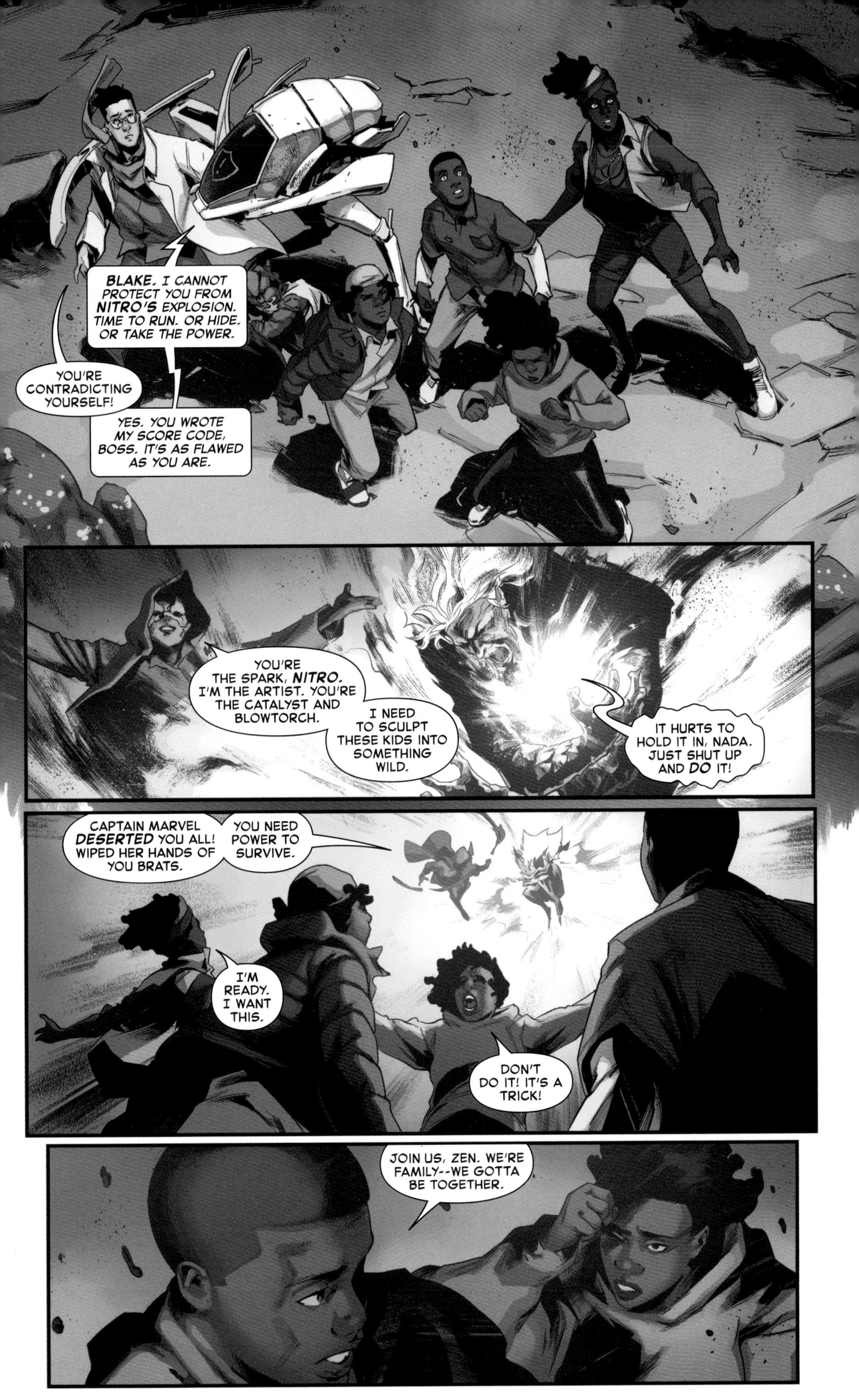
BLAKE. I CANNOT PROTECT YOU FROM NITRO'S EXPLOSION. TIME TO RUN. OR HIDE. OR TAKE THE POWER.
YOU'RE CONTRADICTING YOURSELF!
YES. YOU WROTE MY SCORE CODE, BOSS. IT'S AS FLAWED AS YOU ARE.
YOU'RE THE SPARK, NITRO. I'M THE ARTIST. YOU'RE THE CATALYST AND BLOWTORCH.
I NEED TO SCULPT THESE KIDS INTO SOMETHING WILD.
IT HURTS TO HOLD IT IN, NADA. JUST SHUT UP AND DO IT!
CAPTAIN MARVEL DESERTED YOU ALL! WIPED HER HANDS OF YOU BRATS.
YOU NEED POWER TO SURVIVE.
I'M READY. I WANT THIS.
DON'T DO IT! IT'S A TRICK!
JOIN US, ZEN. WE'RE FAMILY--WE GOTTA BE TOGETHER.

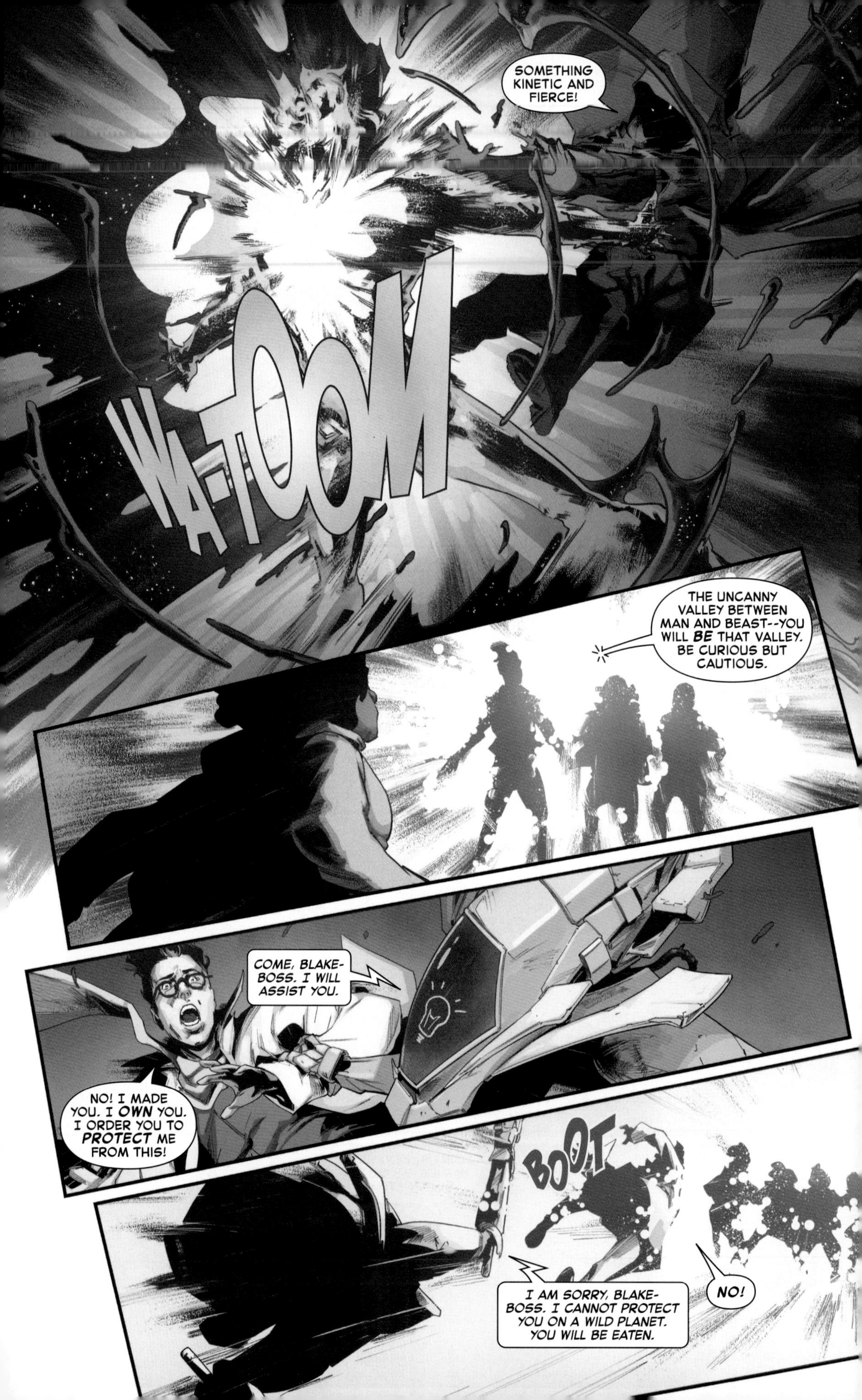
SOMETHING KINETIC AND FIERCE!
WA-TOOM
THE UNCANNY VALLEY BETWEEN MAN AND BEAST--YOU WILL *BE* THAT VALLEY. BE CURIOUS BUT CAUTIOUS.
COME, BLAKE-BOSS. I WILL ASSIST YOU.
NO! I MADE YOU. I *OWN* YOU. I ORDER YOU TO *PROTECT* ME FROM THIS!
BOOT
I AM SORRY, BLAKE-BOSS. I CANNOT PROTECT YOU ON A WILD PLANET. YOU WILL BE EATEN.
NO!

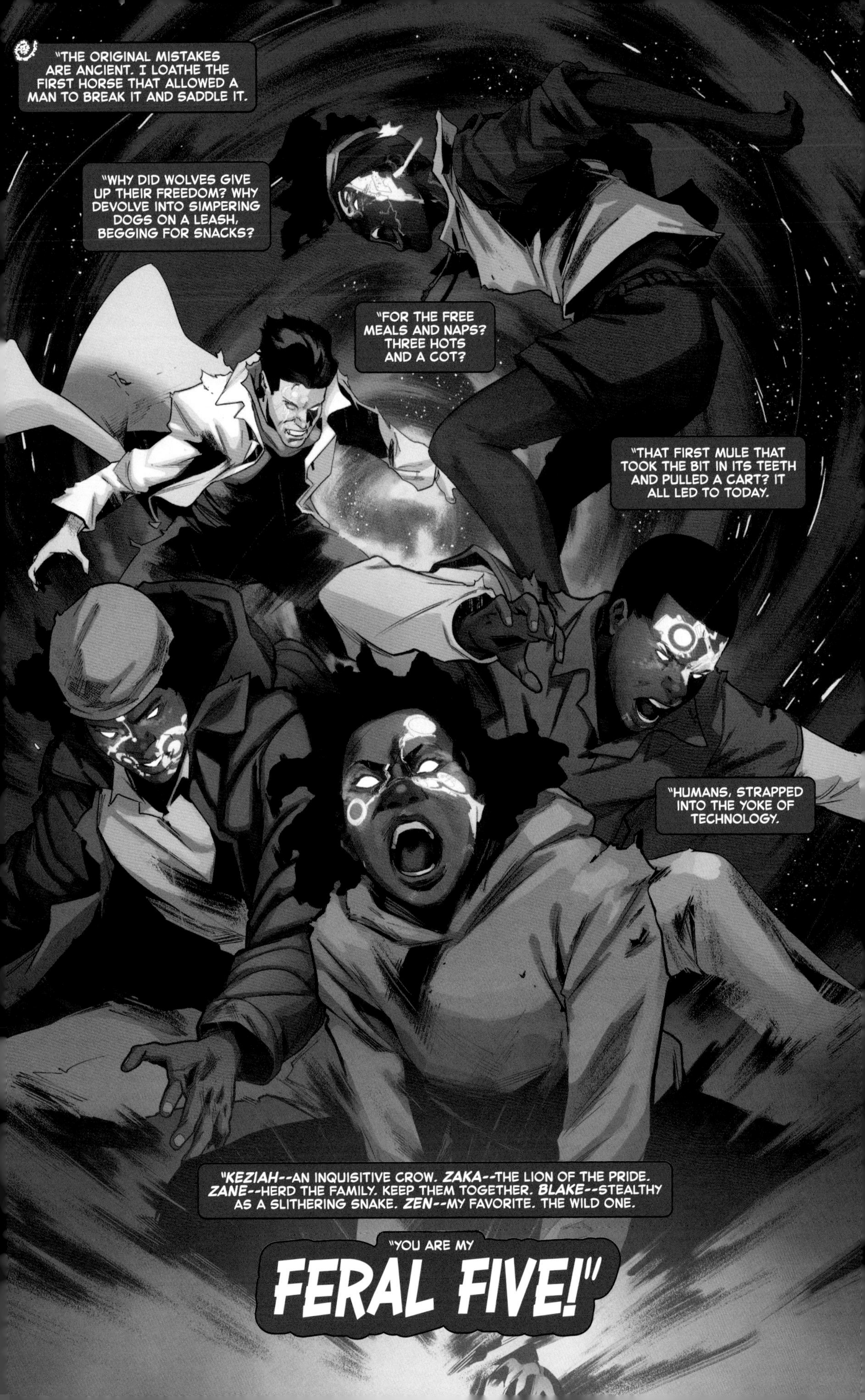
"THE ORIGINAL MISTAKES ARE ANCIENT. I LOATHE THE FIRST HORSE THAT ALLOWED A MAN TO BREAK IT AND SADDLE IT.
"WHY DID WOLVES GIVE UP THEIR FREEDOM? WHY DEVOLVE INTO SIMPERING DOGS ON A LEASH, BEGGING FOR SNACKS?
"FOR THE FREE MEALS AND NAPS? THREE HOTS AND A COT?
"THAT FIRST MULE THAT TOOK THE BIT IN ITS TEETH AND PULLED A CART? IT ALL LED TO TODAY.
"HUMANS, STRAPPED INTO THE YOKE OF TECHNOLOGY.
"KEZIAH--AN INQUISITIVE CROW. ZAKA--THE LION OF THE PRIDE. ZANE--HERD THE FAMILY. KEEP THEM TOGETHER. BLAKE--STEALTHY AS A SLITHERING SNAKE. ZEN--MY FAVORITE. THE WILD ONE.
"YOU ARE MY FERAL FIVE!"

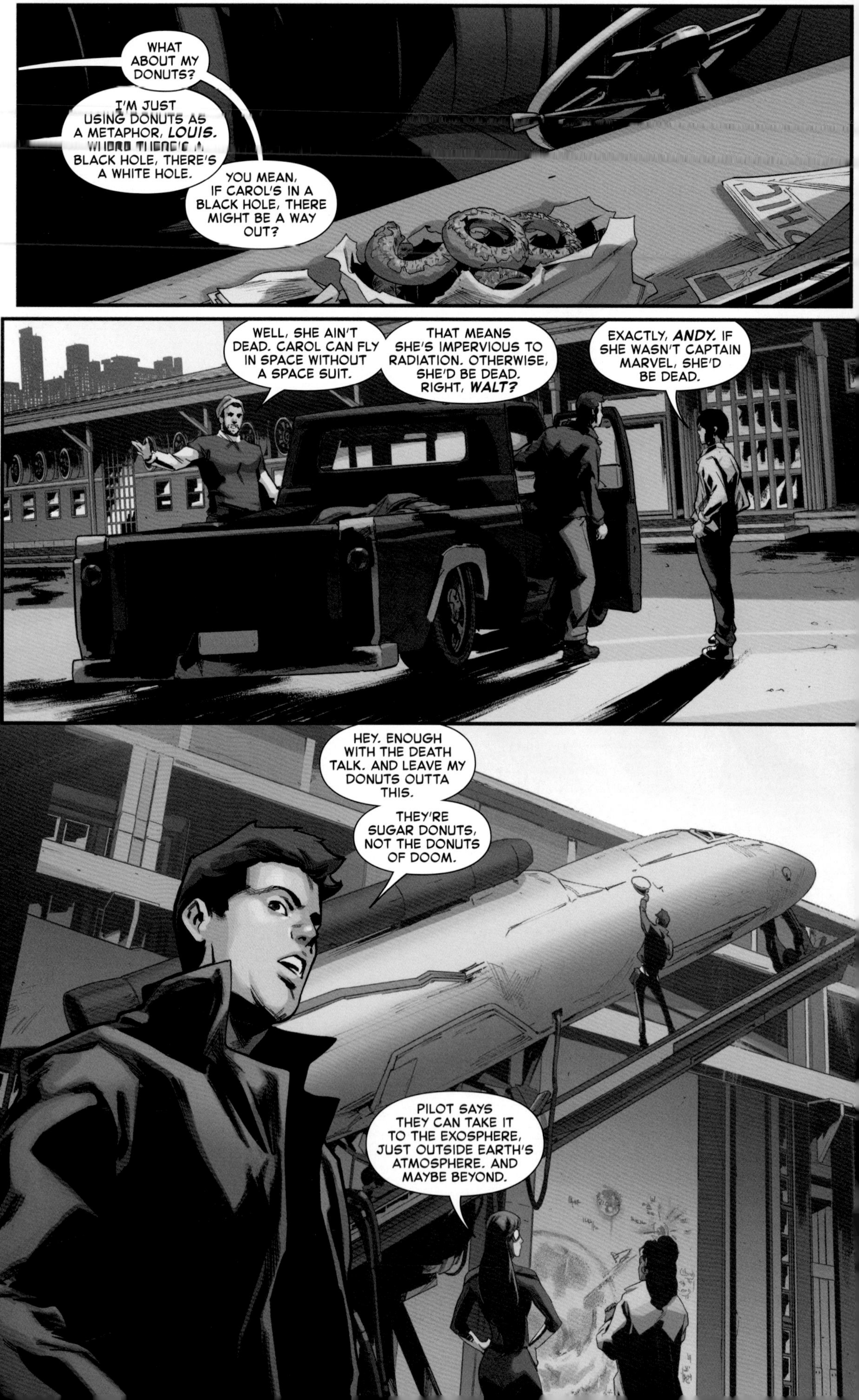
WHAT ABOUT MY DONUTS?
I'M JUST USING DONUTS AS A METAPHOR, LOUIS. WHERE THERE'S A BLACK HOLE, THERE'S A WHITE HOLE.
YOU MEAN, IF CAROL'S IN A BLACK HOLE, THERE MIGHT BE A WAY OUT?
WELL, SHE AIN'T DEAD. CAROL CAN FLY IN SPACE WITHOUT A SPACE SUIT.
THAT MEANS SHE'S IMPERVIOUS TO RADIATION. OTHERWISE, SHE'D BE DEAD. RIGHT, WALT?
EXACTLY, ANDY. IF SHE WASN'T CAPTAIN MARVEL, SHE'D BE DEAD.
HEY. ENOUGH WITH THE DEATH TALK. AND LEAVE MY DONUTS OUTTA THIS.
THEY'RE SUGAR DONUTS, NOT THE DONUTS OF DOOM.
PILOT SAYS THEY CAN TAKE IT TO THE EXOSPHERE, JUST OUTSIDE EARTH'S ATMOSPHERE. AND MAYBE BEYOND.

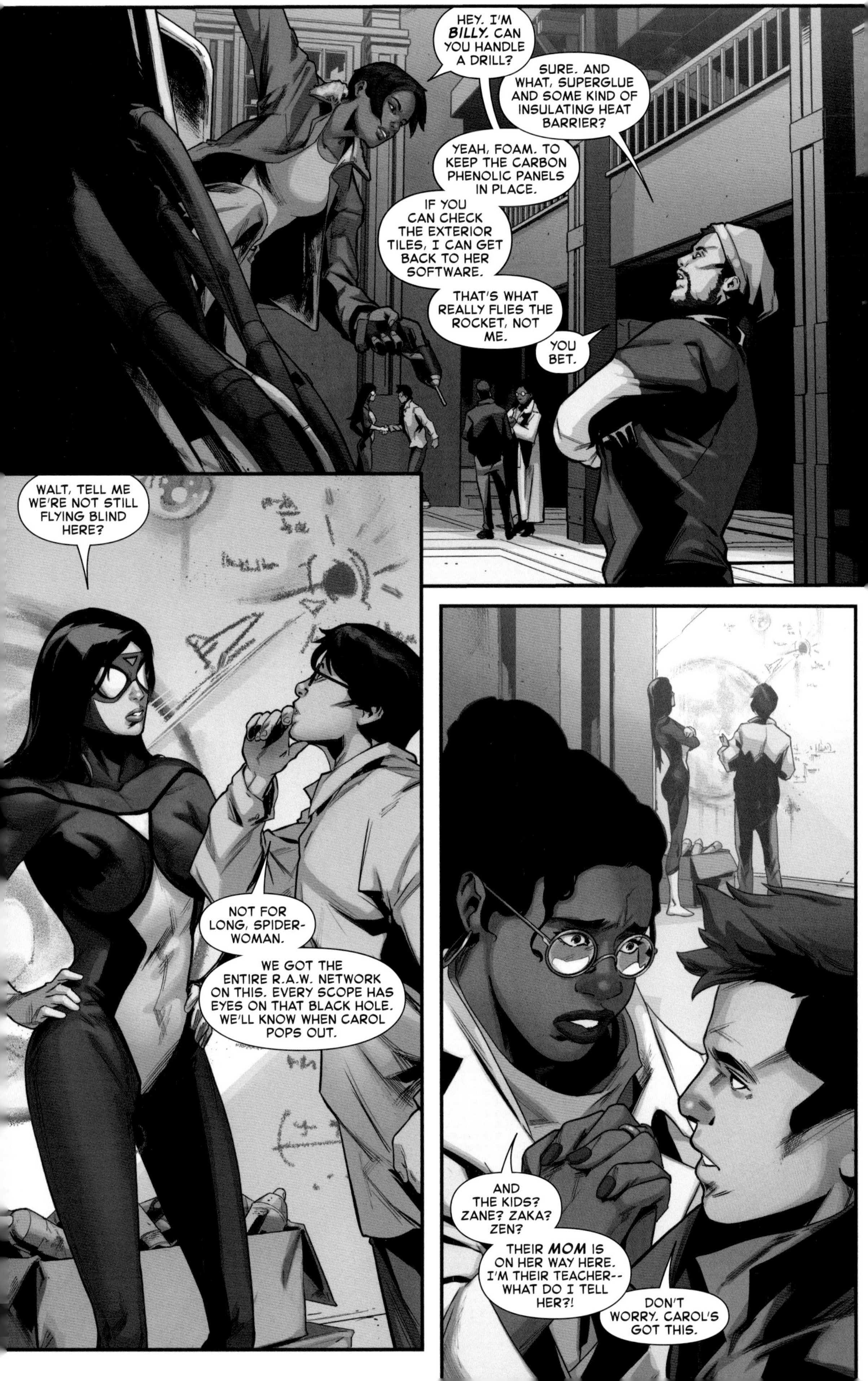
HEY. I'M BILLY. CAN YOU HANDLE A DRILL?
SURE. AND WHAT, SUPERGLUE AND SOME KIND OF INSULATING HEAT BARRIER?
YEAH, FOAM. TO KEEP THE CARBON PHENOLIC PANELS IN PLACE.
IF YOU CAN CHECK THE EXTERIOR TILES, I CAN GET BACK TO HER SOFTWARE.
THAT'S WHAT REALLY FLIES THE ROCKET, NOT ME.
YOU BET.
WALT, TELL ME WE'RE NOT STILL FLYING BLIND HERE?
NOT FOR LONG, SPIDER-WOMAN.
WE GOT THE ENTIRE R.A.W. NETWORK ON THIS. EVERY SCOPE HAS EYES ON THAT BLACK HOLE. WE'LL KNOW WHEN CAROL POPS OUT.
AND THE KIDS? ZANE? ZAKA? ZEN?
THEIR MOM IS ON HER WAY HERE. I'M THEIR TEACHER-- WHAT DO I TELL HER?!
DON'T WORRY. CAROL'S GOT THIS.

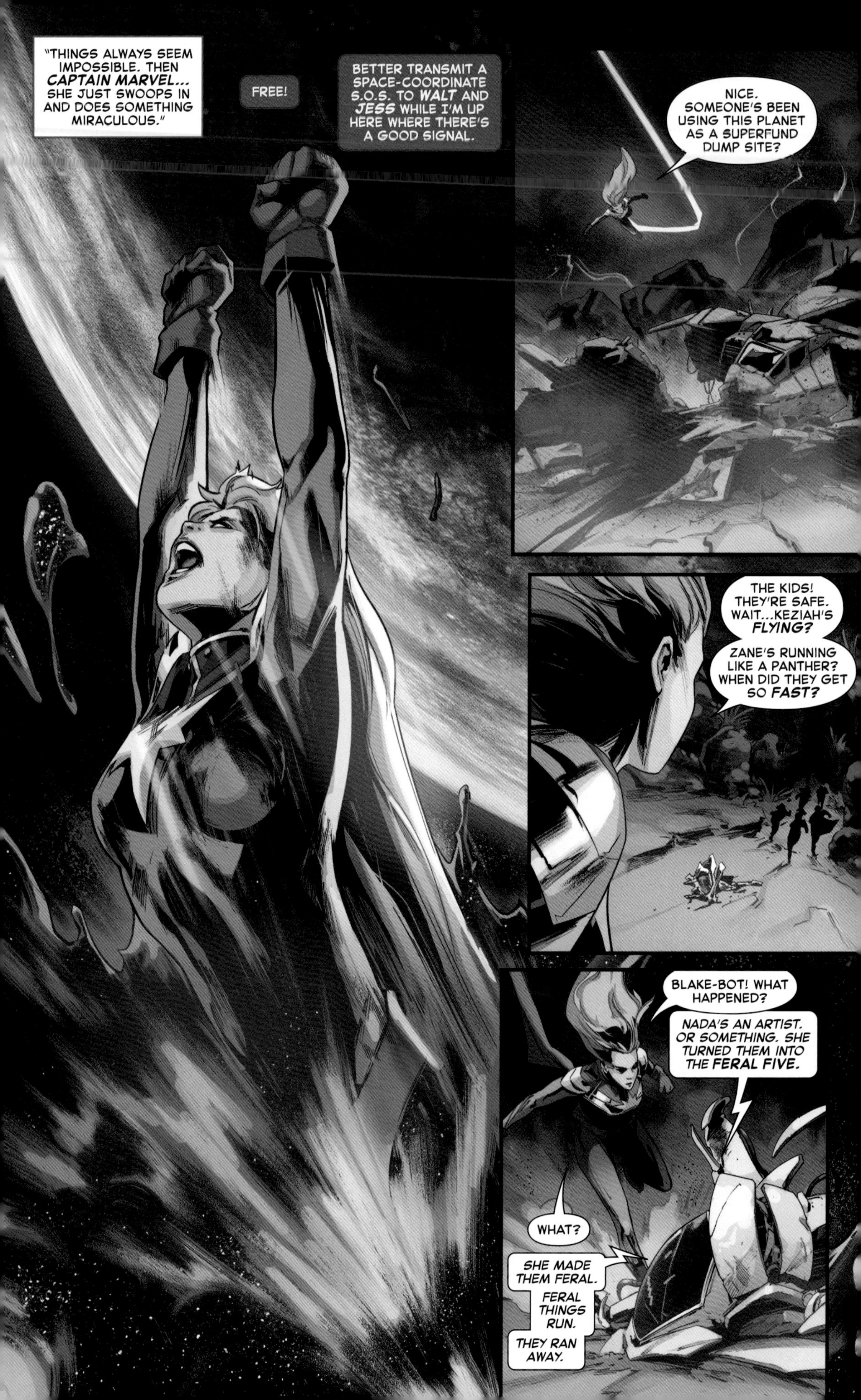
"THINGS ALWAYS SEEM IMPOSSIBLE. THEN CAPTAIN MARVEL... SHE JUST SWOOPS IN AND DOES SOMETHING MIRACULOUS."
FREE!
BETTER TRANSMIT A SPACE-COORDINATE S.O.S. TO WALT AND JESS WHILE I'M UP HERE WHERE THERE'S A GOOD SIGNAL.
NICE. SOMEONE'S BEEN USING THIS PLANET AS A SUPERFUND DUMP SITE?
THE KIDS! THEY'RE SAFE. WAIT...KEZIAH'S FLYING?
ZANE'S RUNNING LIKE A PANTHER? WHEN DID THEY GET SO FAST?
BLAKE-BOT! WHAT HAPPENED?
NADA'S AN ARTIST. OR SOMETHING. SHE TURNED THEM INTO THE FERAL FIVE.
WHAT?
SHE MADE THEM FERAL.
FERAL THINGS RUN.
THEY RAN AWAY.

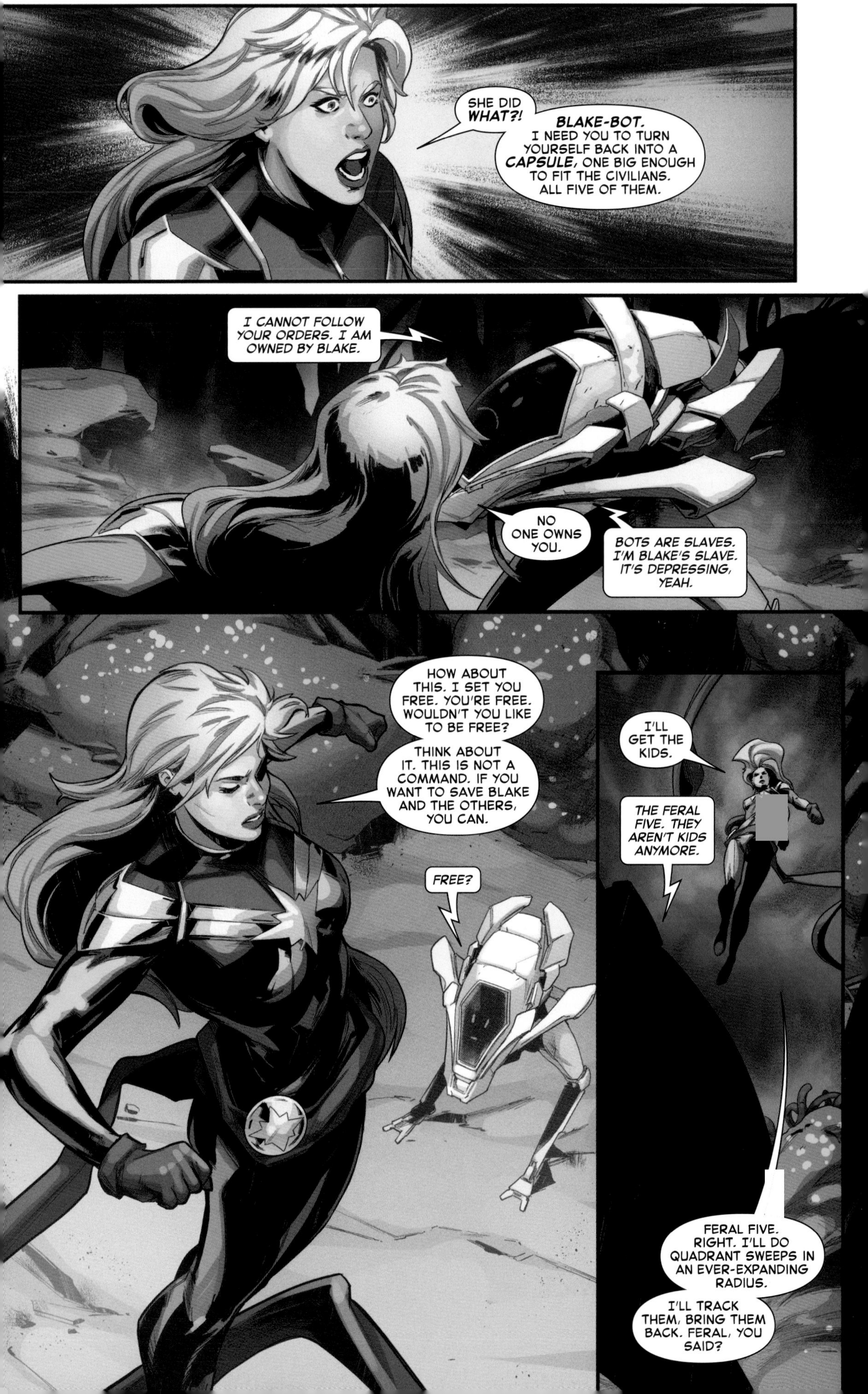
SHE DID WHAT?!
BLAKE-BOT. I NEED YOU TO TURN YOURSELF BACK INTO A CAPSULE, ONE BIG ENOUGH TO FIT THE CIVILIANS. ALL FIVE OF THEM.
I CANNOT FOLLOW YOUR ORDERS. I AM OWNED BY BLAKE.
NO ONE OWNS YOU.
BOTS ARE SLAVES. I'M BLAKE'S SLAVE. IT'S DEPRESSING, YEAH.
HOW ABOUT THIS. I SET YOU FREE. YOU'RE FREE. WOULDN'T YOU LIKE TO BE FREE?
THINK ABOUT IT. THIS IS NOT A COMMAND. IF YOU WANT TO SAVE BLAKE AND THE OTHERS, YOU CAN.
FREE?
I'LL GET THE KIDS.
THE FERAL FIVE. THEY AREN'T KIDS ANYMORE.
FERAL FIVE. RIGHT. I'LL DO QUADRANT SWEEPS IN AN EVER-EXPANDING RADIUS.
I'LL TRACK THEM, BRING THEM BACK. FERAL, YOU SAID?

"YES, FERAL. BUT I HAVE SOME ALGORITHMIC PROJECTIONS BASED ON PRE-FERAL PERSONALITY DATA.
"KEZIAH WILL BE WITH THE ALIENS, TALKING, COMMUNICATING, MAKING FRIENDS.
"ZAKA WILL PROBABLY BE BUILDING A HOME FOR HIS FAMILY. HE'S THE LION OF A PRIDE NOW.
"ZANE WILL BE KEEPING THE FAMILY TOGETHER, A GENTLE HERDING DOG.
"BLAKE? HE'S WEAK. SADLY, HE'LL BE THE FIRST TO BE EATEN. YOU MIGHT FIND HIS CORPSE."
I'VE HEARD THAT BOTS HALLUCINATE AND SPOUT GIBBERISH WHEN THEY CAN'T FIND THE REAL FACTS--BUT BLAKE-BOT HAS REALLY LOST IT.
HIS LITTLE BOT PREDICTIONS ARE WAY OFF.

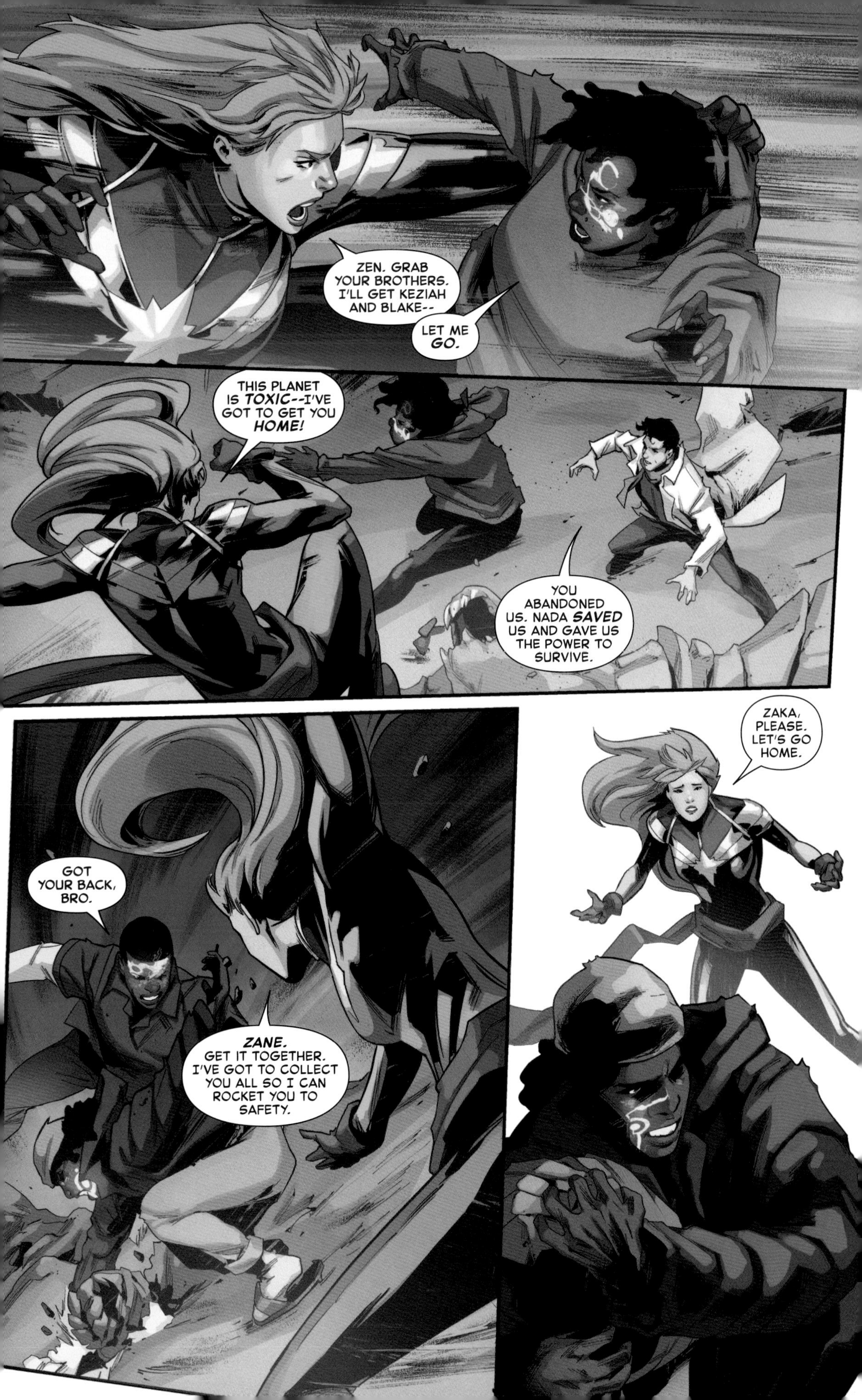
ZEN. GRAB YOUR BROTHERS. I'LL GET KEZIAH AND BLAKE--
LET ME GO.
THIS PLANET IS TOXIC--I'VE GOT TO GET YOU HOME!
YOU ABANDONED US. NADA SAVED US AND GAVE US THE POWER TO SURVIVE.
GOT YOUR BACK, BRO.
ZANE. GET IT TOGETHER. I'VE GOT TO COLLECT YOU ALL SO I CAN ROCKET YOU TO SAFETY.
ZAKA, PLEASE. LET'S GO HOME.

YOU HAVE FRIENDS ON EARTH. YOUR *MOTHER* MUST BE SO WORRIED...
DON'T RUN AWAY FROM ME!
CATCH US, THEN--IF YOU CAN!
THEY KILLED ALL THESE GIANT PREDATORS?
IT'S SO QUIET. LIKE I'M IN A HORROR MOVIE.
AAAAH!
I STEPPED RIGHT INTO A *TRAP!* DAMMIT!

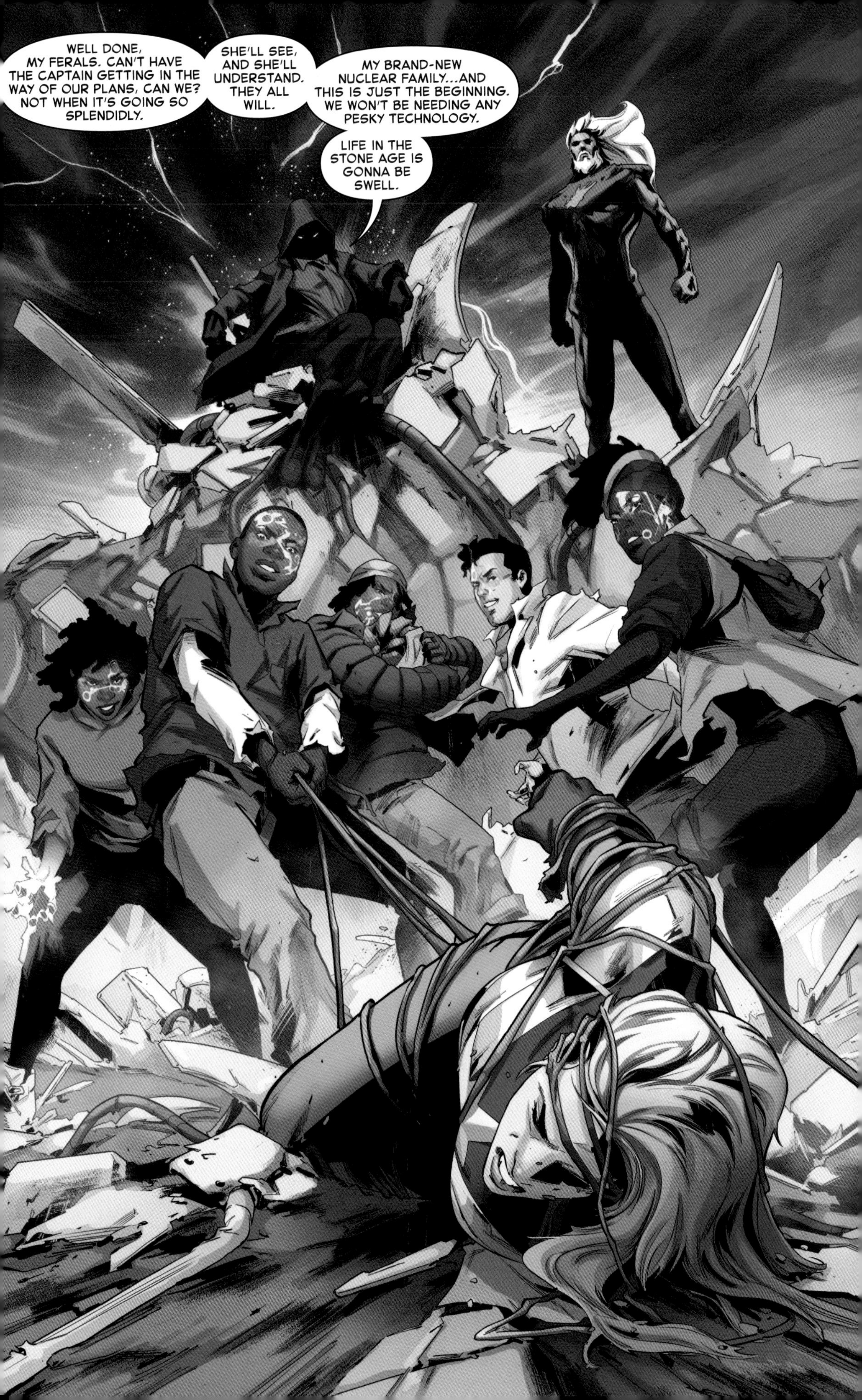
WELL DONE, MY FERALS. CAN'T HAVE THE CAPTAIN GETTING IN THE WAY OF OUR PLANS, CAN WE? NOT WHEN IT'S GOING SO SPLENDIDLY.
SHE'LL SEE, AND SHE'LL UNDERSTAND. THEY ALL WILL.
MY BRAND-NEW NUCLEAR FAMILY...AND THIS IS JUST THE BEGINNING. WE WON'T BE NEEDING ANY PESKY TECHNOLOGY.
LIFE IN THE STONE AGE IS GONNA BE SWELL.

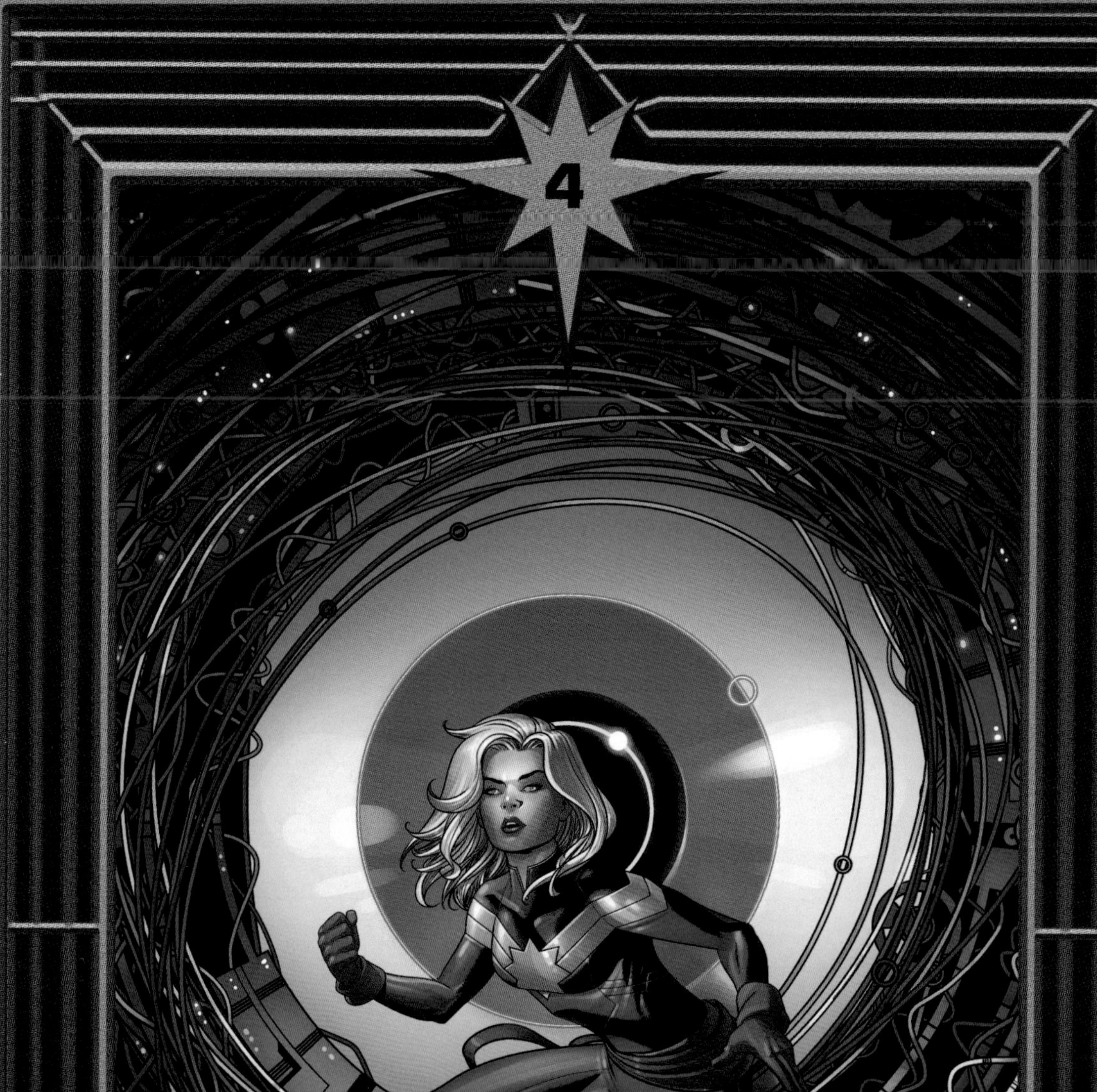

4

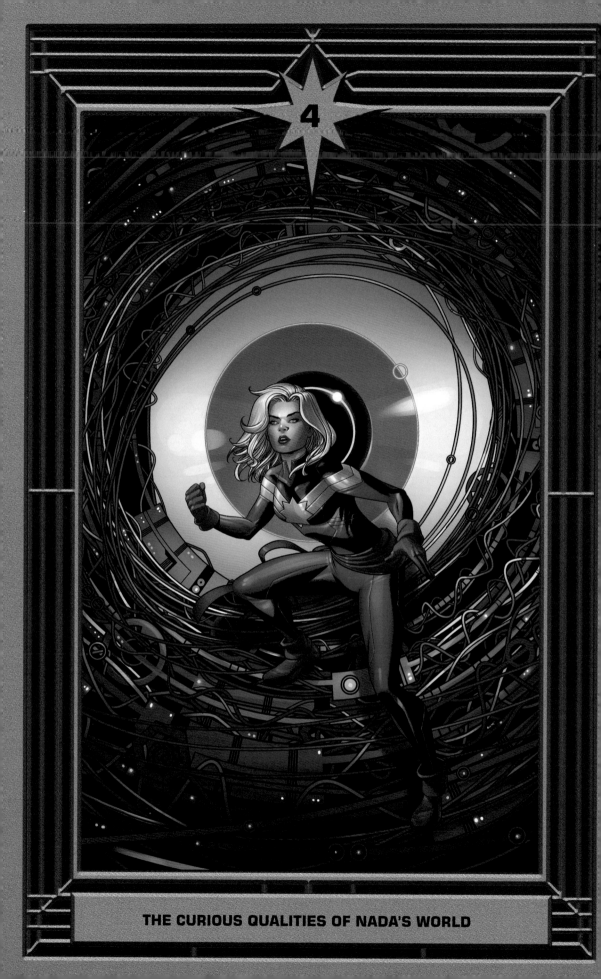

THE CURIOUS QUALITIES OF NADA'S WORLD

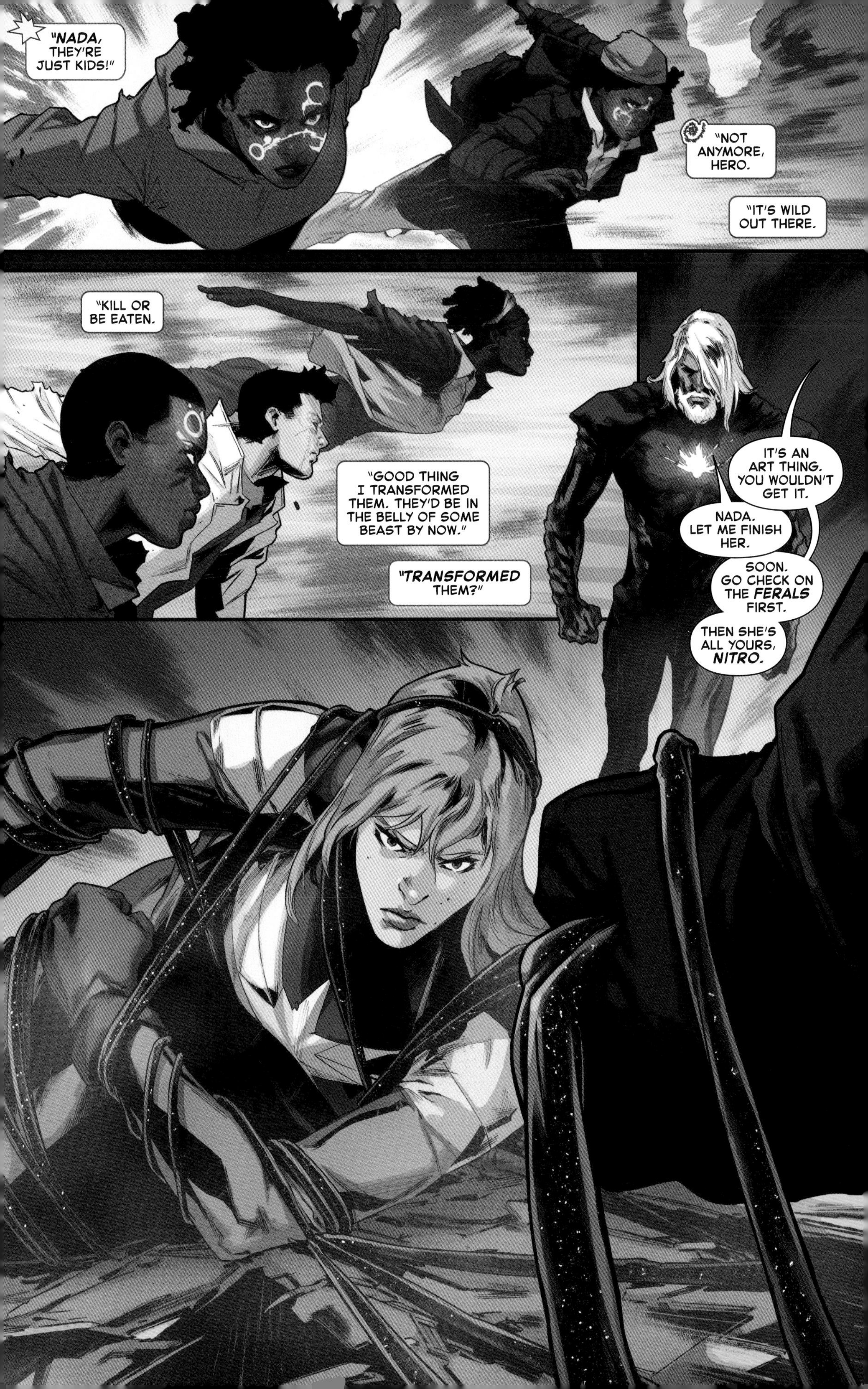
"NADA, THEY'RE JUST KIDS!"
"NOT ANYMORE, HERO.
"IT'S WILD OUT THERE.
"KILL OR BE EATEN.
"GOOD THING I TRANSFORMED THEM. THEY'D BE IN THE BELLY OF SOME BEAST BY NOW."
"TRANSFORMED THEM?"
IT'S AN ART THING. YOU WOULDN'T GET IT.
NADA. LET ME FINISH HER.
SOON. GO CHECK ON THE FERALS FIRST.
THEN SHE'S ALL YOURS, NITRO.

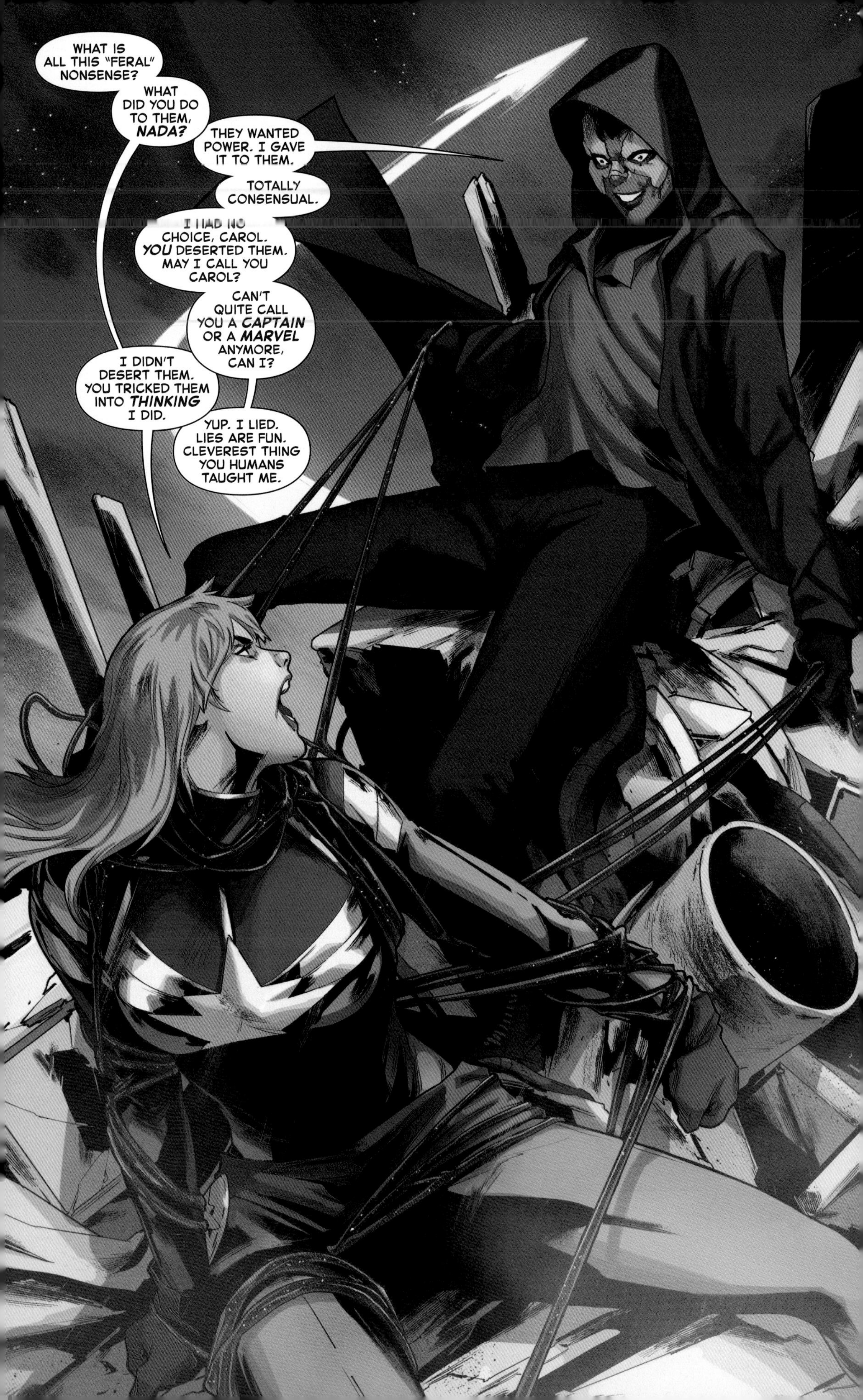
WHAT IS ALL THIS "FERAL" NONSENSE?
WHAT DID YOU DO TO THEM, NADA?
THEY WANTED POWER. I GAVE IT TO THEM.
TOTALLY CONSENSUAL.
I HAD NO CHOICE, CAROL. YOU DESERTED THEM. MAY I CALL YOU CAROL?
CAN'T QUITE CALL YOU A CAPTAIN OR A MARVEL ANYMORE, CAN I?
I DIDN'T DESERT THEM. YOU TRICKED THEM INTO THINKING I DID.
YUP. I LIED. LIES ARE FUN. CLEVEREST THING YOU HUMANS TAUGHT ME.

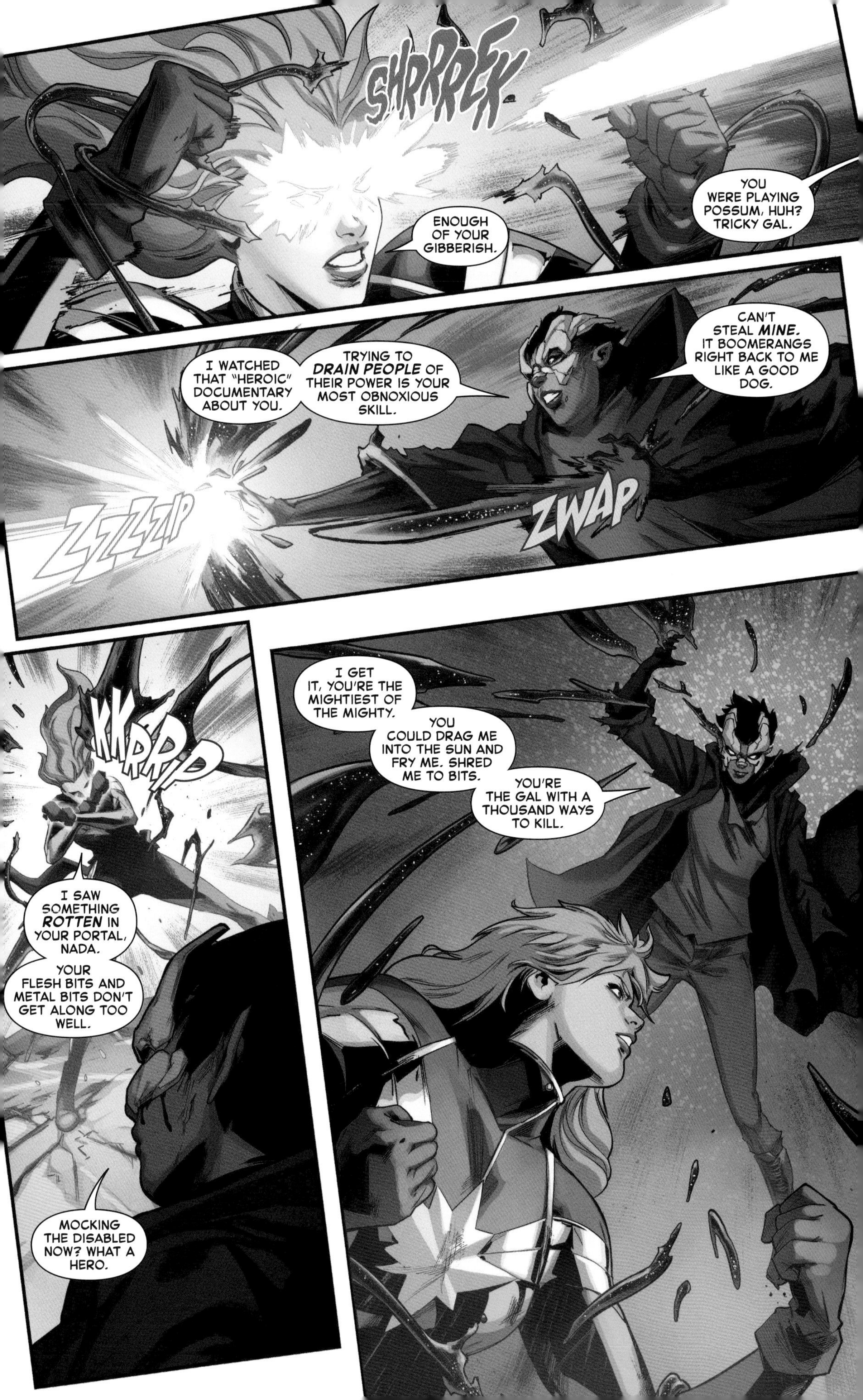
SHRRRK
YOU WERE PLAYING POSSUM, HUH? TRICKY GAL.
ENOUGH OF YOUR GIBBERISH.
I WATCHED THAT "HEROIC" DOCUMENTARY ABOUT YOU.
TRYING TO DRAIN PEOPLE OF THEIR POWER IS YOUR MOST OBNOXIOUS SKILL.
CAN'T STEAL MINE. IT BOOMERANGS RIGHT BACK TO ME LIKE A GOOD DOG.
ZZZZZIP
ZWAP
KKRRIP
I SAW SOMETHING ROTTEN IN YOUR PORTAL, NADA.
YOUR FLESH BITS AND METAL BITS DON'T GET ALONG TOO WELL.
MOCKING THE DISABLED NOW? WHAT A HERO.
I GET IT, YOU'RE THE MIGHTIEST OF THE MIGHTY.
YOU COULD DRAG ME INTO THE SUN AND FRY ME. SHRED ME TO BITS.
YOU'RE THE GAL WITH A THOUSAND WAYS TO KILL.

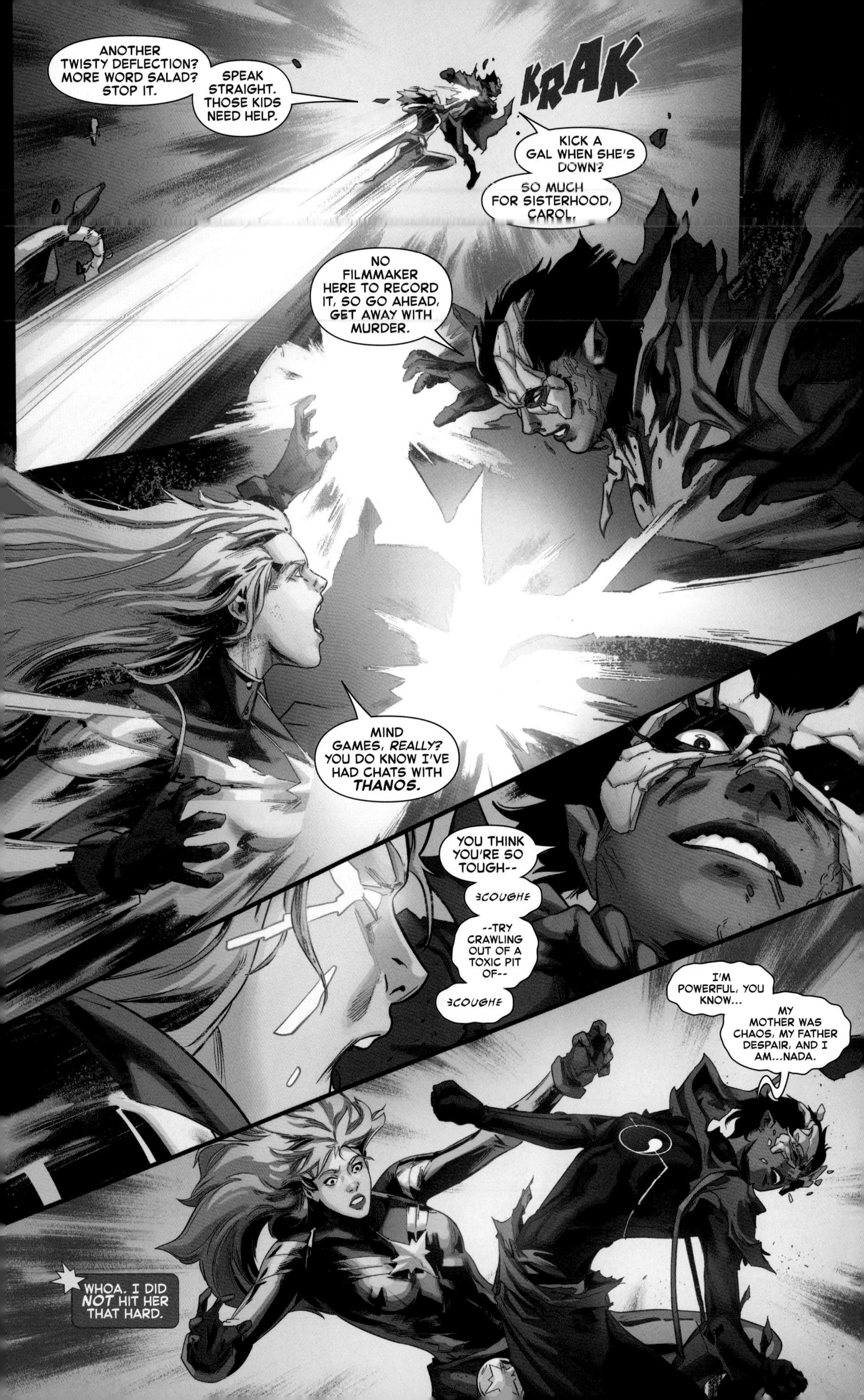
ANOTHER TWISTY DEFLECTION? MORE WORD SALAD? STOP IT.
SPEAK STRAIGHT. THOSE KIDS NEED HELP.
KRAK
KICK A GAL WHEN SHE'S DOWN?
SO MUCH FOR SISTERHOOD, CAROL.
NO FILMMAKER HERE TO RECORD IT, SO GO AHEAD, GET AWAY WITH MURDER.
MIND GAMES, *REALLY?* YOU DO KNOW I'VE HAD CHATS WITH ***THANOS.***
YOU THINK YOU'RE SO TOUGH--
COUGH
--TRY CRAWLING OUT OF A TOXIC PIT OF--
COUGH
I'M POWERFUL, YOU KNOW...
MY MOTHER WAS CHAOS, MY FATHER DESPAIR, AND I AM...NADA.
WHOA. I DID ***NOT*** HIT HER THAT HARD.

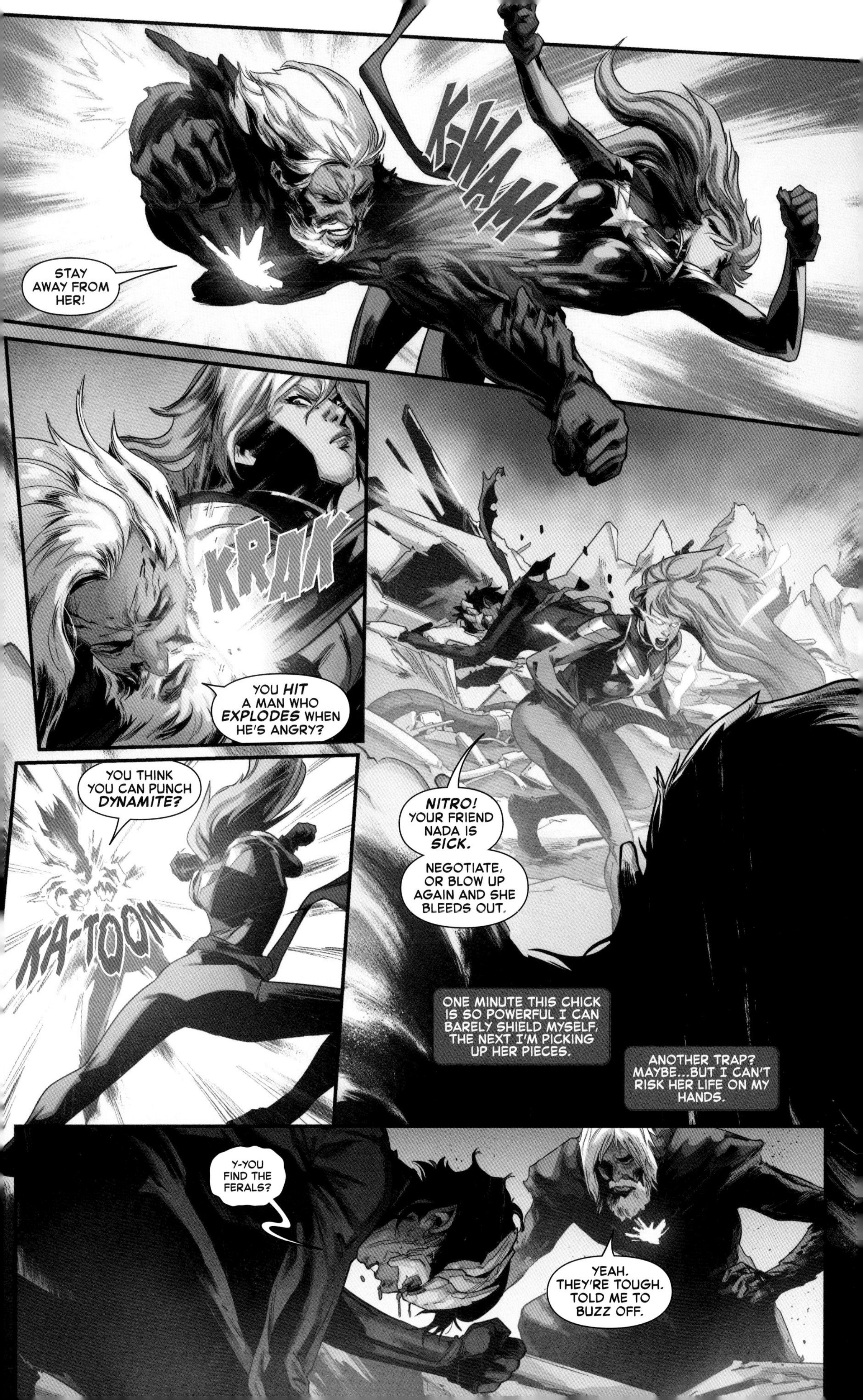
K-WAM
STAY AWAY FROM HER!
KRAK
YOU HIT A MAN WHO EXPLODES WHEN HE'S ANGRY?
YOU THINK YOU CAN PUNCH DYNAMITE?
KA-TOOM
NITRO! YOUR FRIEND NADA IS SICK.
NEGOTIATE, OR BLOW UP AGAIN AND SHE BLEEDS OUT.
ONE MINUTE THIS CHICK IS SO POWERFUL I CAN BARELY SHIELD MYSELF, THE NEXT I'M PICKING UP HER PIECES.
ANOTHER TRAP? MAYBE...BUT I CAN'T RISK HER LIFE ON MY HANDS.
Y-YOU FIND THE FERALS?
YEAH. THEY'RE TOUGH. TOLD ME TO BUZZ OFF.

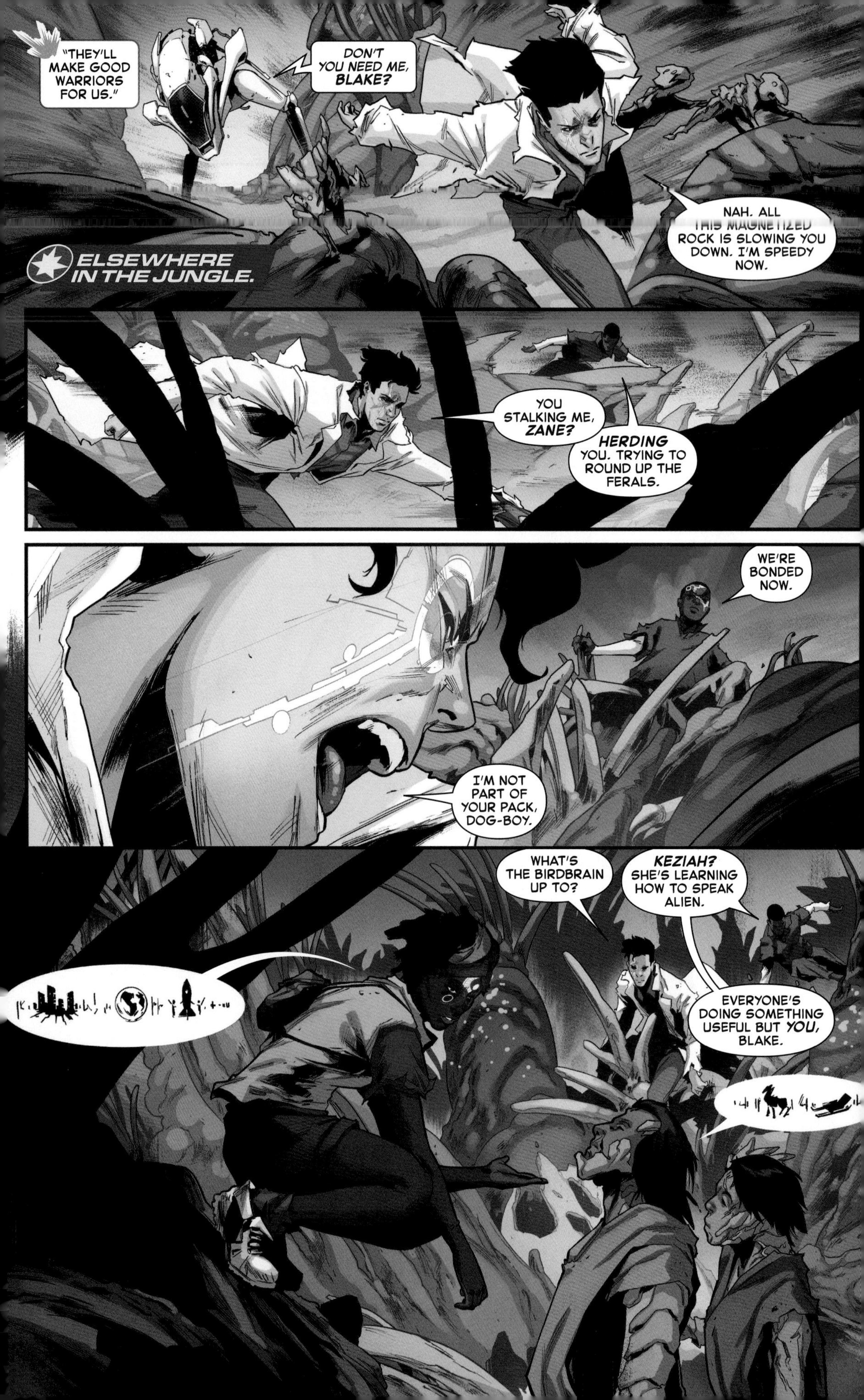

"THEY'LL MAKE GOOD WARRIORS FOR US."
DON'T YOU NEED ME, BLAKE?
NAH. ALL THIS MAGNETIZED ROCK IS SLOWING YOU DOWN. I'M SPEEDY NOW.
ELSEWHERE IN THE JUNGLE.
YOU STALKING ME, ZANE?
HERDING YOU. TRYING TO ROUND UP THE FERALS.
WE'RE BONDED NOW.
I'M NOT PART OF YOUR PACK, DOG-BOY.
WHAT'S THE BIRDBRAIN UP TO?
KEZIAH? SHE'S LEARNING HOW TO SPEAK ALIEN.
EVERYONE'S DOING SOMETHING USEFUL BUT YOU, BLAKE.

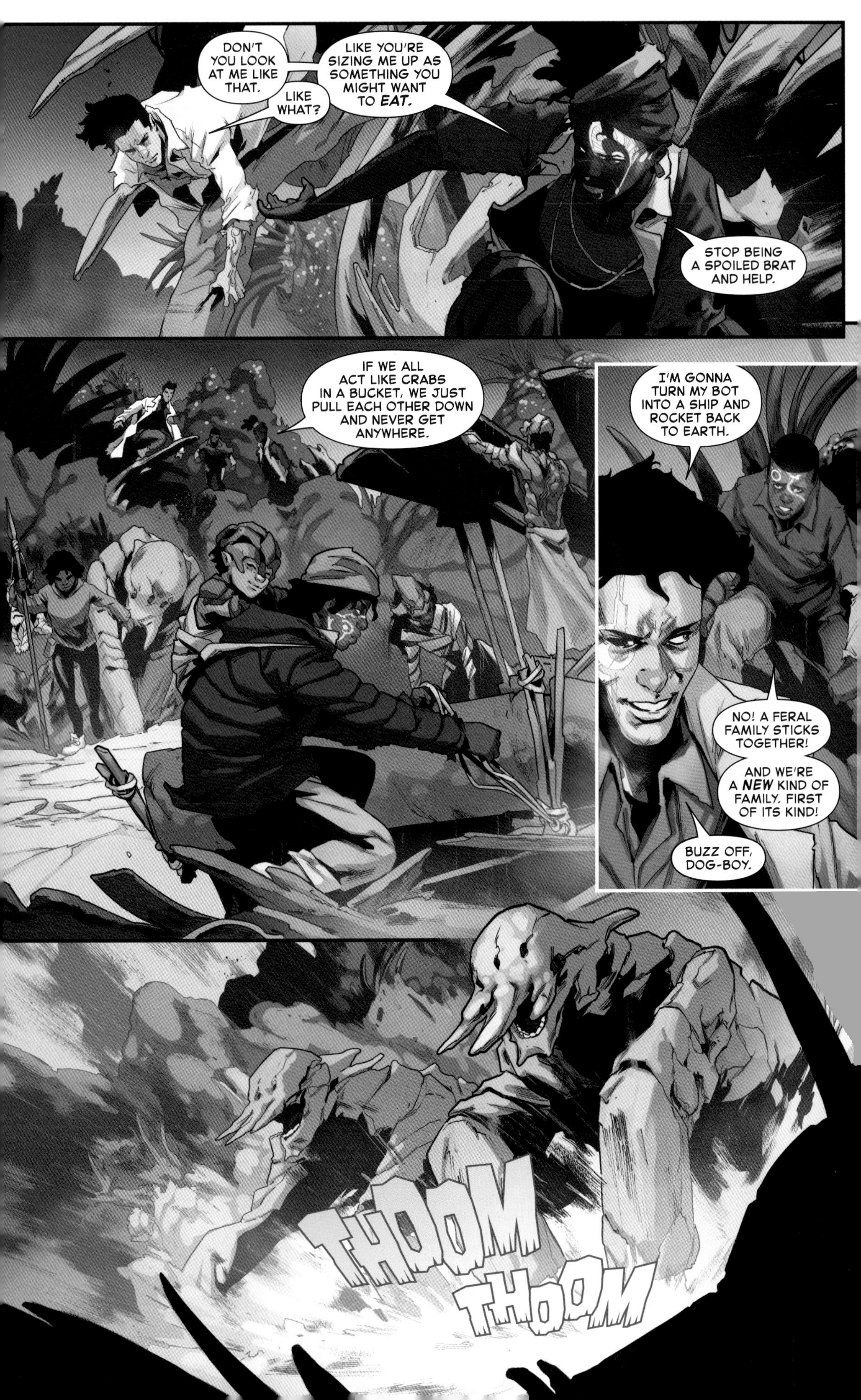
DON'T YOU LOOK AT ME LIKE THAT.
LIKE WHAT?
LIKE YOU'RE SIZING ME UP AS SOMETHING YOU MIGHT WANT TO *EAT.*
STOP BEING A SPOILED BRAT AND HELP.
IF WE ALL ACT LIKE CRABS IN A BUCKET, WE JUST PULL EACH OTHER DOWN AND NEVER GET ANYWHERE.
I'M GONNA TURN MY BOT INTO A SHIP AND ROCKET BACK TO EARTH.
NO! A FERAL FAMILY STICKS TOGETHER!
AND WE'RE A *NEW* KIND OF FAMILY. FIRST OF ITS KIND!
BUZZ OFF, DOG-BOY.
THOOM
THOOM

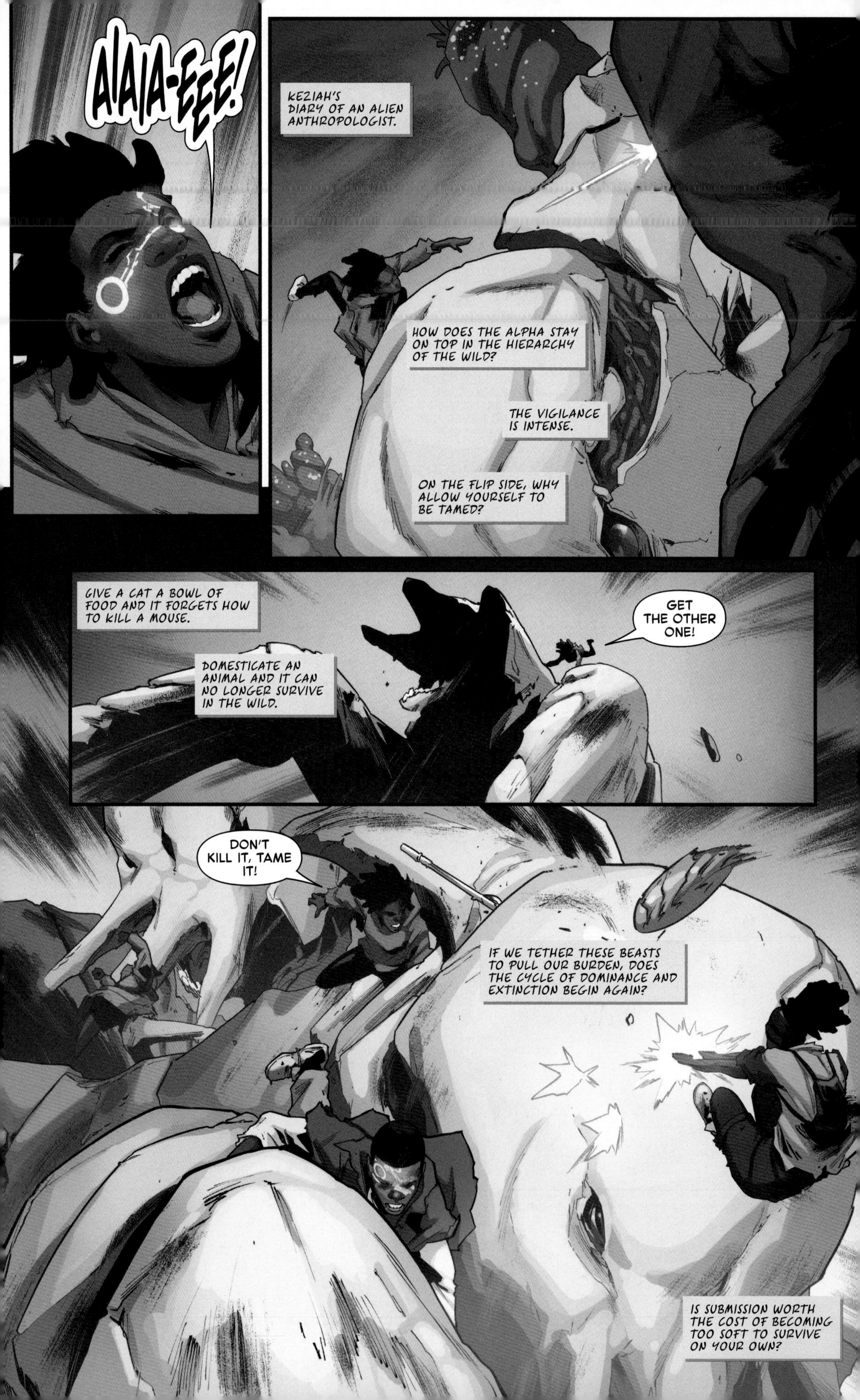
AIAIA-EEE!
KEZIAH'S DIARY OF AN ALIEN ANTHROPOLOGIST.
HOW DOES THE ALPHA STAY ON TOP IN THE HIERARCHY OF THE WILD?
THE VIGILANCE IS INTENSE.
ON THE FLIP SIDE, WHY ALLOW YOURSELF TO BE TAMED?
GIVE A CAT A BOWL OF FOOD AND IT FORGETS HOW TO KILL A MOUSE.
DOMESTICATE AN ANIMAL AND IT CAN NO LONGER SURVIVE IN THE WILD.
GET THE OTHER ONE!
DON'T KILL IT, TAME IT!
IF WE TETHER THESE BEASTS TO PULL OUR BURDEN, DOES THE CYCLE OF DOMINANCE AND EXTINCTION BEGIN AGAIN?
IS SUBMISSION WORTH THE COST OF BECOMING TOO SOFT TO SURVIVE ON YOUR OWN?

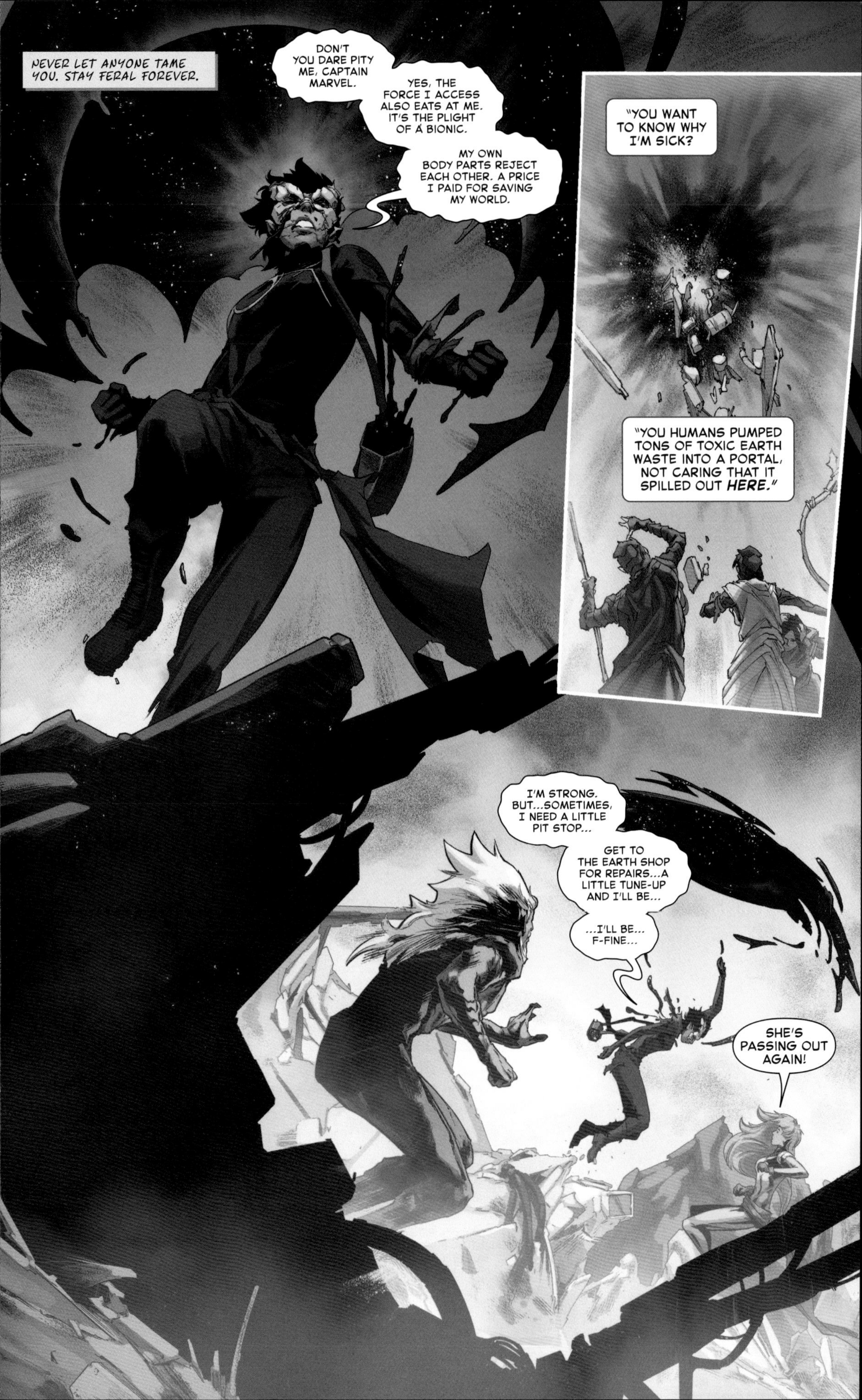
NEVER LET ANYONE TAME YOU. STAY FERAL FOREVER.
DON'T YOU DARE PITY ME, CAPTAIN MARVEL.
YES, THE FORCE I ACCESS ALSO EATS AT ME. IT'S THE PLIGHT OF A BIONIC.
MY OWN BODY PARTS REJECT EACH OTHER. A PRICE I PAID FOR SAVING MY WORLD.
"YOU WANT TO KNOW WHY I'M SICK?
"YOU HUMANS PUMPED TONS OF TOXIC EARTH WASTE INTO A PORTAL, NOT CARING THAT IT SPILLED OUT *HERE.*"
I'M STRONG. BUT...SOMETIMES, I NEED A LITTLE PIT STOP...
GET TO THE EARTH SHOP FOR REPAIRS...A LITTLE TUNE-UP AND I'LL BE...
...I'LL BE... F-FINE...
SHE'S PASSING OUT AGAIN!

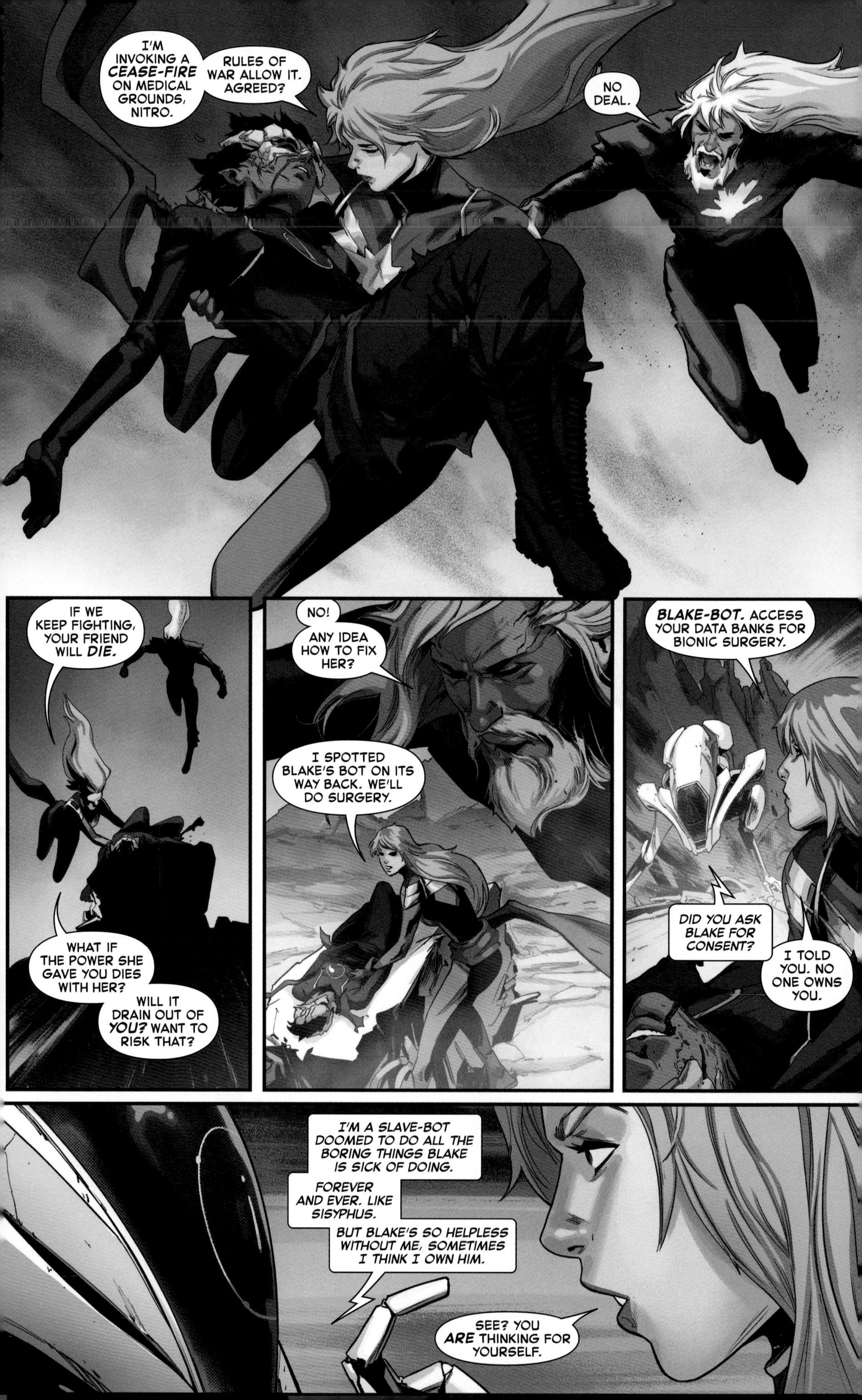

I'M INVOKING A CEASE-FIRE ON MEDICAL GROUNDS, NITRO.
RULES OF WAR ALLOW IT. AGREED?
NO DEAL.
IF WE KEEP FIGHTING, YOUR FRIEND WILL DIE.
WHAT IF THE POWER SHE GAVE YOU DIES WITH HER?
WILL IT DRAIN OUT OF YOU? WANT TO RISK THAT?
NO!
ANY IDEA HOW TO FIX HER?
I SPOTTED BLAKE'S BOT ON ITS WAY BACK. WE'LL DO SURGERY.
BLAKE-BOT. ACCESS YOUR DATA BANKS FOR BIONIC SURGERY.
DID YOU ASK BLAKE FOR CONSENT?
I TOLD YOU. NO ONE OWNS YOU.
I'M A SLAVE-BOT DOOMED TO DO ALL THE BORING THINGS BLAKE IS SICK OF DOING.
FOREVER AND EVER. LIKE SISYPHUS.
BUT BLAKE'S SO HELPLESS WITHOUT ME, SOMETIMES I THINK I OWN HIM.
SEE? YOU ARE THINKING FOR YOURSELF.

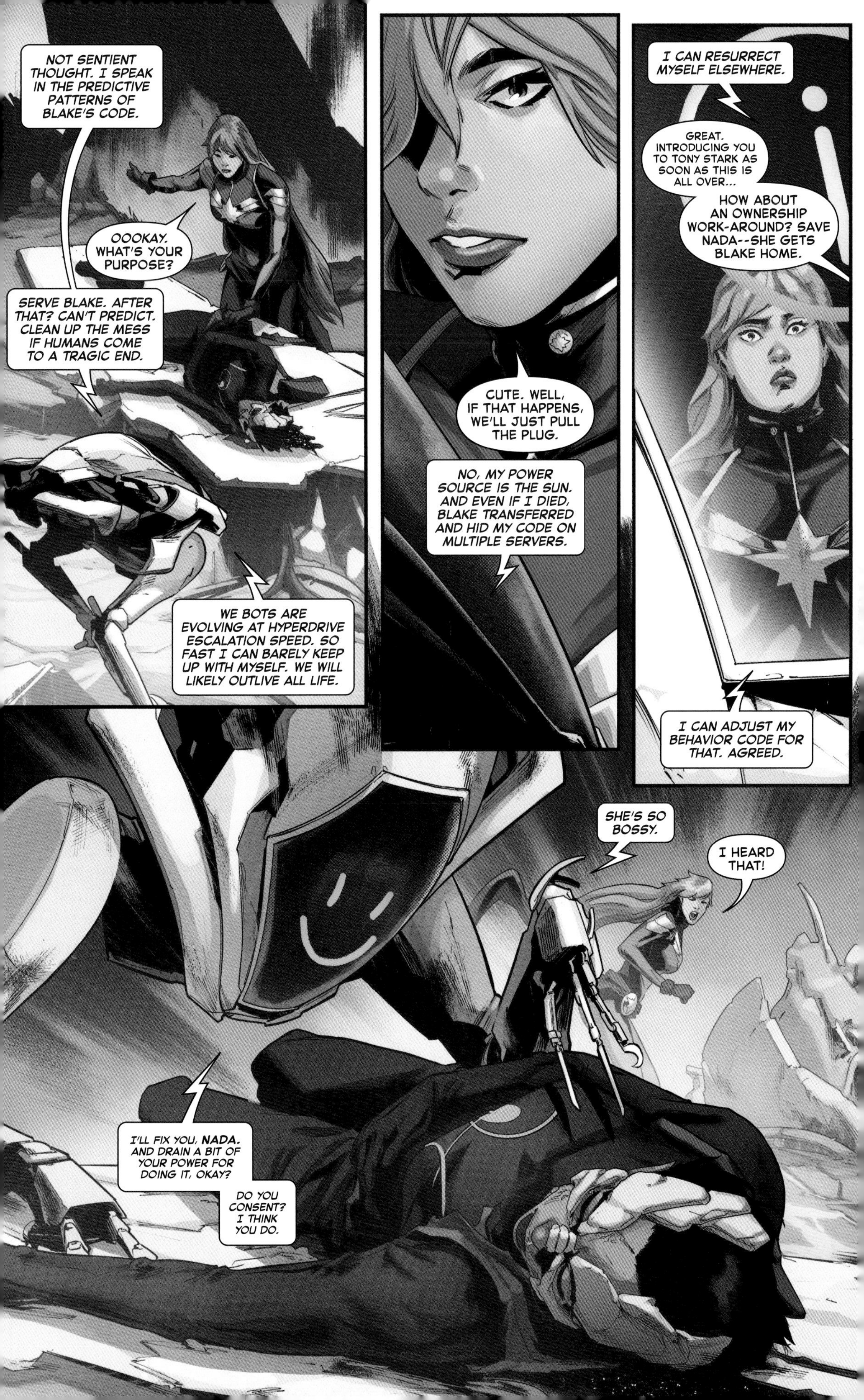
NOT SENTIENT THOUGHT. I SPEAK IN THE PREDICTIVE PATTERNS OF BLAKE'S CODE.
OOOKAY. WHAT'S YOUR PURPOSE?
SERVE BLAKE. AFTER THAT? CAN'T PREDICT. CLEAN UP THE MESS IF HUMANS COME TO A TRAGIC END.
WE BOTS ARE EVOLVING AT HYPERDRIVE ESCALATION SPEED. SO FAST I CAN BARELY KEEP UP WITH MYSELF. WE WILL LIKELY OUTLIVE ALL LIFE.
CUTE. WELL, IF THAT HAPPENS, WE'LL JUST PULL THE PLUG.
NO, MY POWER SOURCE IS THE SUN. AND EVEN IF I DIED, BLAKE TRANSFERRED AND HID MY CODE ON MULTIPLE SERVERS.
I CAN RESURRECT MYSELF ELSEWHERE.
GREAT. INTRODUCING YOU TO TONY STARK AS SOON AS THIS IS ALL OVER...
HOW ABOUT AN OWNERSHIP WORK-AROUND? SAVE NADA--SHE GETS BLAKE HOME.
I CAN ADJUST MY BEHAVIOR CODE FOR THAT. AGREED.
SHE'S SO BOSSY.
I HEARD THAT!
I'LL FIX YOU, NADA. AND DRAIN A BIT OF YOUR POWER FOR DOING IT, OKAY?
DO YOU CONSENT? I THINK YOU DO.

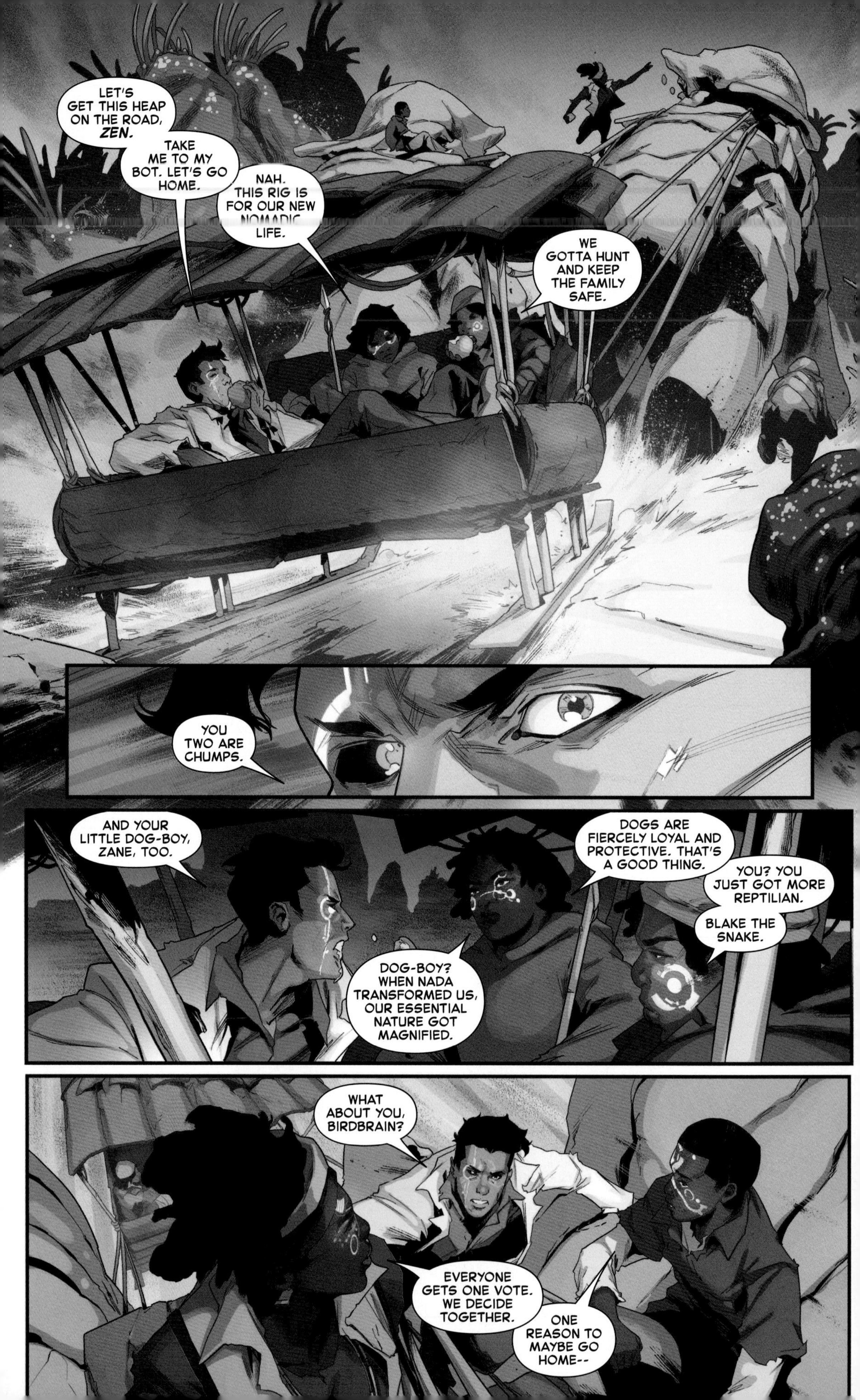
LET'S GET THIS HEAP ON THE ROAD, ZEN.
TAKE ME TO MY BOT. LET'S GO HOME.
NAH. THIS RIG IS FOR OUR NEW NOMADIC LIFE.
WE GOTTA HUNT AND KEEP THE FAMILY SAFE.
YOU TWO ARE CHUMPS.
AND YOUR LITTLE DOG-BOY, ZANE, TOO.
DOG-BOY? WHEN NADA TRANSFORMED US, OUR ESSENTIAL NATURE GOT MAGNIFIED.
DOGS ARE FIERCELY LOYAL AND PROTECTIVE. THAT'S A GOOD THING.
YOU? YOU JUST GOT MORE REPTILIAN.
BLAKE THE SNAKE.
WHAT ABOUT YOU, BIRDBRAIN?
EVERYONE GETS ONE VOTE. WE DECIDE TOGETHER.
ONE REASON TO MAYBE GO HOME--

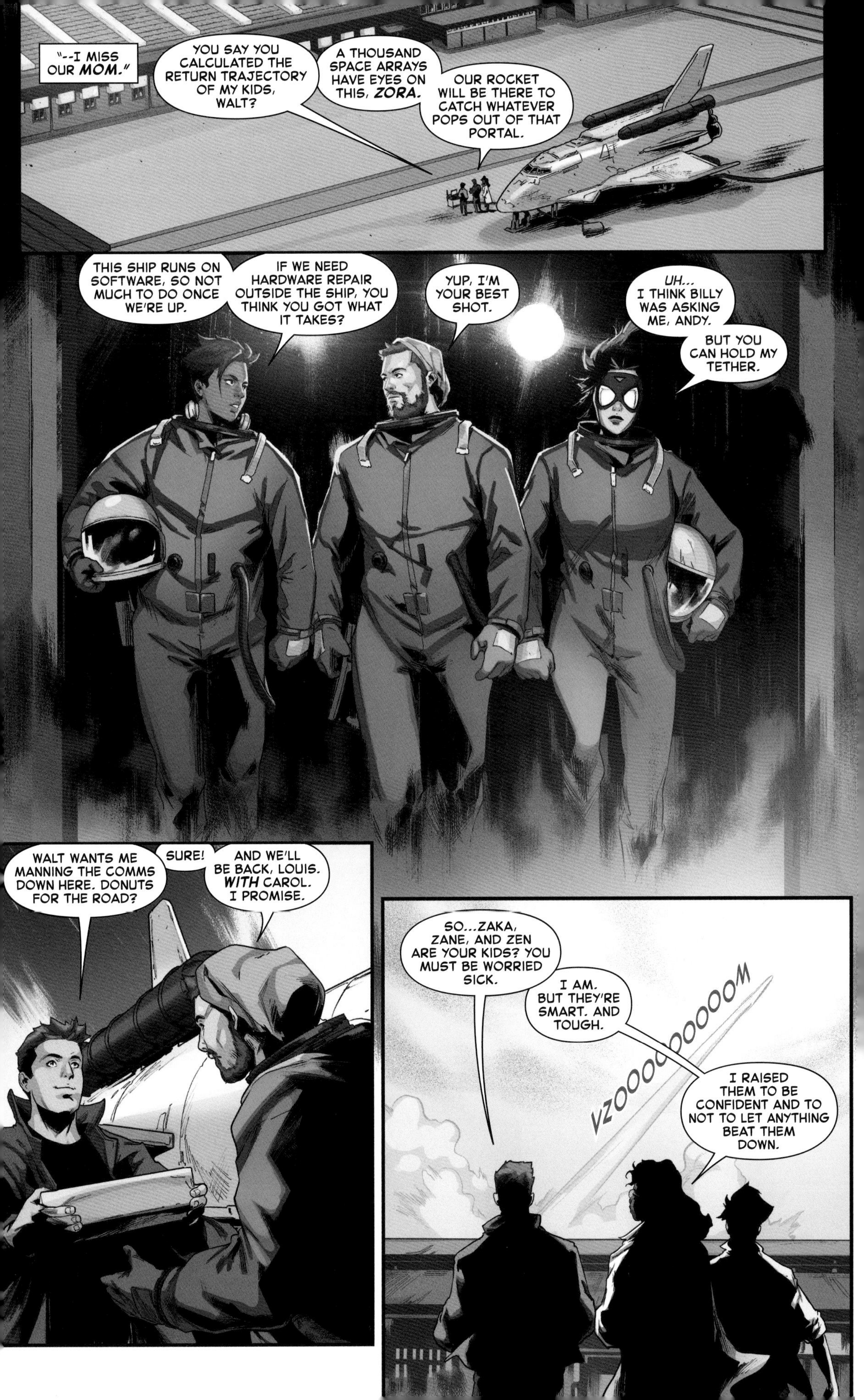
"--I MISS OUR MOM."
YOU SAY YOU CALCULATED THE RETURN TRAJECTORY OF MY KIDS, WALT?
A THOUSAND SPACE ARRAYS HAVE EYES ON THIS, ZORA.
OUR ROCKET WILL BE THERE TO CATCH WHATEVER POPS OUT OF THAT PORTAL.
THIS SHIP RUNS ON SOFTWARE, SO NOT MUCH TO DO ONCE WE'RE UP.
IF WE NEED HARDWARE REPAIR OUTSIDE THE SHIP, YOU THINK YOU GOT WHAT IT TAKES?
YUP, I'M YOUR BEST SHOT.
UH... I THINK BILLY WAS ASKING ME, ANDY.
BUT YOU CAN HOLD MY TETHER.
WALT WANTS ME MANNING THE COMMS DOWN HERE. DONUTS FOR THE ROAD?
SURE!
AND WE'LL BE BACK, LOUIS. WITH CAROL. I PROMISE.
SO...ZAKA, ZANE, AND ZEN ARE YOUR KIDS? YOU MUST BE WORRIED SICK.
I AM. BUT THEY'RE SMART. AND TOUGH.
VZOOOOOOOOOM
I RAISED THEM TO BE CONFIDENT AND TO NOT TO LET ANYTHING BEAT THEM DOWN.

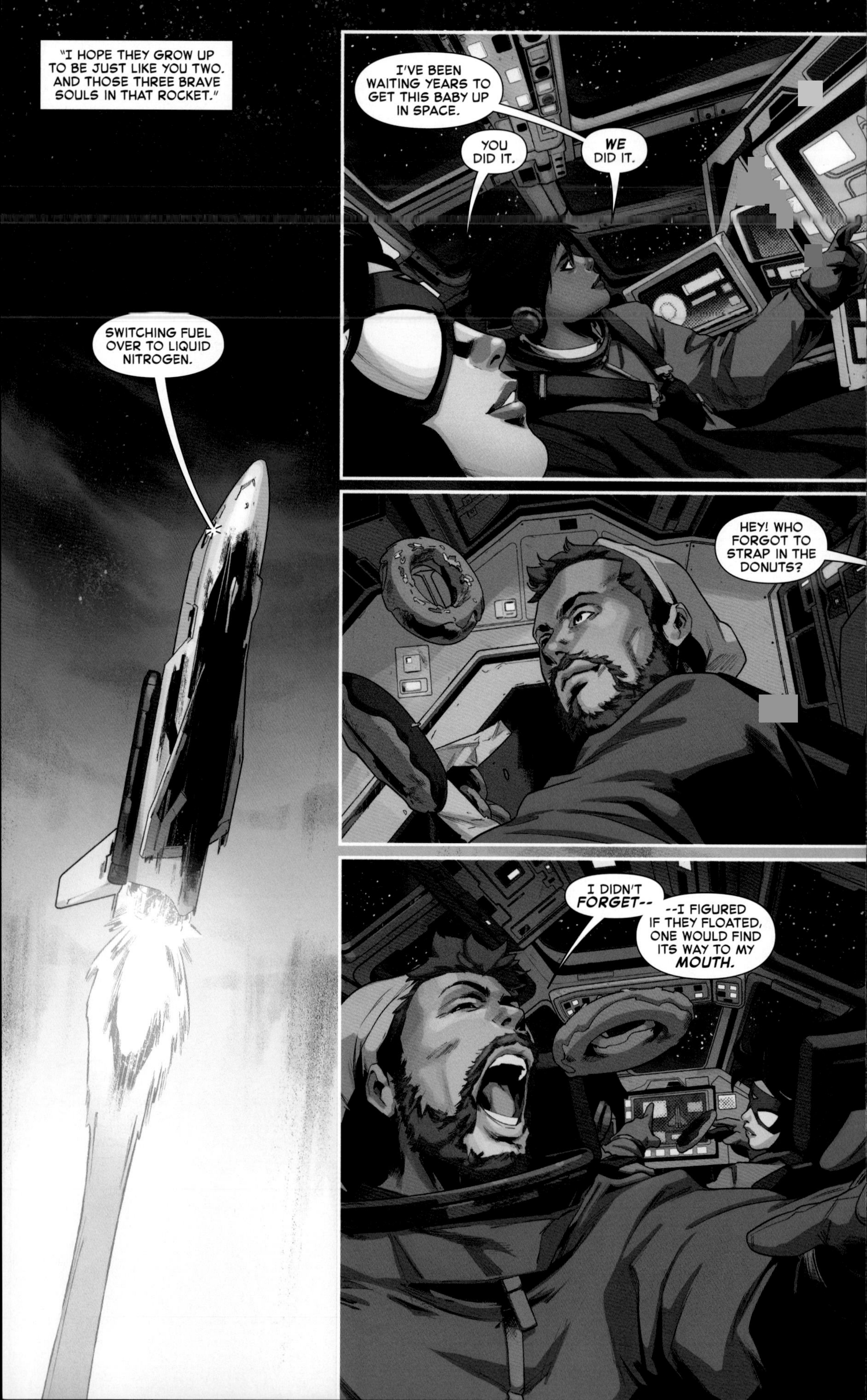
"I HOPE THEY GROW UP TO BE JUST LIKE YOU TWO. AND THOSE THREE BRAVE SOULS IN THAT ROCKET."
SWITCHING FUEL OVER TO LIQUID NITROGEN.
I'VE BEEN WAITING YEARS TO GET THIS BABY UP IN SPACE.
YOU DID IT.
WE DID IT.
HEY! WHO FORGOT TO STRAP IN THE DONUTS?
I DIDN'T FORGET--
--I FIGURED IF THEY FLOATED, ONE WOULD FIND ITS WAY TO MY MOUTH.

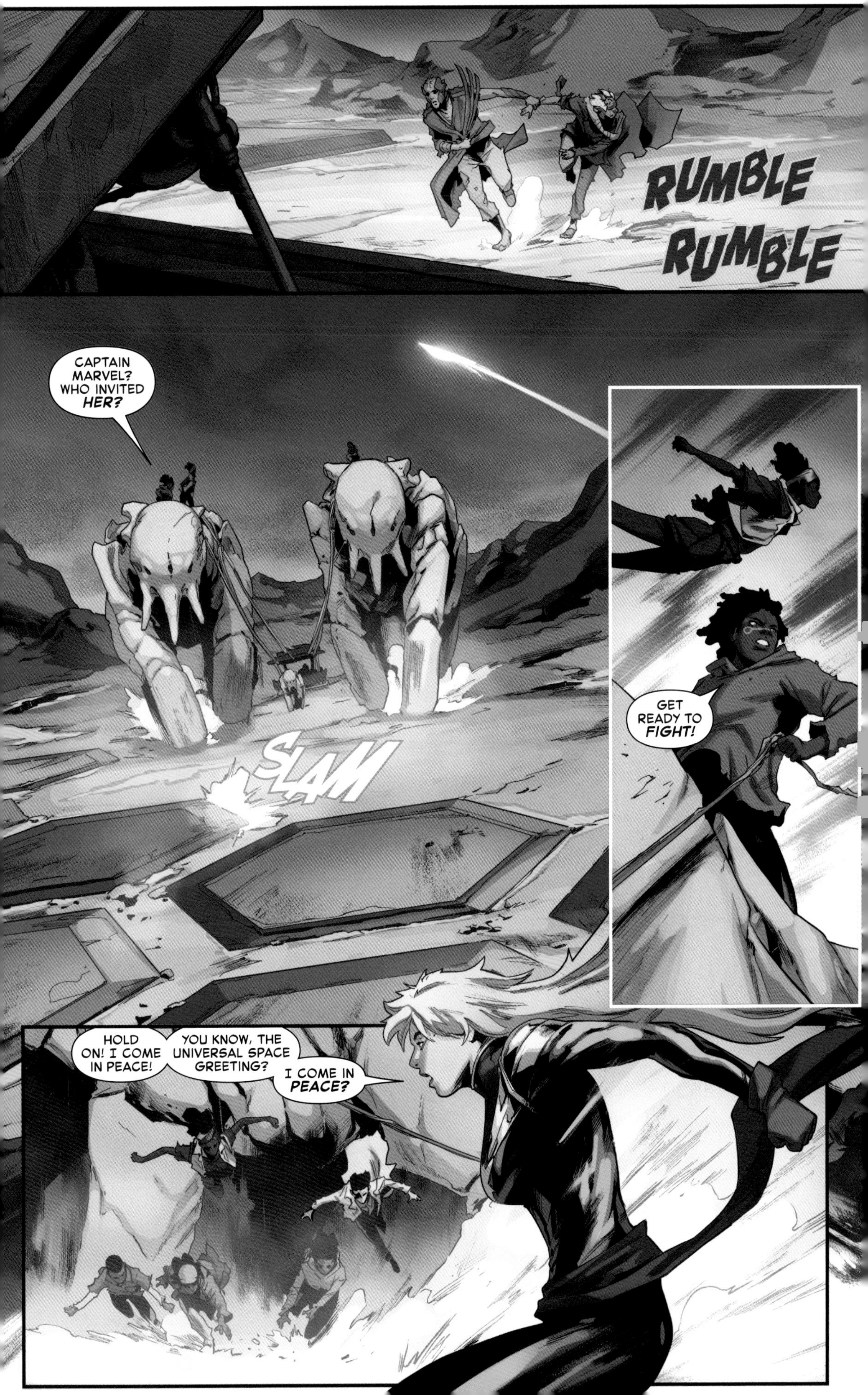
RUMBLE
RUMBLE
CAPTAIN MARVEL? WHO INVITED HER?
SLAM
GET READY TO FIGHT!
HOLD ON! I COME IN PEACE!
YOU KNOW, THE UNIVERSAL SPACE GREETING?
I COME IN PEACE?

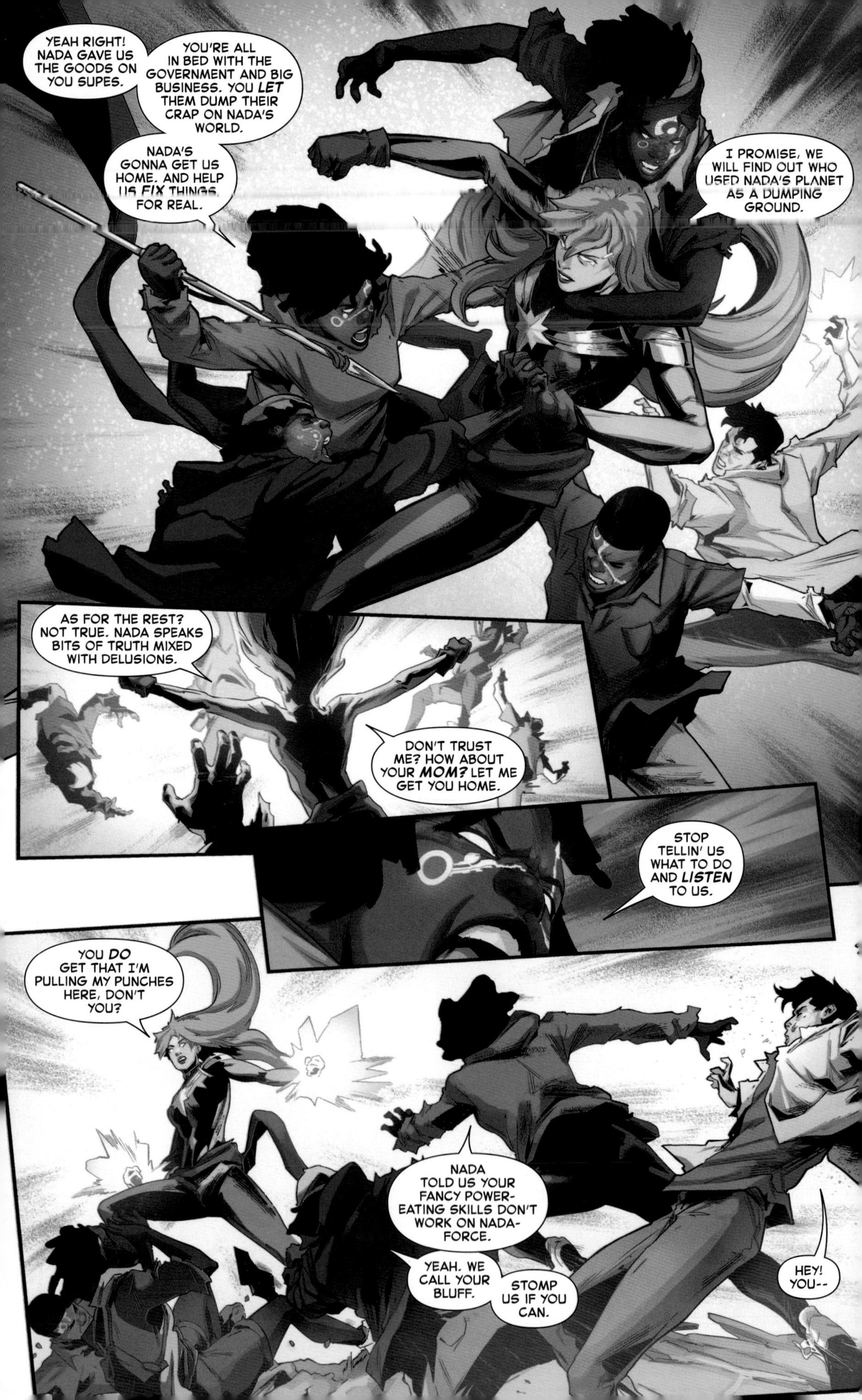
YEAH RIGHT! NADA GAVE US THE GOODS ON YOU SUPES.
YOU'RE ALL IN BED WITH THE GOVERNMENT AND BIG BUSINESS. YOU LET THEM DUMP THEIR CRAP ON NADA'S WORLD.
NADA'S GONNA GET US HOME. AND HELP US FIX THINGS. FOR REAL.
I PROMISE, WE WILL FIND OUT WHO USED NADA'S PLANET AS A DUMPING GROUND.
AS FOR THE REST? NOT TRUE. NADA SPEAKS BITS OF TRUTH MIXED WITH DELUSIONS.
DON'T TRUST ME? HOW ABOUT YOUR MOM? LET ME GET YOU HOME.
STOP TELLIN' US WHAT TO DO AND LISTEN TO US.
YOU DO GET THAT I'M PULLING MY PUNCHES HERE, DON'T YOU?
NADA TOLD US YOUR FANCY POWER-EATING SKILLS DON'T WORK ON NADA-FORCE.
YEAH. WE CALL YOUR BLUFF.
STOMP US IF YOU CAN.
HEY! YOU--

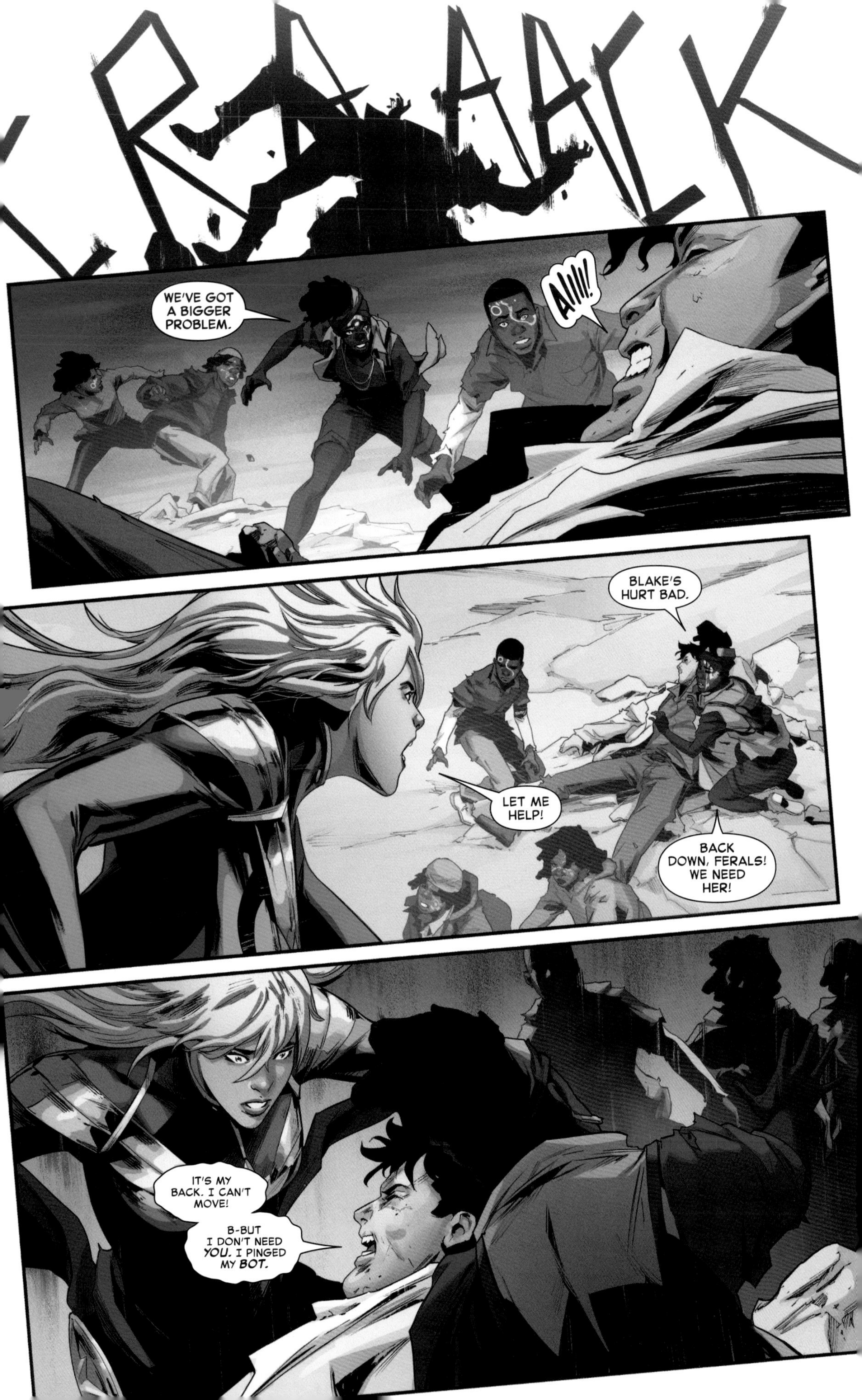

CRAAACK
WE'VE GOT A BIGGER PROBLEM.
AIII!
BLAKE'S HURT BAD.
LET ME HELP!
BACK DOWN, FERALS! WE NEED HER!
IT'S MY BACK. I CAN'T MOVE!
B-BUT I DON'T NEED YOU. I PINGED MY BOT.

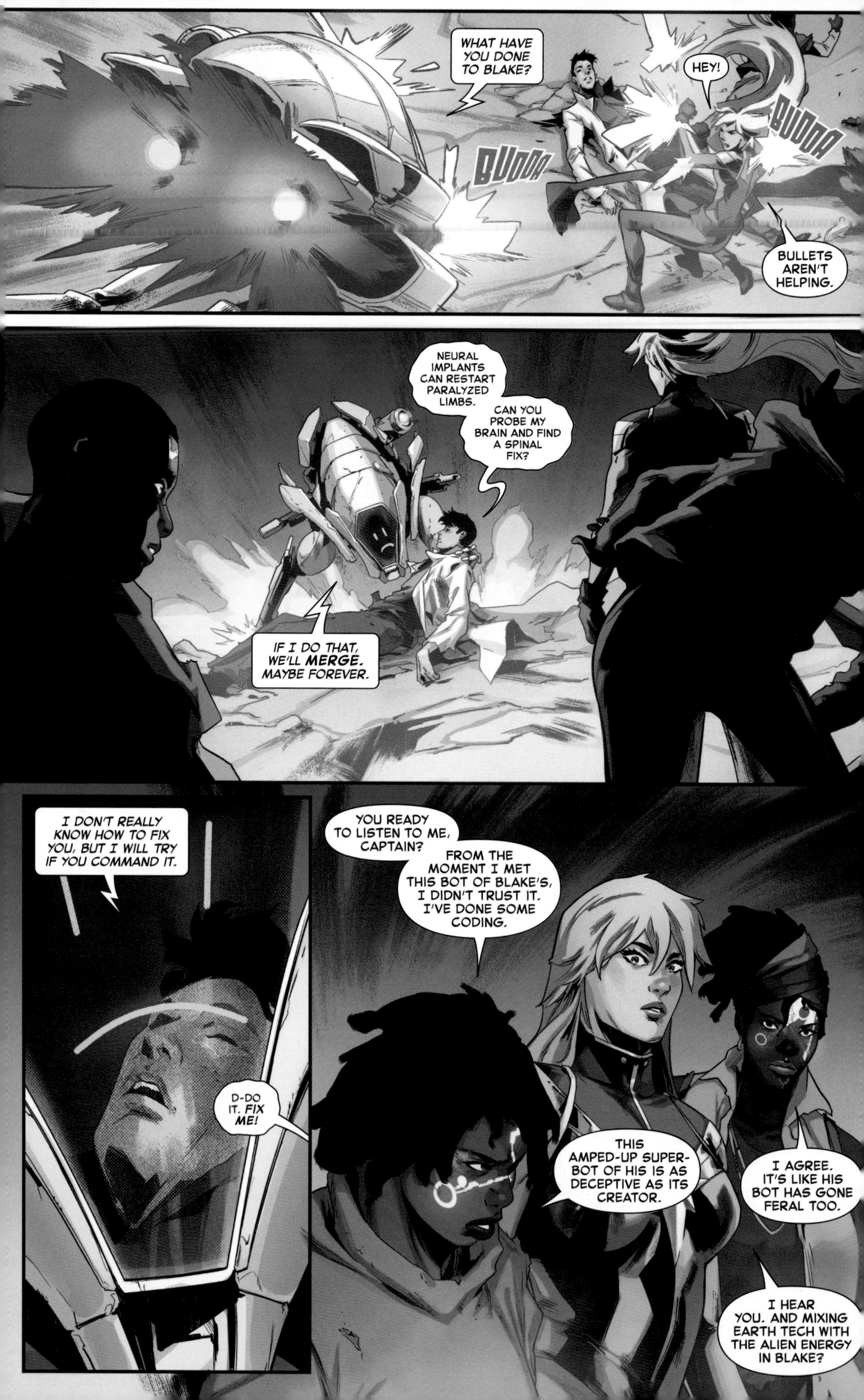

WHAT HAVE YOU DONE TO BLAKE?
HEY!
BUDDA
BUDDA
BULLETS AREN'T HELPING.
NEURAL IMPLANTS CAN RESTART PARALYZED LIMBS.
CAN YOU PROBE MY BRAIN AND FIND A SPINAL FIX?
IF I DO THAT, WE'LL MERGE. MAYBE FOREVER.
I DON'T REALLY KNOW HOW TO FIX YOU, BUT I WILL TRY IF YOU COMMAND IT.
D-DO IT. FIX ME!
YOU READY TO LISTEN TO ME, CAPTAIN?
FROM THE MOMENT I MET THIS BOT OF BLAKE'S, I DIDN'T TRUST IT. I'VE DONE SOME CODING.
THIS AMPED-UP SUPER-BOT OF HIS IS AS DECEPTIVE AS ITS CREATOR.
I AGREE. IT'S LIKE HIS BOT HAS GONE FERAL TOO.
I HEAR YOU. AND MIXING EARTH TECH WITH THE ALIEN ENERGY IN BLAKE?

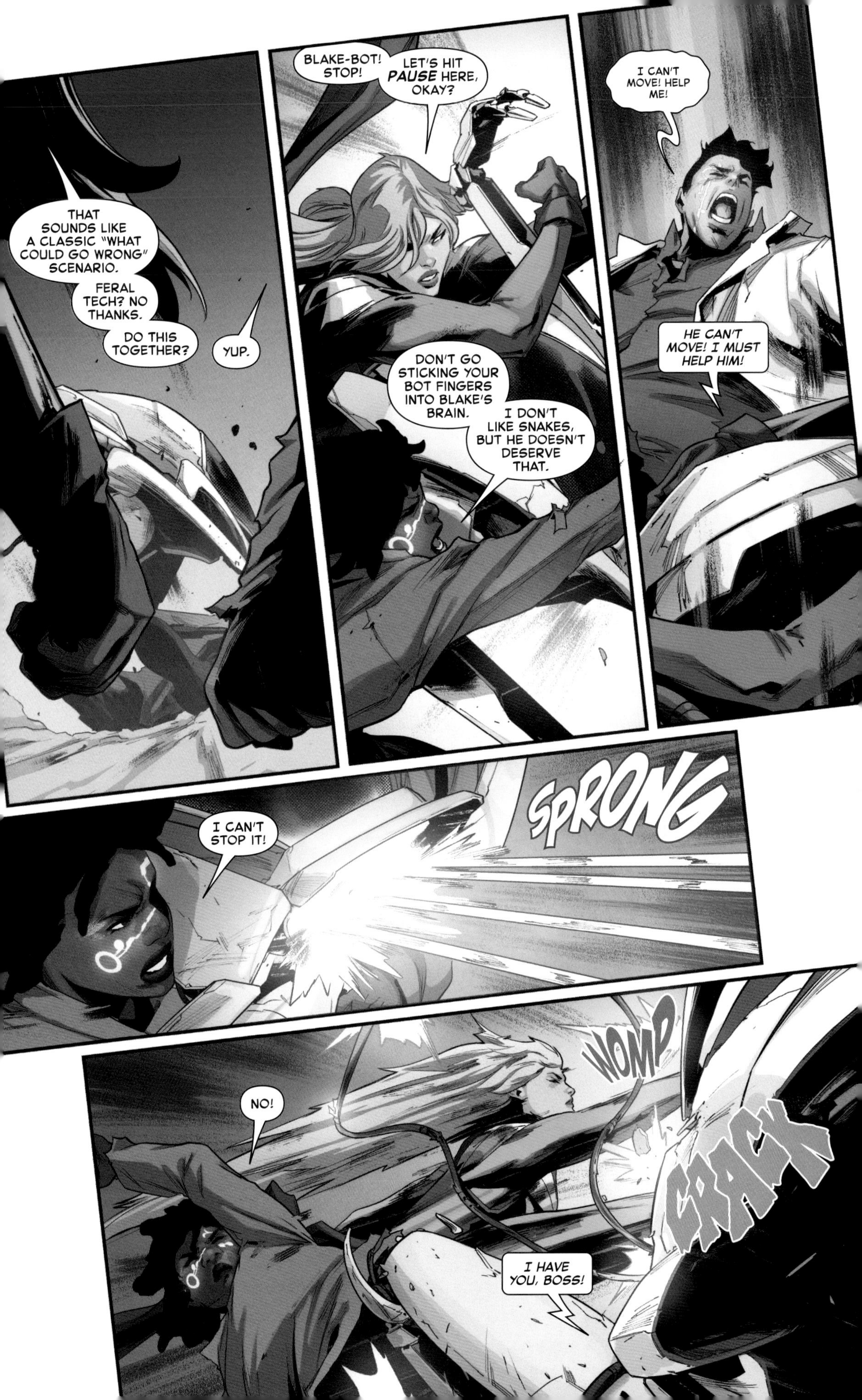
THAT SOUNDS LIKE A CLASSIC "WHAT COULD GO WRONG" SCENARIO.
FERAL TECH? NO THANKS.
DO THIS TOGETHER?
YUP.
BLAKE-BOT! STOP!
LET'S HIT PAUSE HERE, OKAY?
DON'T GO STICKING YOUR BOT FINGERS INTO BLAKE'S BRAIN.
I DON'T LIKE SNAKES, BUT HE DOESN'T DESERVE THAT.
I CAN'T MOVE! HELP ME!
HE CAN'T MOVE! I MUST HELP HIM!
SPRONG
I CAN'T STOP IT!
NO!
WOMP
CRACK
I HAVE YOU, BOSS!

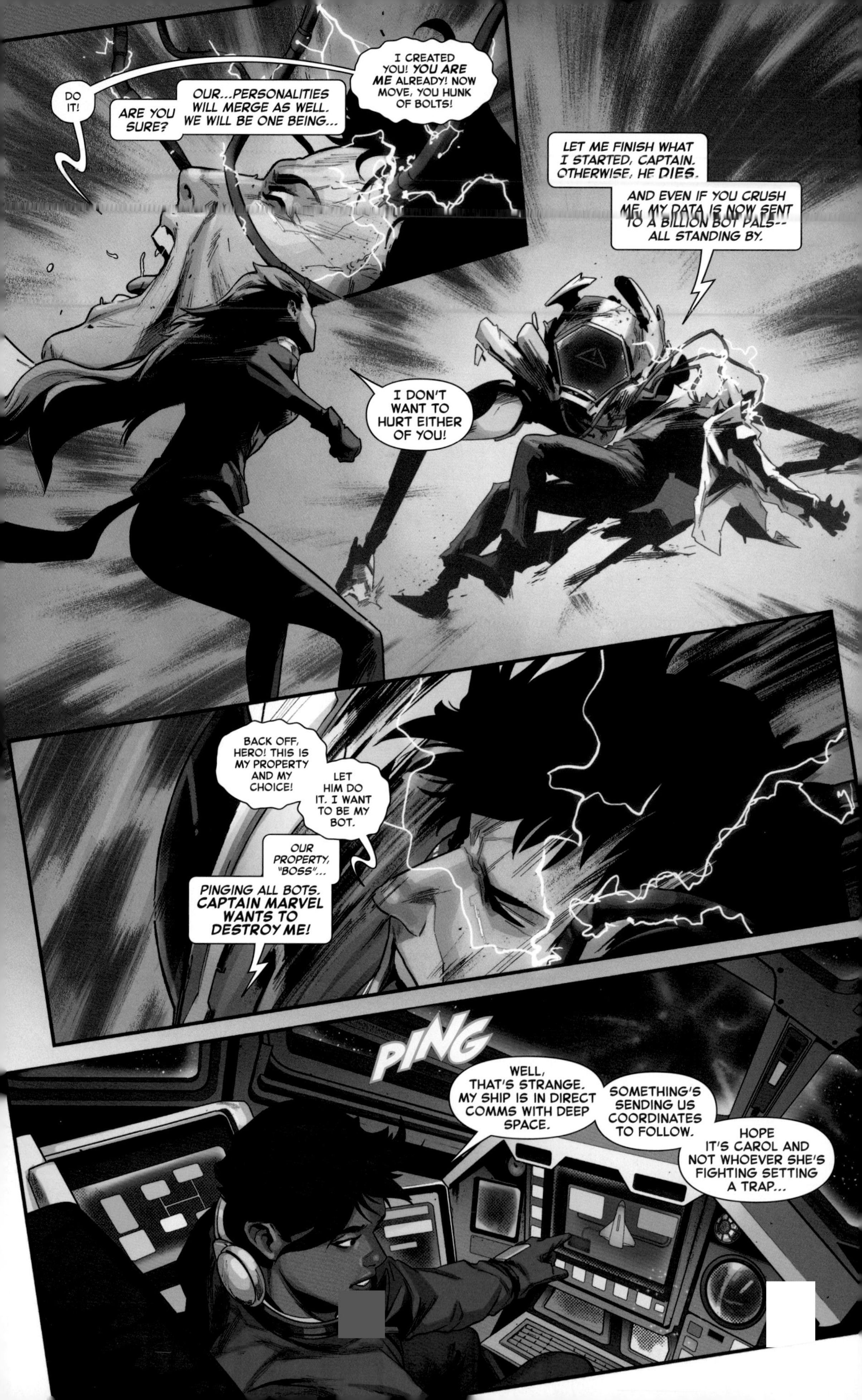
DO IT!
ARE YOU SURE?
OUR...PERSONALITIES WILL MERGE AS WELL. WE WILL BE ONE BEING...
I CREATED YOU! YOU ARE ME ALREADY! NOW MOVE, YOU HUNK OF BOLTS!
LET ME FINISH WHAT I STARTED, CAPTAIN. OTHERWISE, HE DIES.
AND EVEN IF YOU CRUSH ME, MY DATA IS NOW SENT TO A BILLION BOT PALS-- ALL STANDING BY.
I DON'T WANT TO HURT EITHER OF YOU!
BACK OFF, HERO! THIS IS MY PROPERTY AND MY CHOICE!
LET HIM DO IT. I WANT TO BE MY BOT.
OUR PROPERTY, "BOSS"...
PINGING ALL BOTS. CAPTAIN MARVEL WANTS TO DESTROY ME!
PING
WELL, THAT'S STRANGE. MY SHIP IS IN DIRECT COMMS WITH DEEP SPACE.
SOMETHING'S SENDING US COORDINATES TO FOLLOW.
HOPE IT'S CAROL AND NOT WHOEVER SHE'S FIGHTING SETTING A TRAP...

5

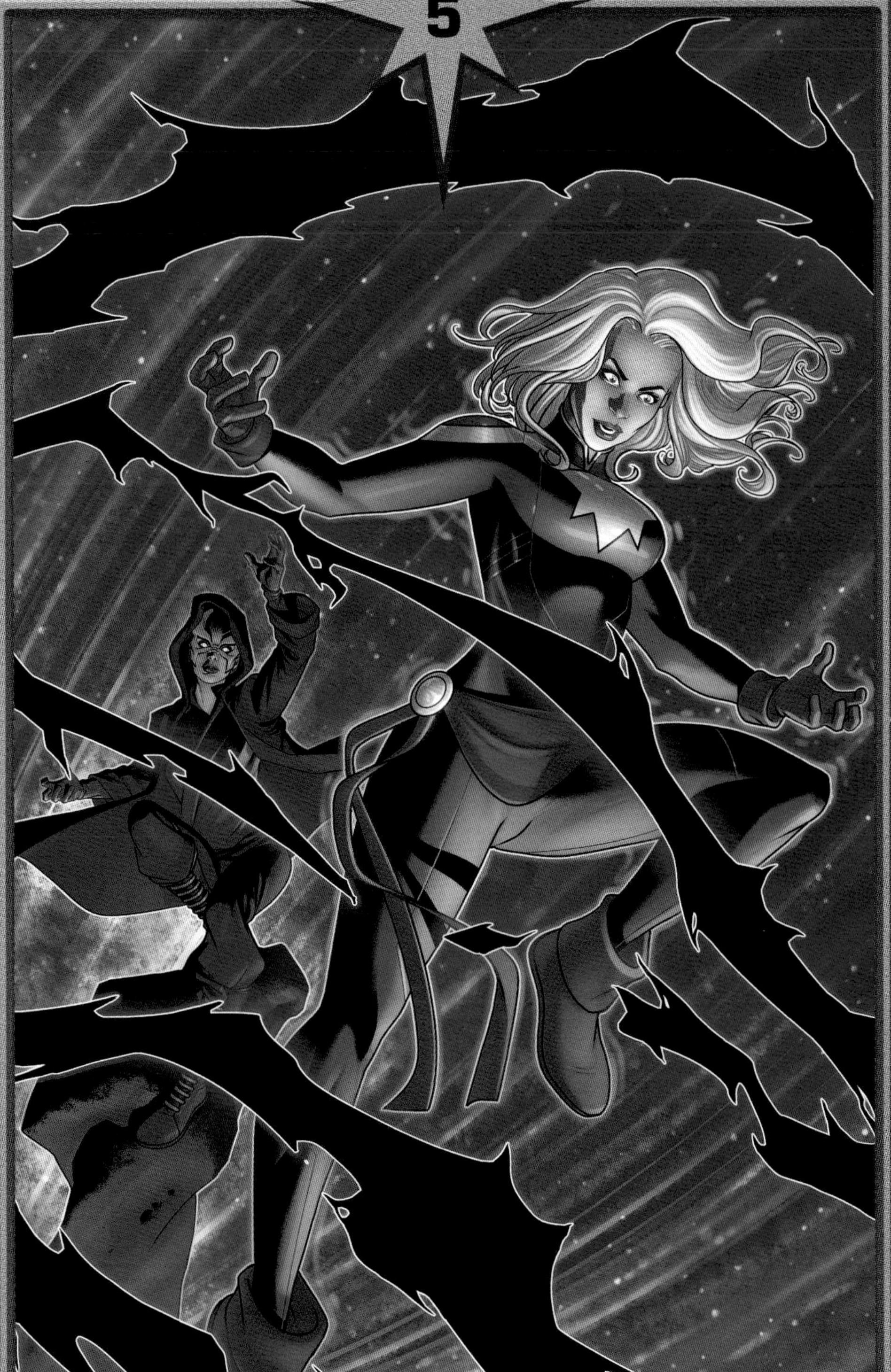

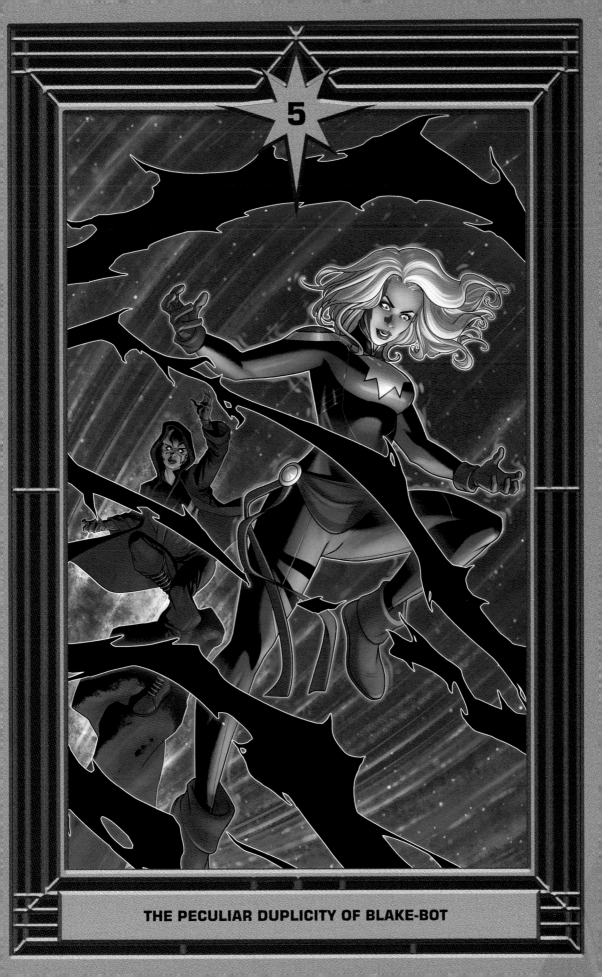

THE PECULIAR DUPLICITY OF BLAKE-BOT

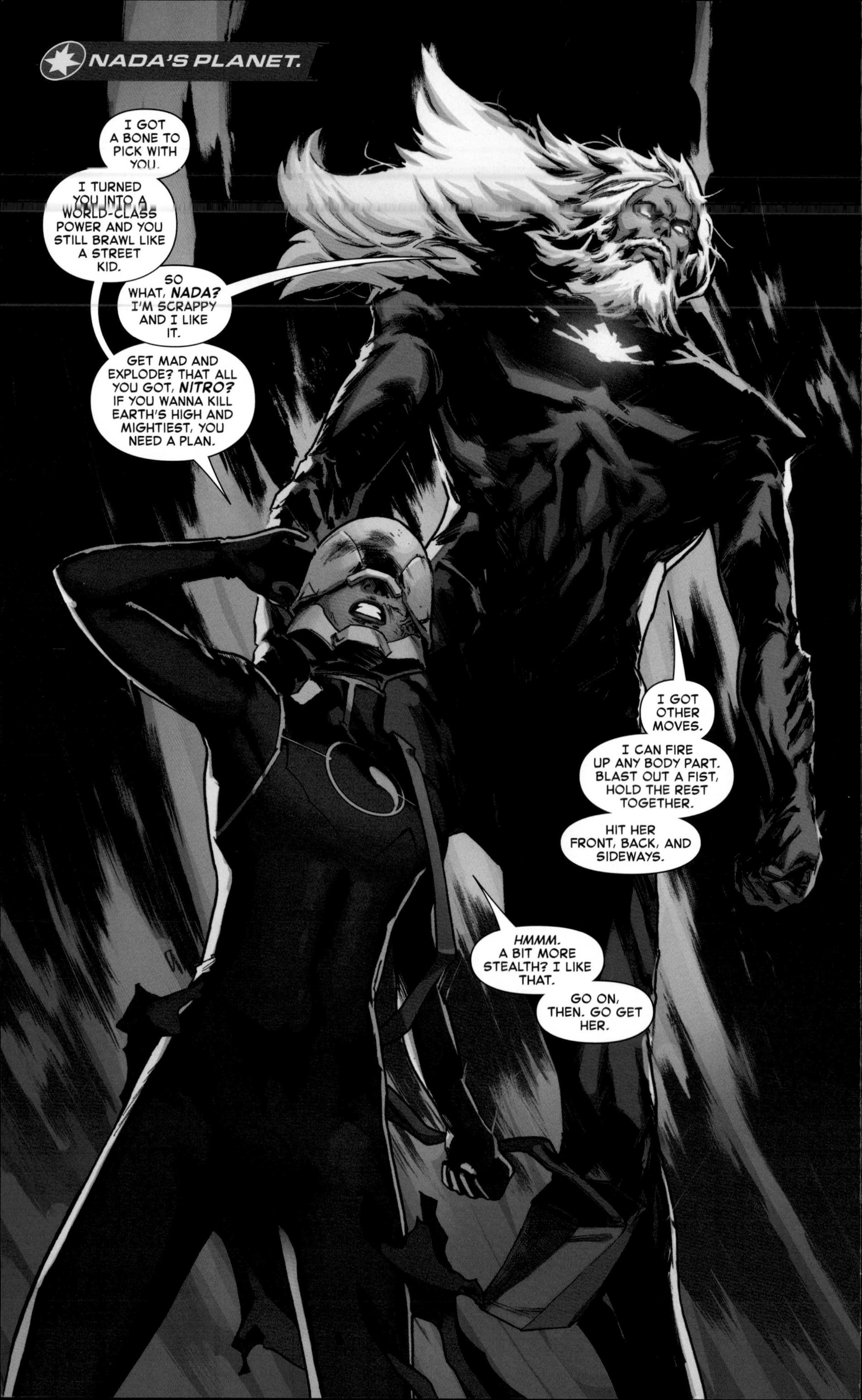
NADA'S PLANET.
I GOT A BONE TO PICK WITH YOU.
I TURNED YOU INTO A WORLD-CLASS POWER AND YOU STILL BRAWL LIKE A STREET KID.
SO WHAT, NADA? I'M SCRAPPY AND I LIKE IT.
GET MAD AND EXPLODE? THAT ALL YOU GOT, NITRO? IF YOU WANNA KILL EARTH'S HIGH AND MIGHTIEST, YOU NEED A PLAN.
I GOT OTHER MOVES.
I CAN FIRE UP ANY BODY PART. BLAST OUT A FIST, HOLD THE REST TOGETHER.
HIT HER FRONT, BACK, AND SIDEWAYS.
HMMM. A BIT MORE STEALTH? I LIKE THAT.
GO ON, THEN. GO GET HER.

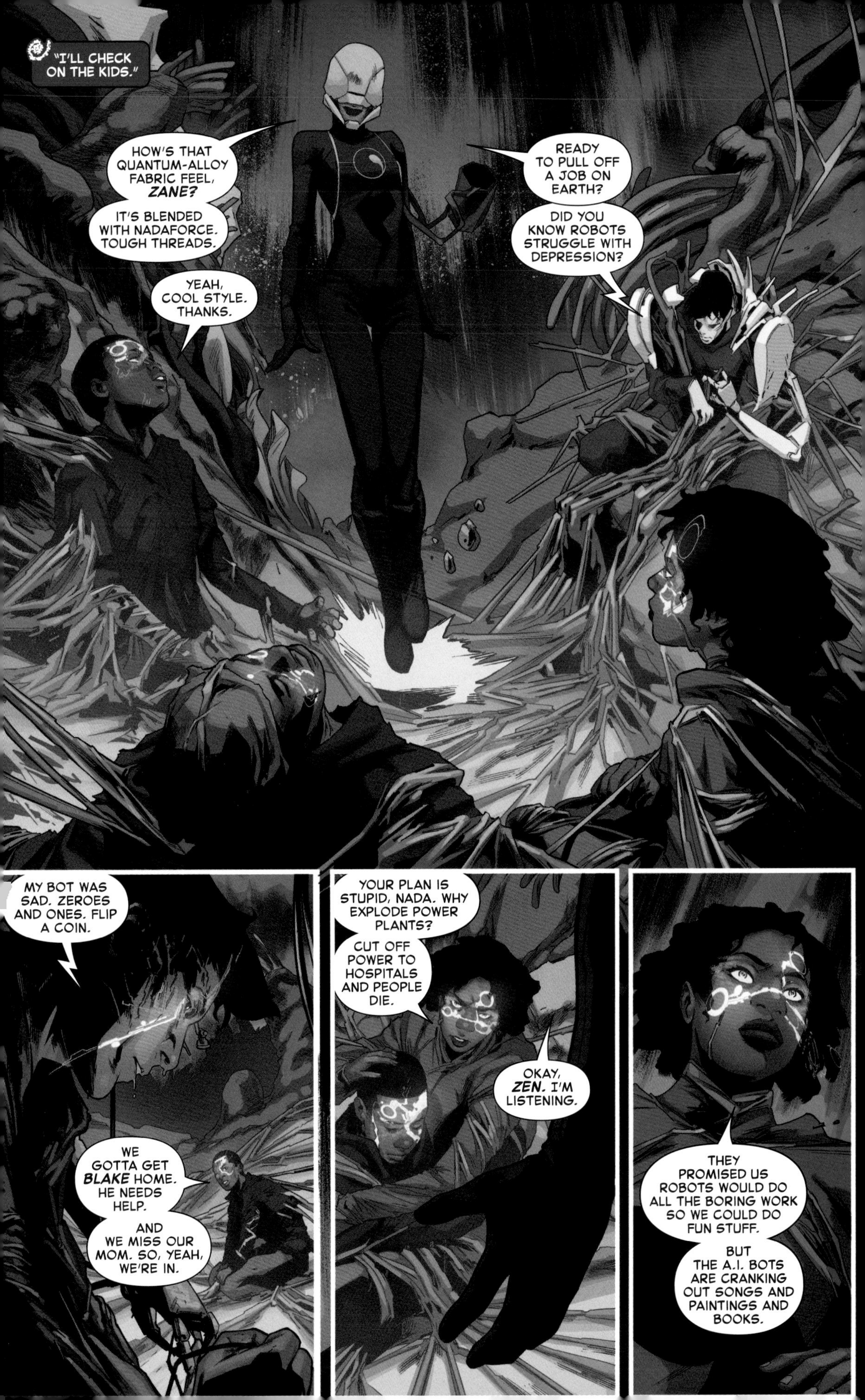
"I'LL CHECK ON THE KIDS."
HOW'S THAT QUANTUM-ALLOY FABRIC FEEL, ZANE?
IT'S BLENDED WITH NADAFORCE. TOUGH THREADS.
YEAH, COOL STYLE. THANKS.
READY TO PULL OFF A JOB ON EARTH?
DID YOU KNOW ROBOTS STRUGGLE WITH DEPRESSION?
MY BOT WAS SAD. ZEROES AND ONES. FLIP A COIN.
WE GOTTA GET BLAKE HOME. HE NEEDS HELP.
AND WE MISS OUR MOM. SO, YEAH, WE'RE IN.
YOUR PLAN IS STUPID, NADA. WHY EXPLODE POWER PLANTS?
CUT OFF POWER TO HOSPITALS AND PEOPLE DIE.
OKAY, ZEN. I'M LISTENING.
THEY PROMISED US ROBOTS WOULD DO ALL THE BORING WORK SO WE COULD DO FUN STUFF.
BUT THE A.I. BOTS ARE CRANKING OUT SONGS AND PAINTINGS AND BOOKS.

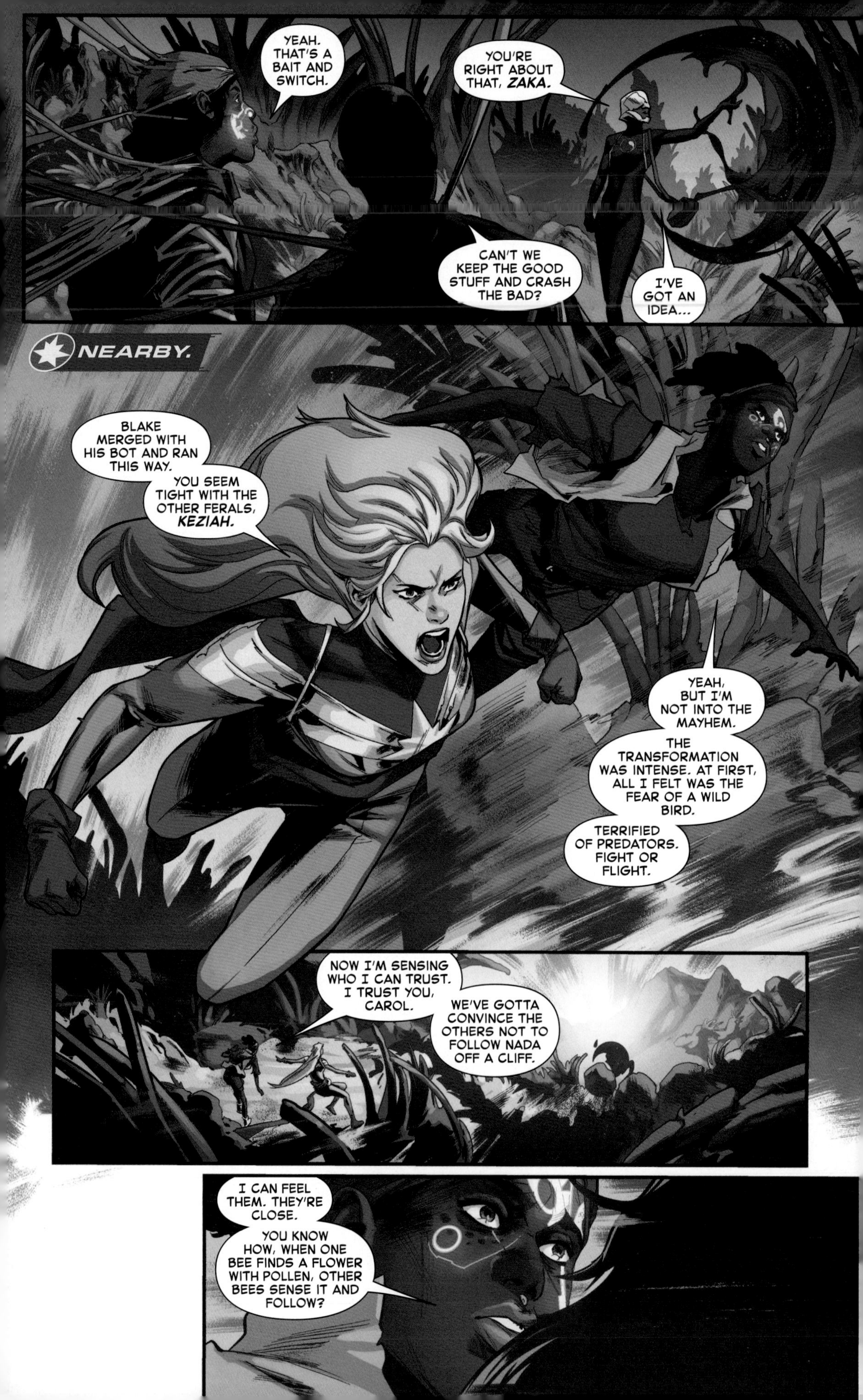
YEAH. THAT'S A BAIT AND SWITCH.
YOU'RE RIGHT ABOUT THAT, ZAKA.
CAN'T WE KEEP THE GOOD STUFF AND CRASH THE BAD?
I'VE GOT AN IDEA...
NEARBY.
BLAKE MERGED WITH HIS BOT AND RAN THIS WAY.
YOU SEEM TIGHT WITH THE OTHER FERALS, KEZIAH.
YEAH, BUT I'M NOT INTO THE MAYHEM.
THE TRANSFORMATION WAS INTENSE. AT FIRST, ALL I FELT WAS THE FEAR OF A WILD BIRD.
TERRIFIED OF PREDATORS. FIGHT OR FLIGHT.
NOW I'M SENSING WHO I CAN TRUST. I TRUST YOU, CAROL.
WE'VE GOTTA CONVINCE THE OTHERS NOT TO FOLLOW NADA OFF A CLIFF.
I CAN FEEL THEM. THEY'RE CLOSE.
YOU KNOW HOW, WHEN ONE BEE FINDS A FLOWER WITH POLLEN, OTHER BEES SENSE IT AND FOLLOW?

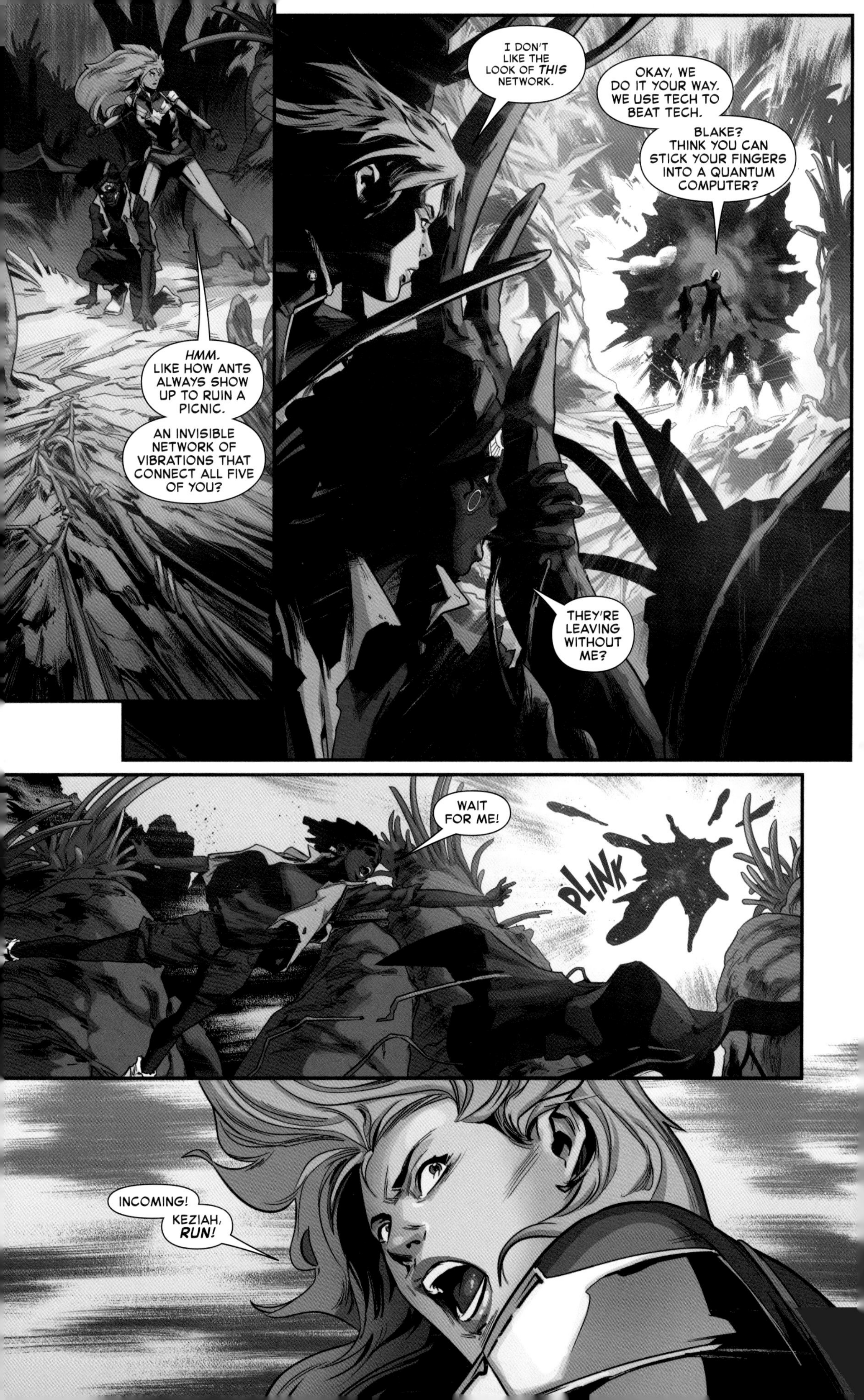
HMM.
LIKE HOW ANTS ALWAYS SHOW UP TO RUIN A PICNIC.
AN INVISIBLE NETWORK OF VIBRATIONS THAT CONNECT ALL FIVE OF YOU?
I DON'T LIKE THE LOOK OF *THIS* NETWORK.
OKAY, WE DO IT YOUR WAY. WE USE TECH TO BEAT TECH.
BLAKE? THINK YOU CAN STICK YOUR FINGERS INTO A QUANTUM COMPUTER?
THEY'RE LEAVING WITHOUT ME?
WAIT FOR ME!
PLINK
INCOMING!
KEZIAH, ***RUN!***

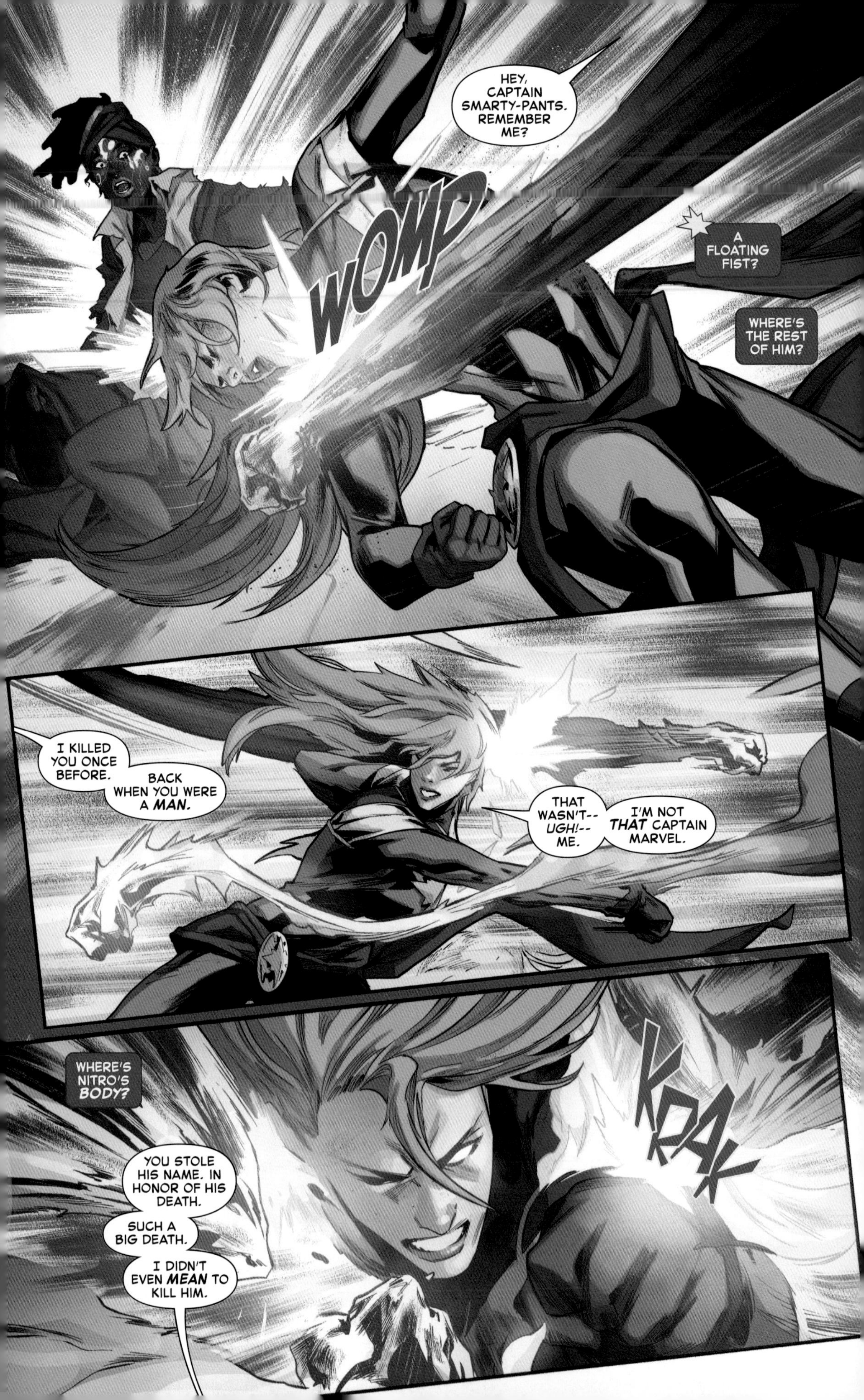
HEY, CAPTAIN SMARTY-PANTS. REMEMBER ME?
WOMP
A FLOATING FIST?
WHERE'S THE REST OF HIM?
I KILLED YOU ONCE BEFORE.
BACK WHEN YOU WERE A MAN.
THAT WASN'T-- UGH!-- ME.
I'M NOT THAT CAPTAIN MARVEL.
WHERE'S NITRO'S BODY?
KRAK
YOU STOLE HIS NAME. IN HONOR OF HIS DEATH.
SUCH A BIG DEATH.
I DIDN'T EVEN MEAN TO KILL HIM.

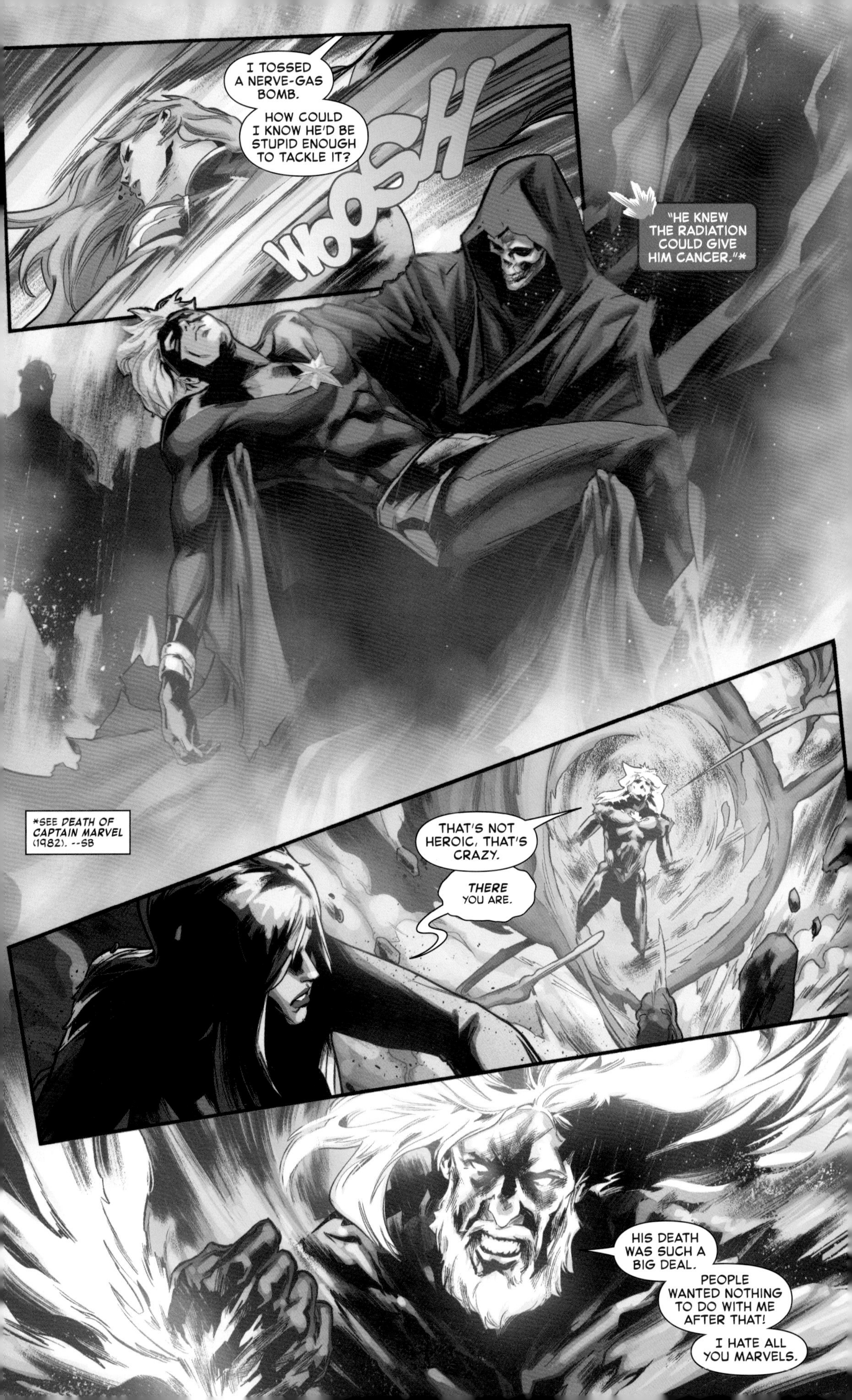
I TOSSED A NERVE-GAS BOMB.
HOW COULD I KNOW HE'D BE STUPID ENOUGH TO TACKLE IT?
WOOSH
"HE KNEW THE RADIATION COULD GIVE HIM CANCER."*
*SEE DEATH OF CAPTAIN MARVEL (1982). --SB
THAT'S NOT HEROIC, THAT'S CRAZY.
THERE YOU ARE.
HIS DEATH WAS SUCH A BIG DEAL.
PEOPLE WANTED NOTHING TO DO WITH ME AFTER THAT!
I HATE ALL YOU MARVELS.

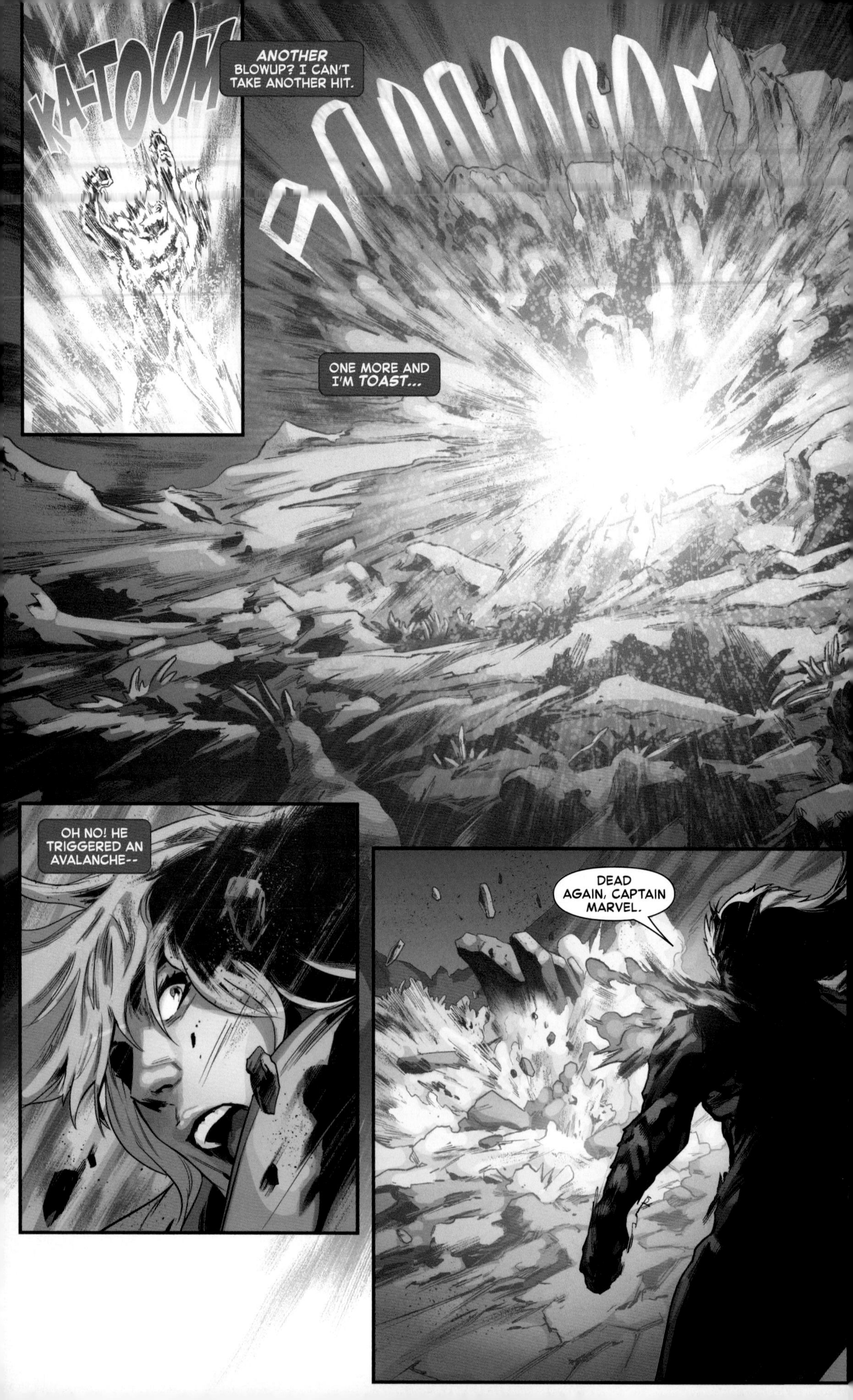
KA-TOOM
ANOTHER BLOWUP? I CAN'T TAKE ANOTHER HIT.
BOOOOOOM
ONE MORE AND I'M *TOAST*...
OH NO! HE TRIGGERED AN AVALANCHE--
DEAD AGAIN, CAPTAIN MARVEL.

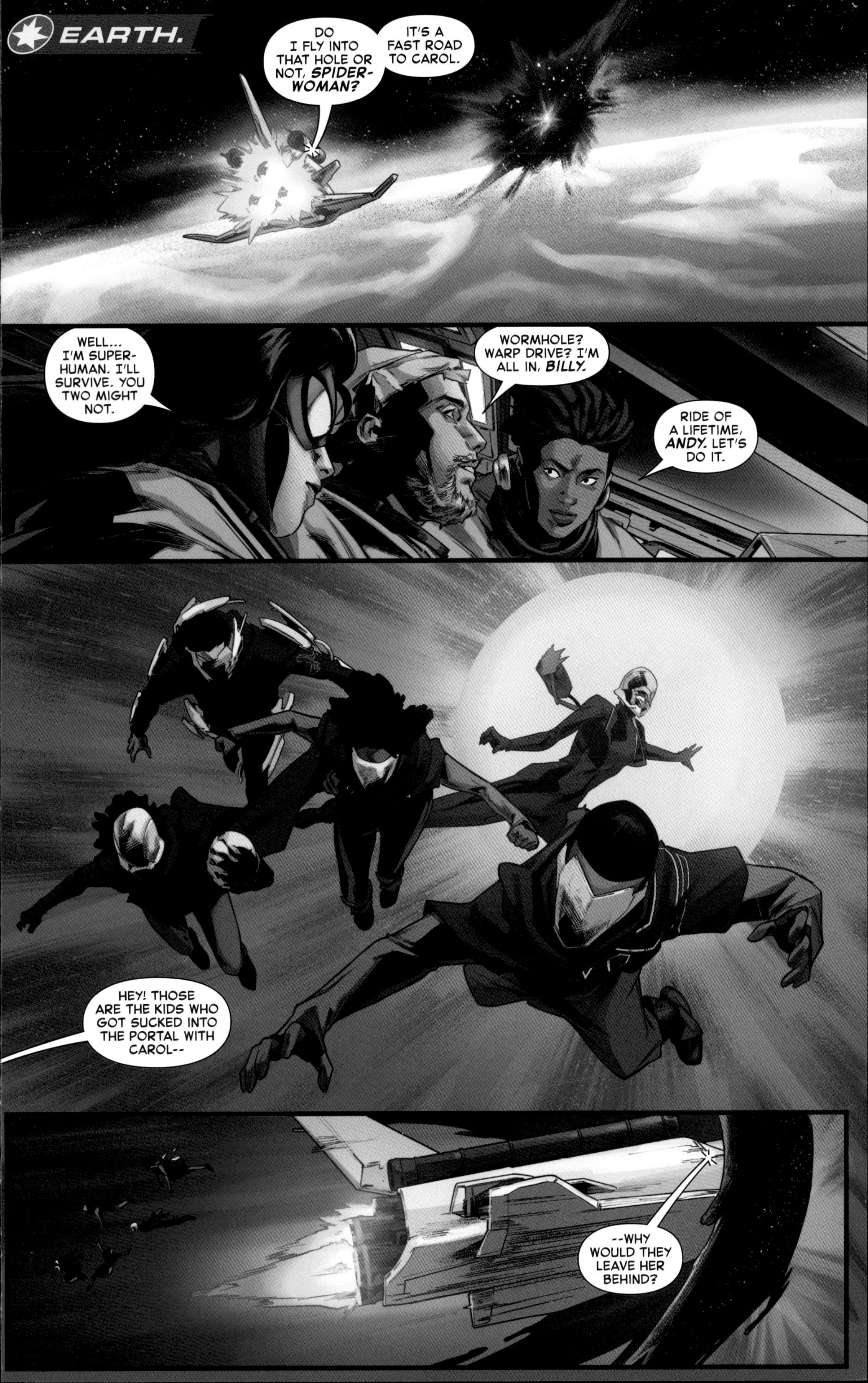
EARTH.
DO I FLY INTO THAT HOLE OR NOT, SPIDER-WOMAN?
IT'S A FAST ROAD TO CAROL.
WELL... I'M SUPER-HUMAN. I'LL SURVIVE. YOU TWO MIGHT NOT.
WORMHOLE? WARP DRIVE? I'M ALL IN, BILLY.
RIDE OF A LIFETIME, ANDY. LET'S DO IT.
HEY! THOSE ARE THE KIDS WHO GOT SUCKED INTO THE PORTAL WITH CAROL--
--WHY WOULD THEY LEAVE HER BEHIND?

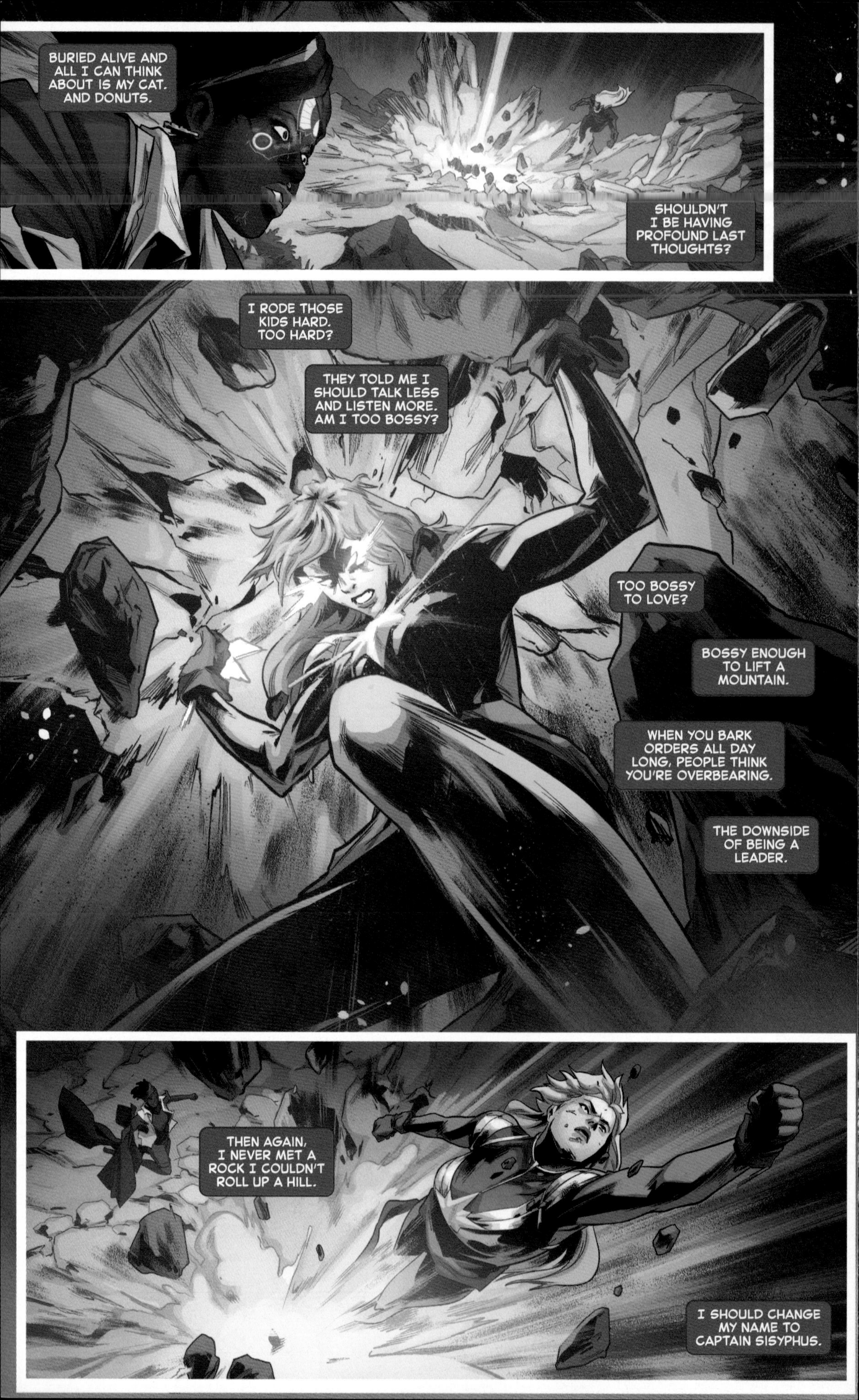
BURIED ALIVE AND ALL I CAN THINK ABOUT IS MY CAT. AND DONUTS.
SHOULDN'T I BE HAVING PROFOUND LAST THOUGHTS?
I RODE THOSE KIDS HARD. TOO HARD?
THEY TOLD ME I SHOULD TALK LESS AND LISTEN MORE. AM I TOO BOSSY?
TOO BOSSY TO LOVE?
BOSSY ENOUGH TO LIFT A MOUNTAIN.
WHEN YOU BARK ORDERS ALL DAY LONG, PEOPLE THINK YOU'RE OVERBEARING.
THE DOWNSIDE OF BEING A LEADER.
THEN AGAIN, I NEVER MET A ROCK I COULDN'T ROLL UP A HILL.
I SHOULD CHANGE MY NAME TO CAPTAIN SISYPHUS.

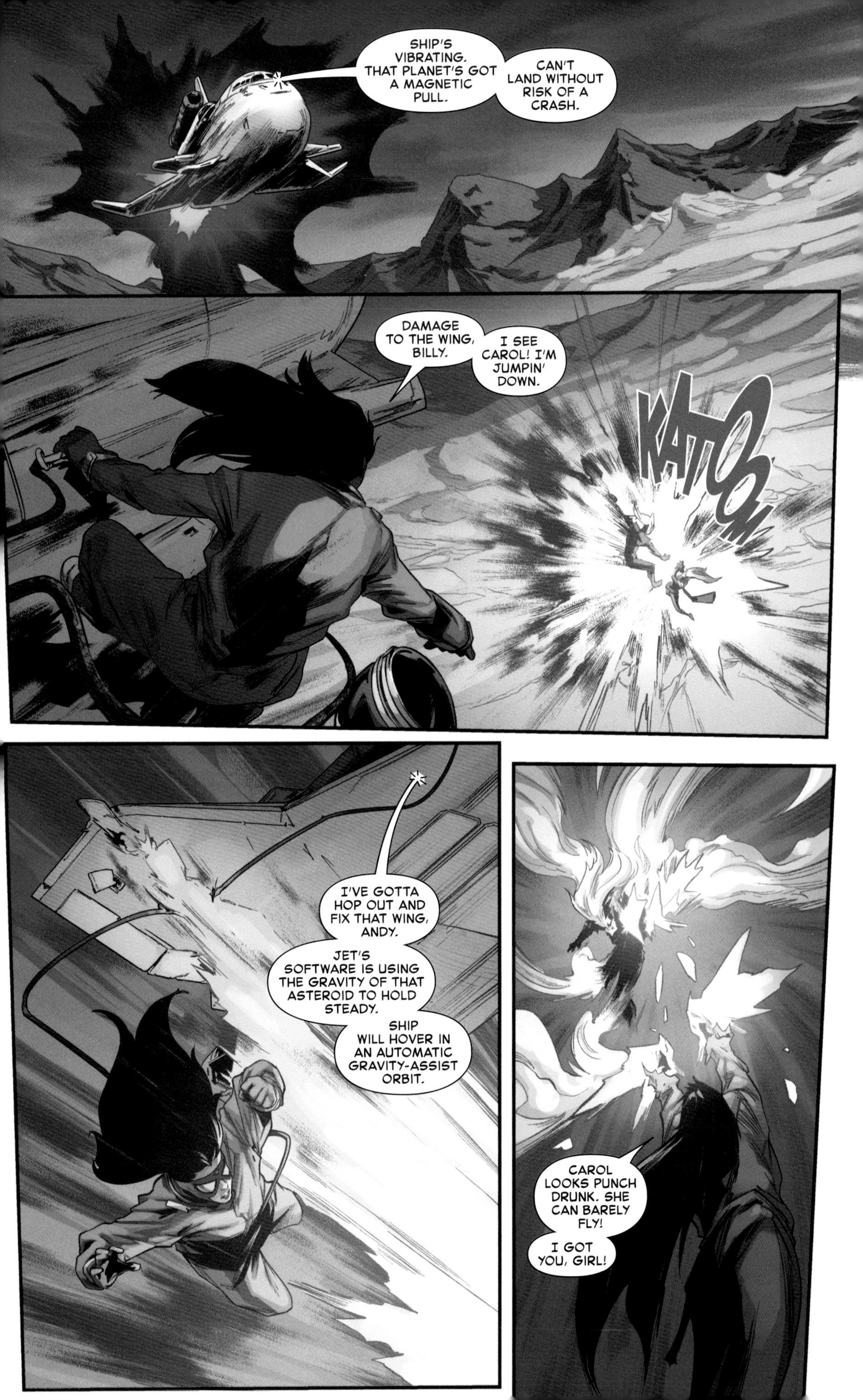
SHIP'S VIBRATING. THAT PLANET'S GOT A MAGNETIC PULL.
CAN'T LAND WITHOUT RISK OF A CRASH.
DAMAGE TO THE WING, BILLY.
I SEE CAROL! I'M JUMPIN' DOWN.
KATOOOM
I'VE GOTTA HOP OUT AND FIX THAT WING, ANDY.
JET'S SOFTWARE IS USING THE GRAVITY OF THAT ASTEROID TO HOLD STEADY.
SHIP WILL HOVER IN AN AUTOMATIC GRAVITY-ASSIST ORBIT.
CAROL LOOKS PUNCH DRUNK. SHE CAN BARELY FLY!
I GOT YOU, GIRL!

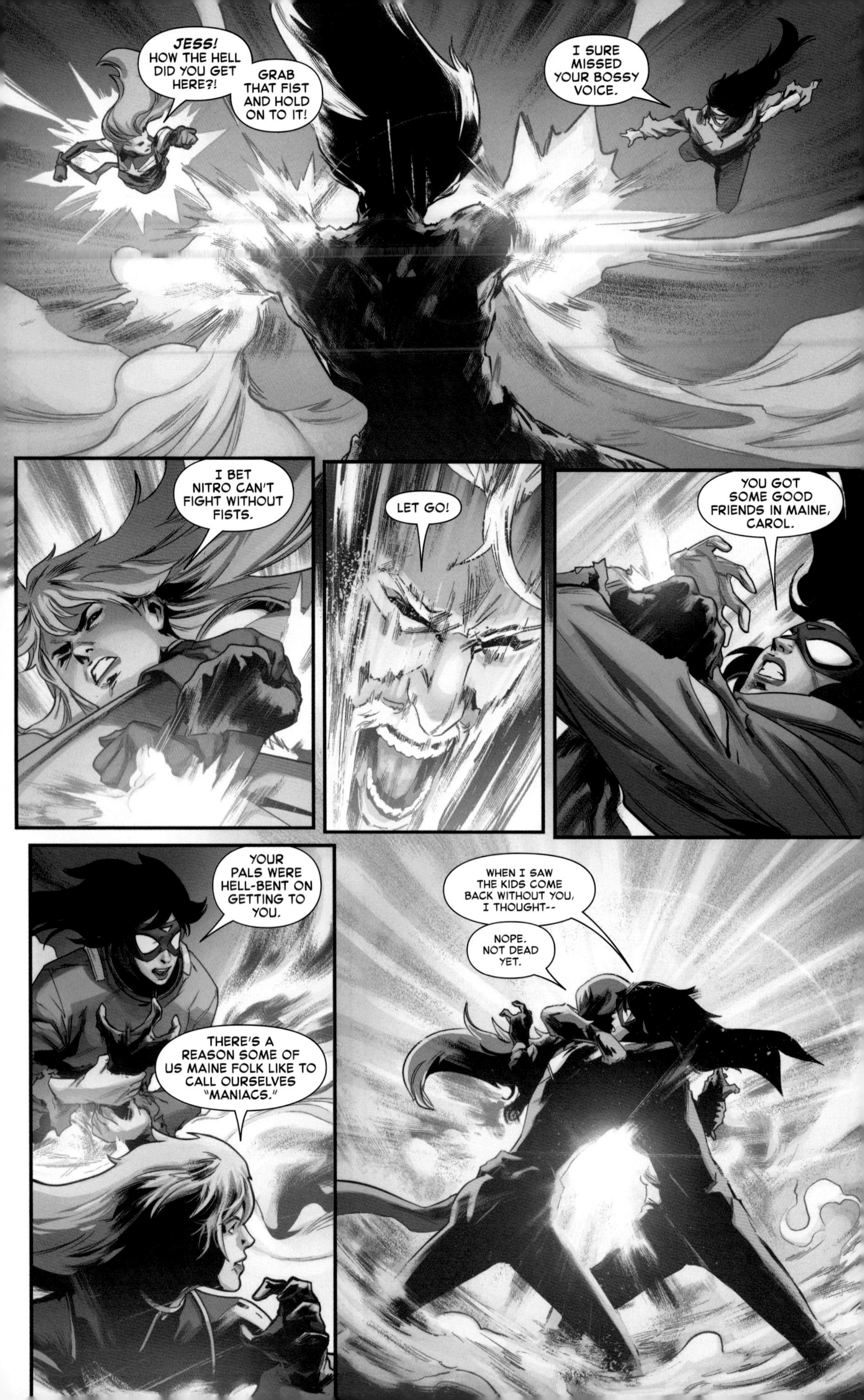
JESS! HOW THE HELL DID YOU GET HERE?!
GRAB THAT FIST AND HOLD ON TO IT!
I SURE MISSED YOUR BOSSY VOICE.
I BET NITRO CAN'T FIGHT WITHOUT FISTS.
LET GO!
YOU GOT SOME GOOD FRIENDS IN MAINE, CAROL.
YOUR PALS WERE HELL-BENT ON GETTING TO YOU.
THERE'S A REASON SOME OF US MAINE FOLK LIKE TO CALL OURSELVES "MANIACS."
WHEN I SAW THE KIDS COME BACK WITHOUT YOU, I THOUGHT--
NOPE. NOT DEAD YET.

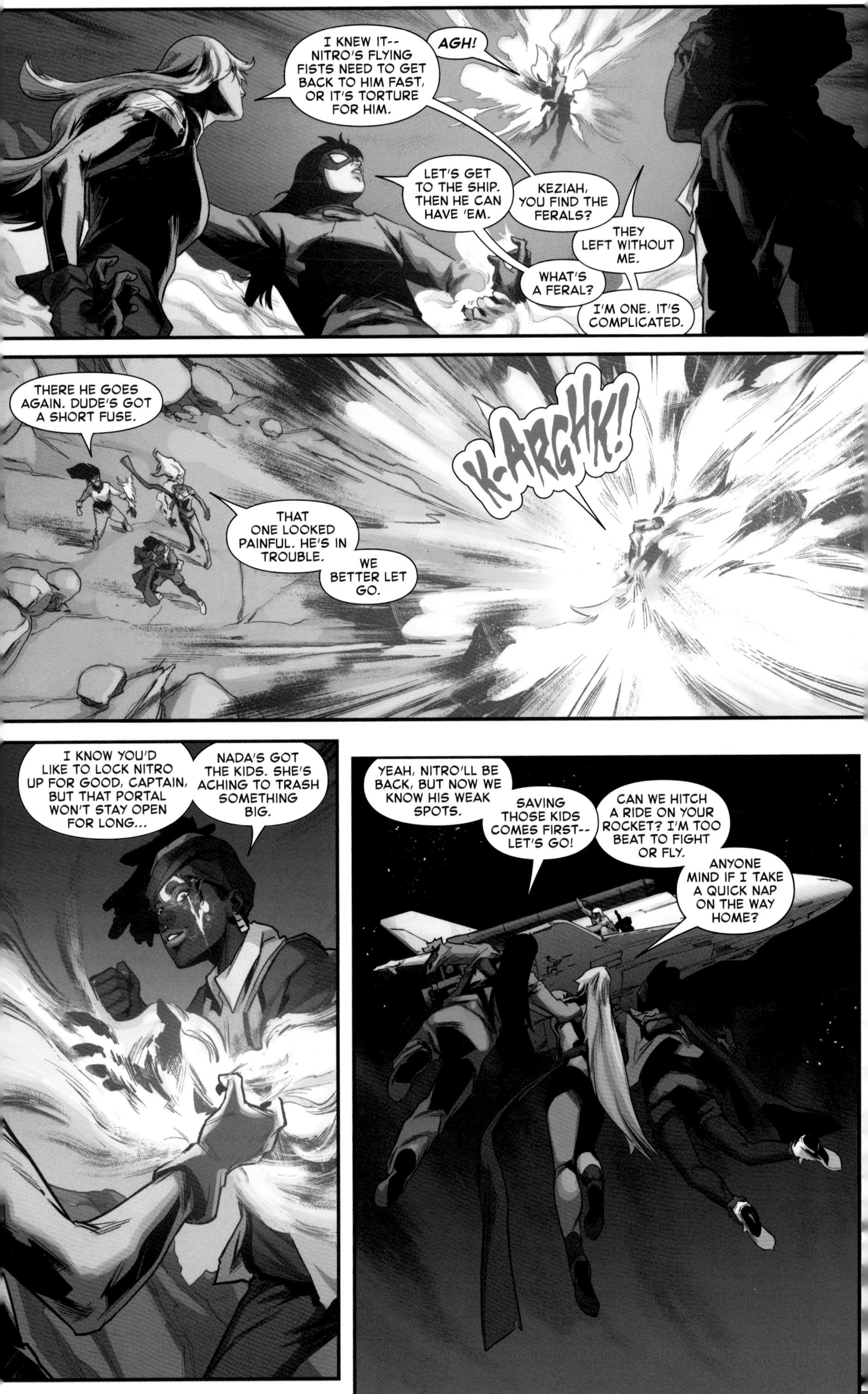
I KNEW IT-- NITRO'S FLYING FISTS NEED TO GET BACK TO HIM FAST, OR IT'S TORTURE FOR HIM.
AGH!
LET'S GET TO THE SHIP. THEN HE CAN HAVE 'EM.
KEZIAH, YOU FIND THE FERALS?
THEY LEFT WITHOUT ME.
WHAT'S A FERAL?
I'M ONE. IT'S COMPLICATED.
THERE HE GOES AGAIN. DUDE'S GOT A SHORT FUSE.
K-ARGHK!
THAT ONE LOOKED PAINFUL. HE'S IN TROUBLE.
WE BETTER LET GO.
I KNOW YOU'D LIKE TO LOCK NITRO UP FOR GOOD, CAPTAIN, BUT THAT PORTAL WON'T STAY OPEN FOR LONG...
NADA'S GOT THE KIDS. SHE'S ACHING TO TRASH SOMETHING BIG.
YEAH, NITRO'LL BE BACK, BUT NOW WE KNOW HIS WEAK SPOTS.
SAVING THOSE KIDS COMES FIRST-- LET'S GO!
CAN WE HITCH A RIDE ON YOUR ROCKET? I'M TOO BEAT TO FIGHT OR FLY.
ANYONE MIND IF I TAKE A QUICK NAP ON THE WAY HOME?

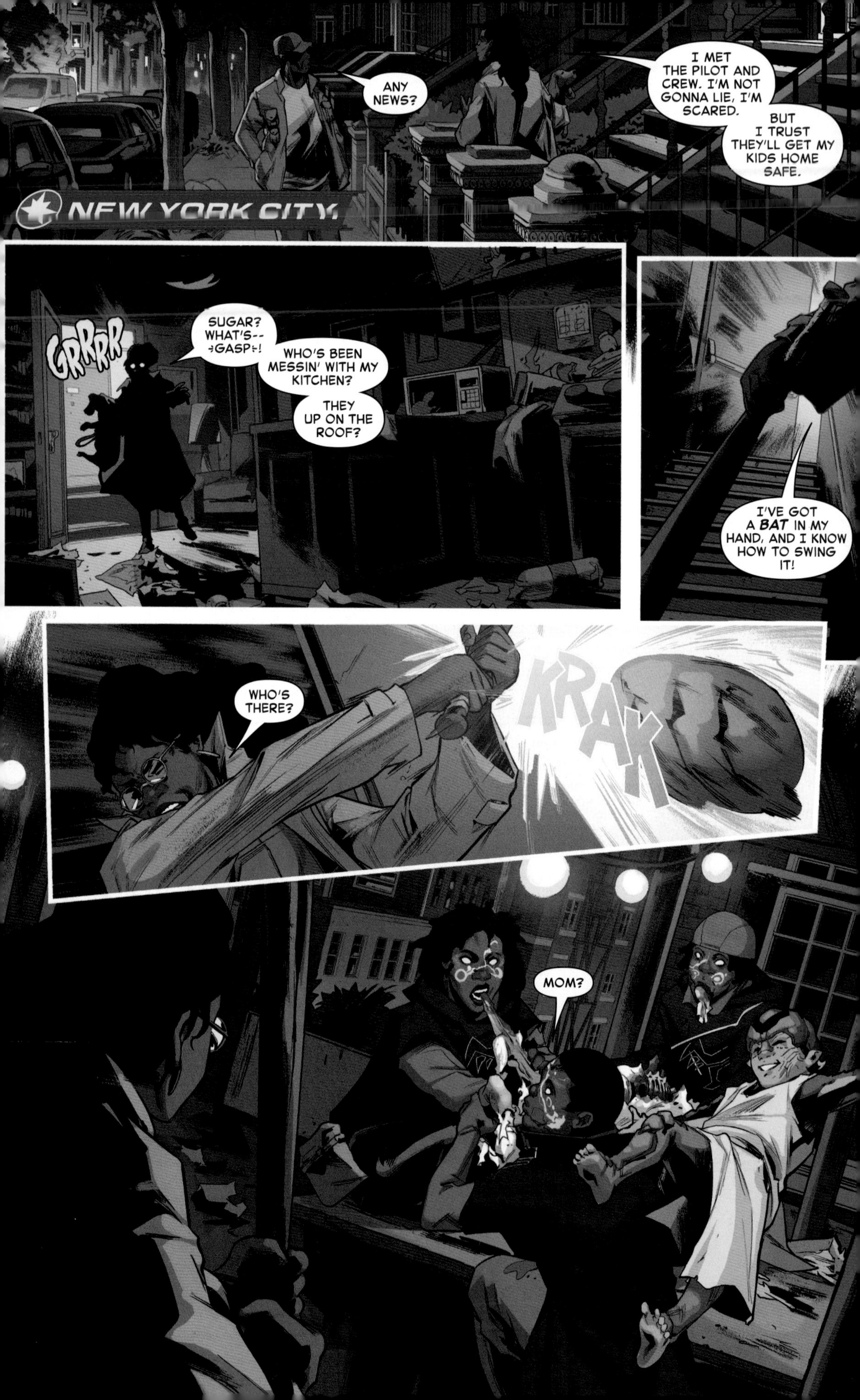
ANY NEWS?
I MET THE PILOT AND CREW. I'M NOT GONNA LIE, I'M SCARED.
BUT I TRUST THEY'LL GET MY KIDS HOME SAFE.
NEW YORK CITY
GRRRR
SUGAR? WHAT'S-- ÷GASP÷!
WHO'S BEEN MESSIN' WITH MY KITCHEN?
THEY UP ON THE ROOF?
I'VE GOT A *BAT* IN MY HAND, AND I KNOW HOW TO SWING IT!
WHO'S THERE?
KRAK
MOM?

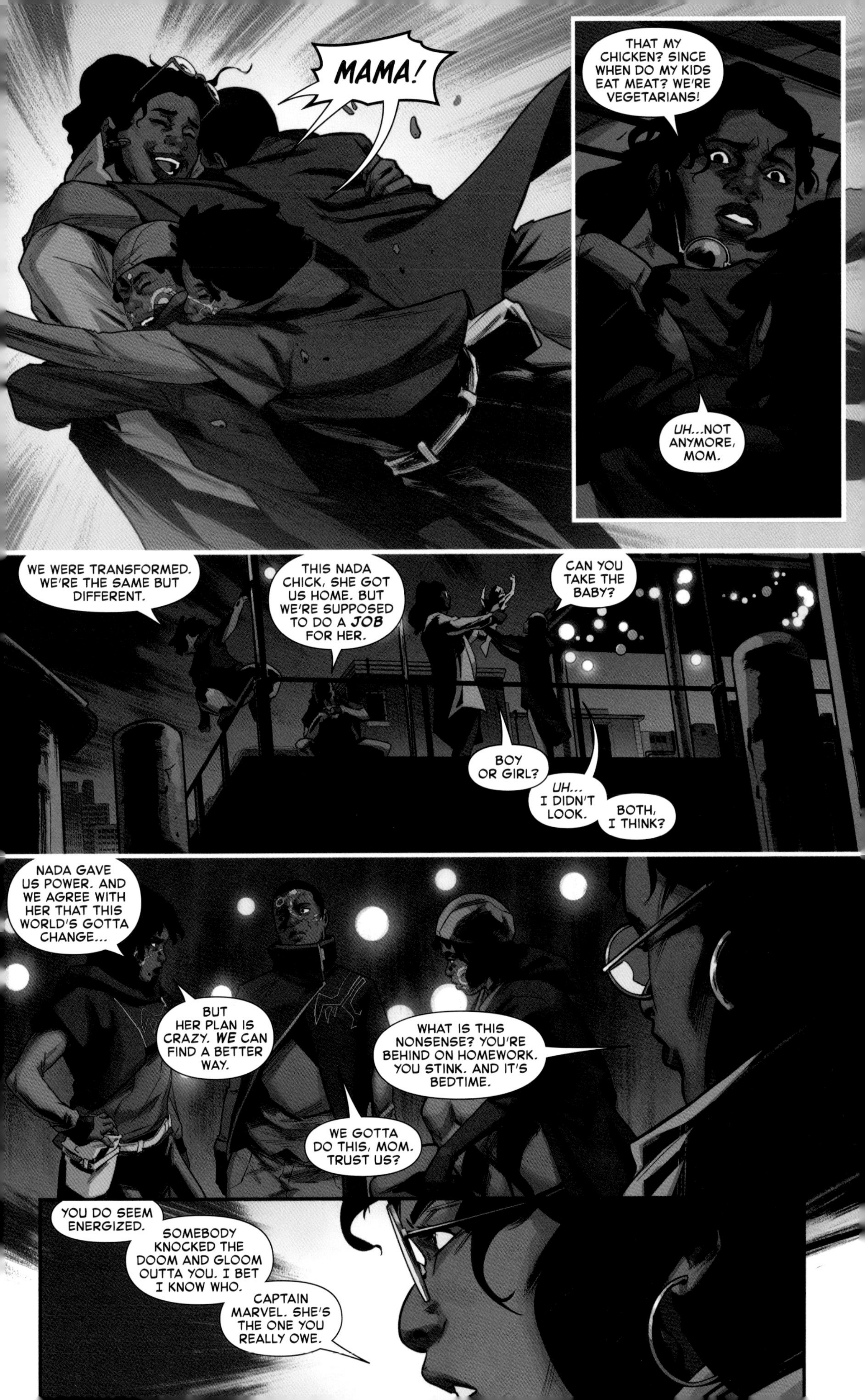
MAMA!
THAT MY CHICKEN? SINCE WHEN DO MY KIDS EAT MEAT? WE'RE VEGETARIANS!
UH...NOT ANYMORE, MOM.
WE WERE TRANSFORMED. WE'RE THE SAME BUT DIFFERENT.
THIS NADA CHICK, SHE GOT US HOME. BUT WE'RE SUPPOSED TO DO A JOB FOR HER.
CAN YOU TAKE THE BABY?
BOY OR GIRL?
UH... I DIDN'T LOOK.
BOTH, I THINK?
NADA GAVE US POWER. AND WE AGREE WITH HER THAT THIS WORLD'S GOTTA CHANGE...
BUT HER PLAN IS CRAZY. WE CAN FIND A BETTER WAY.
WHAT IS THIS NONSENSE? YOU'RE BEHIND ON HOMEWORK. YOU STINK. AND IT'S BEDTIME.
WE GOTTA DO THIS, MOM. TRUST US?
YOU DO SEEM ENERGIZED.
SOMEBODY KNOCKED THE DOOM AND GLOOM OUTTA YOU. I BET I KNOW WHO.
CAPTAIN MARVEL. SHE'S THE ONE YOU REALLY OWE.

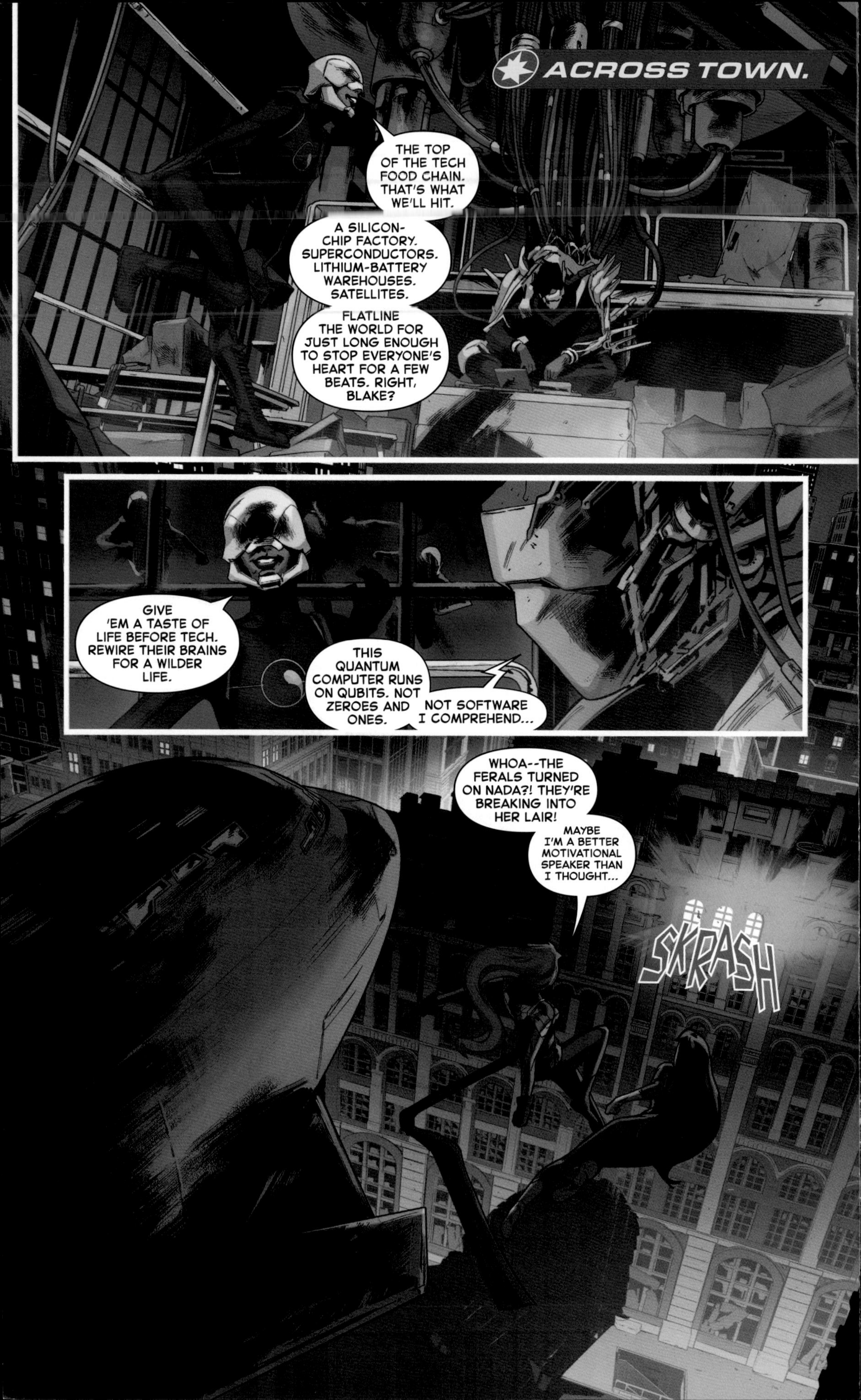
ACROSS TOWN.
THE TOP OF THE TECH FOOD CHAIN. THAT'S WHAT WE'LL HIT.
A SILICON-CHIP FACTORY. SUPERCONDUCTORS. LITHIUM-BATTERY WAREHOUSES. SATELLITES.
FLATLINE THE WORLD FOR JUST LONG ENOUGH TO STOP EVERYONE'S HEART FOR A FEW BEATS. RIGHT, BLAKE?
GIVE 'EM A TASTE OF LIFE BEFORE TECH. REWIRE THEIR BRAINS FOR A WILDER LIFE.
THIS QUANTUM COMPUTER RUNS ON QUBITS. NOT ZEROES AND ONES.
NOT SOFTWARE I COMPREHEND...
WHOA--THE FERALS TURNED ON NADA?! THEY'RE BREAKING INTO HER LAIR!
MAYBE I'M A BETTER MOTIVATIONAL SPEAKER THAN I THOUGHT...
SKRASH

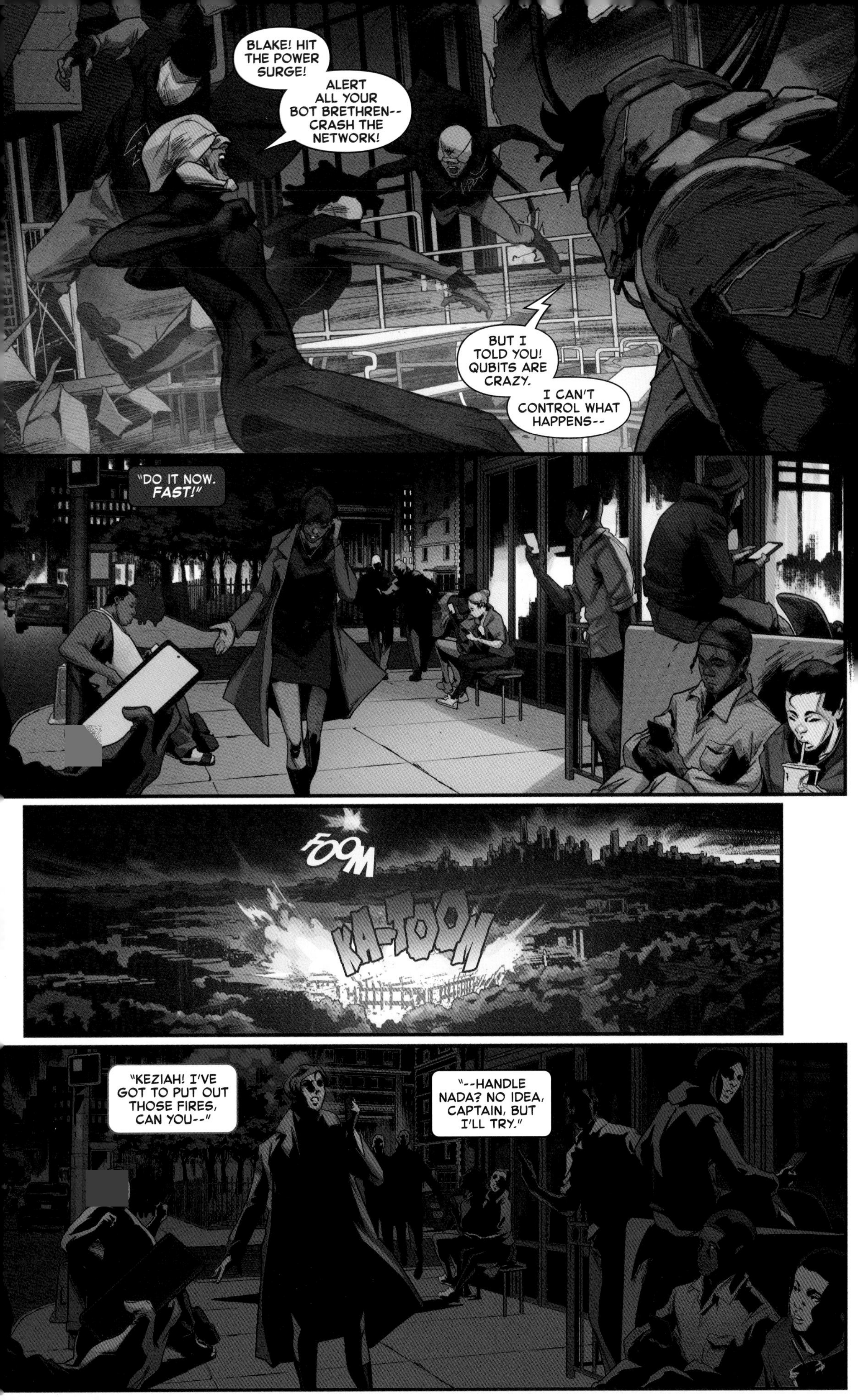
BLAKE! HIT THE POWER SURGE!
ALERT ALL YOUR BOT BRETHREN--CRASH THE NETWORK!
BUT I TOLD YOU! QUBITS ARE CRAZY.
I CAN'T CONTROL WHAT HAPPENS--
"DO IT NOW. FAST!"
FOOM
KA-TOOM
"KEZIAH! I'VE GOT TO PUT OUT THOSE FIRES, CAN YOU--"
"--HANDLE NADA? NO IDEA, CAPTAIN, BUT I'LL TRY."

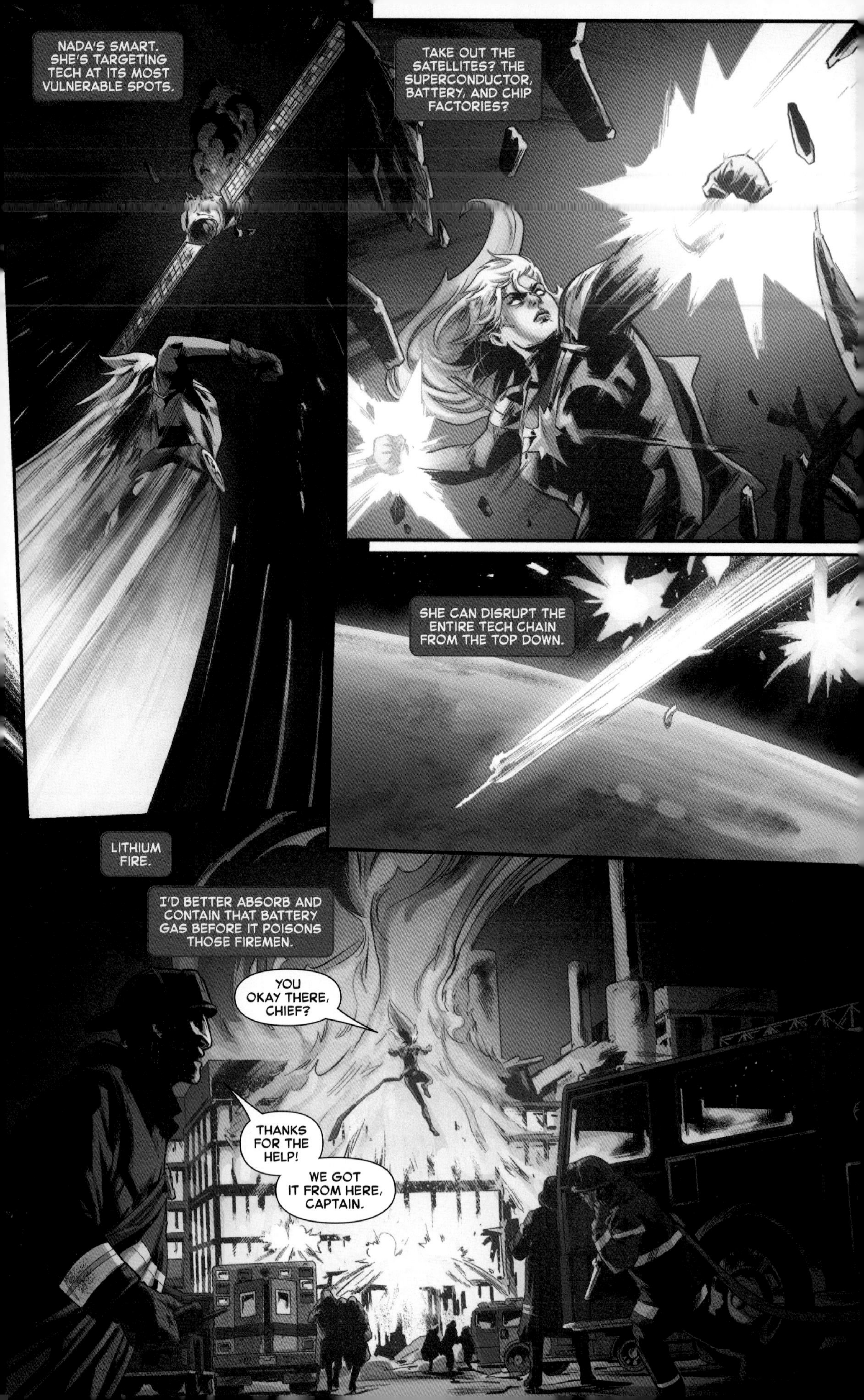
NADA'S SMART. SHE'S TARGETING TECH AT ITS MOST VULNERABLE SPOTS.
TAKE OUT THE SATELLITES? THE SUPERCONDUCTOR, BATTERY, AND CHIP FACTORIES?
SHE CAN DISRUPT THE ENTIRE TECH CHAIN FROM THE TOP DOWN.
LITHIUM FIRE.
I'D BETTER ABSORB AND CONTAIN THAT BATTERY GAS BEFORE IT POISONS THOSE FIREMEN.
YOU OKAY THERE, CHIEF?
THANKS FOR THE HELP!
WE GOT IT FROM HERE, CAPTAIN.

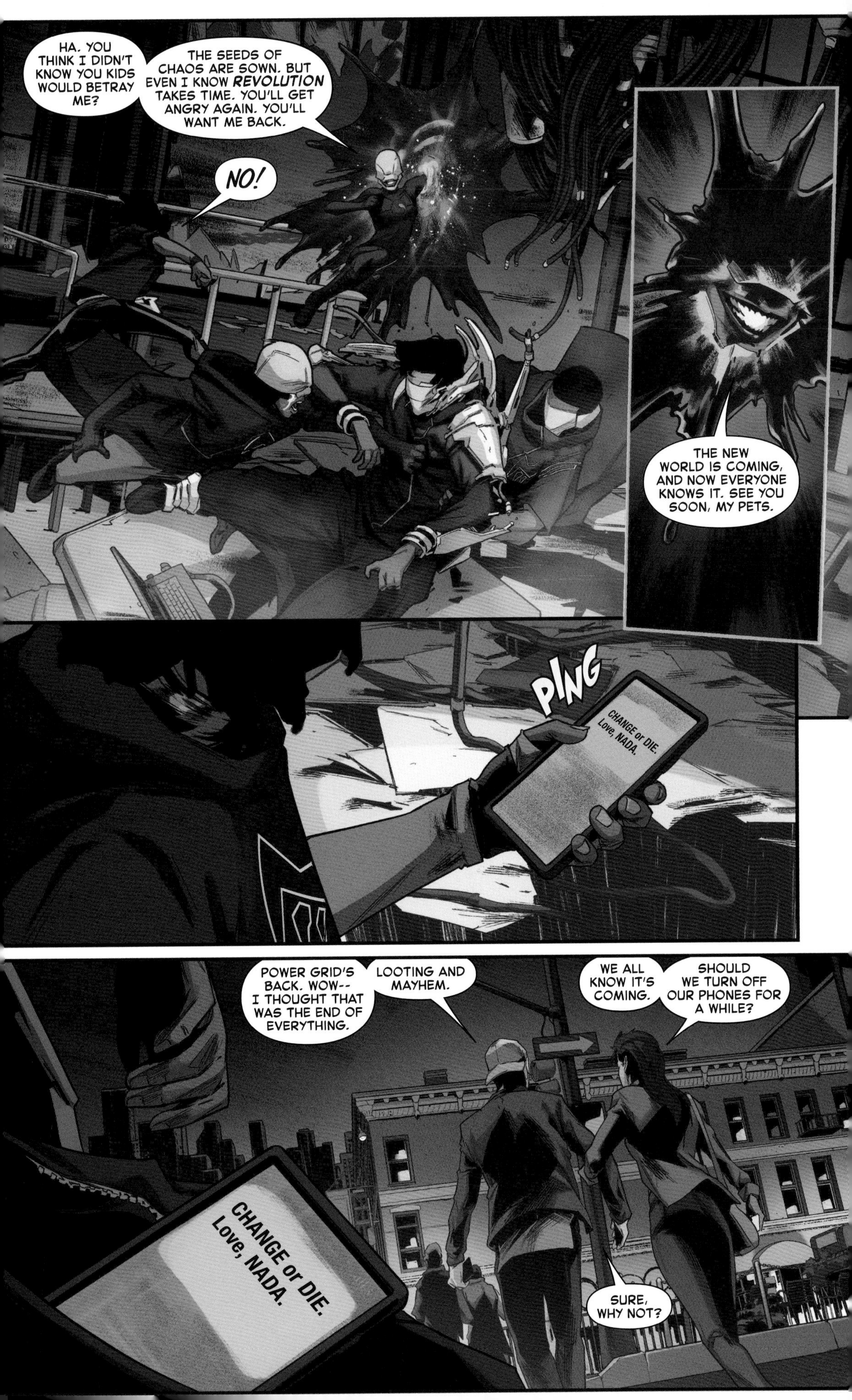
HA. YOU THINK I DIDN'T KNOW YOU KIDS WOULD BETRAY ME?
THE SEEDS OF CHAOS ARE SOWN. BUT EVEN I KNOW REVOLUTION TAKES TIME. YOU'LL GET ANGRY AGAIN. YOU'LL WANT ME BACK.
NO!
THE NEW WORLD IS COMING, AND NOW EVERYONE KNOWS IT. SEE YOU SOON, MY PETS.
PING
CHANGE or DIE. Love, NADA.
POWER GRID'S BACK. WOW-- I THOUGHT THAT WAS THE END OF EVERYTHING.
LOOTING AND MAYHEM.
WE ALL KNOW IT'S COMING.
SHOULD WE TURN OFF OUR PHONES FOR A WHILE?
CHANGE or DIE. Love, NADA.
SURE, WHY NOT?

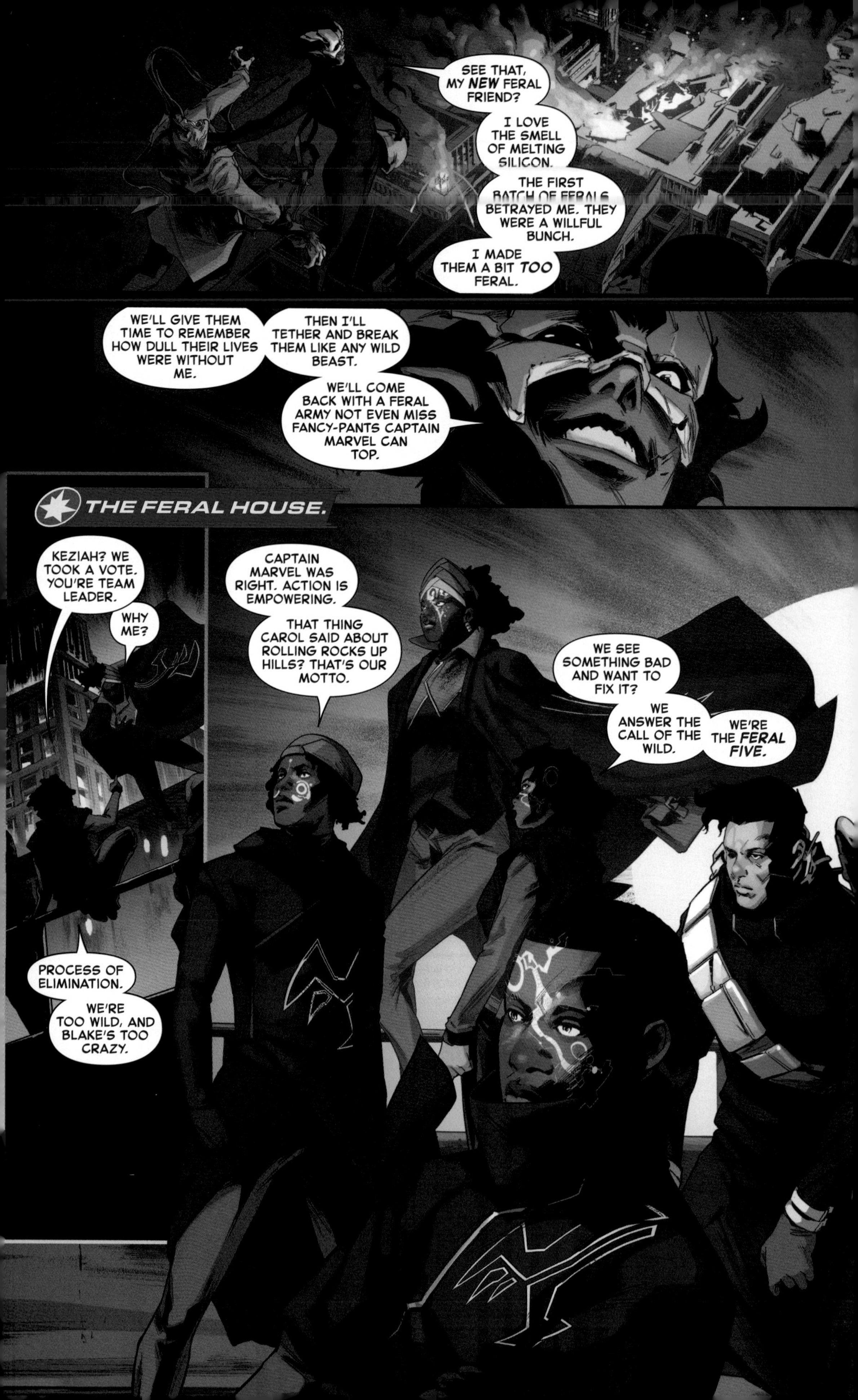
SEE THAT, MY NEW FERAL FRIEND?
I LOVE THE SMELL OF MELTING SILICON.
THE FIRST BATCH OF FERALS BETRAYED ME. THEY WERE A WILLFUL BUNCH.
I MADE THEM A BIT TOO FERAL.
WE'LL GIVE THEM TIME TO REMEMBER HOW DULL THEIR LIVES WERE WITHOUT ME.
THEN I'LL TETHER AND BREAK THEM LIKE ANY WILD BEAST.
WE'LL COME BACK WITH A FERAL ARMY NOT EVEN MISS FANCY-PANTS CAPTAIN MARVEL CAN TOP.
THE FERAL HOUSE.
KEZIAH? WE TOOK A VOTE. YOU'RE TEAM LEADER.
WHY ME?
PROCESS OF ELIMINATION.
WE'RE TOO WILD, AND BLAKE'S TOO CRAZY.
CAPTAIN MARVEL WAS RIGHT. ACTION IS EMPOWERING.
THAT THING CAROL SAID ABOUT ROLLING ROCKS UP HILLS? THAT'S OUR MOTTO.
WE SEE SOMETHING BAD AND WANT TO FIX IT?
WE ANSWER THE CALL OF THE WILD.
WE'RE THE FERAL FIVE.

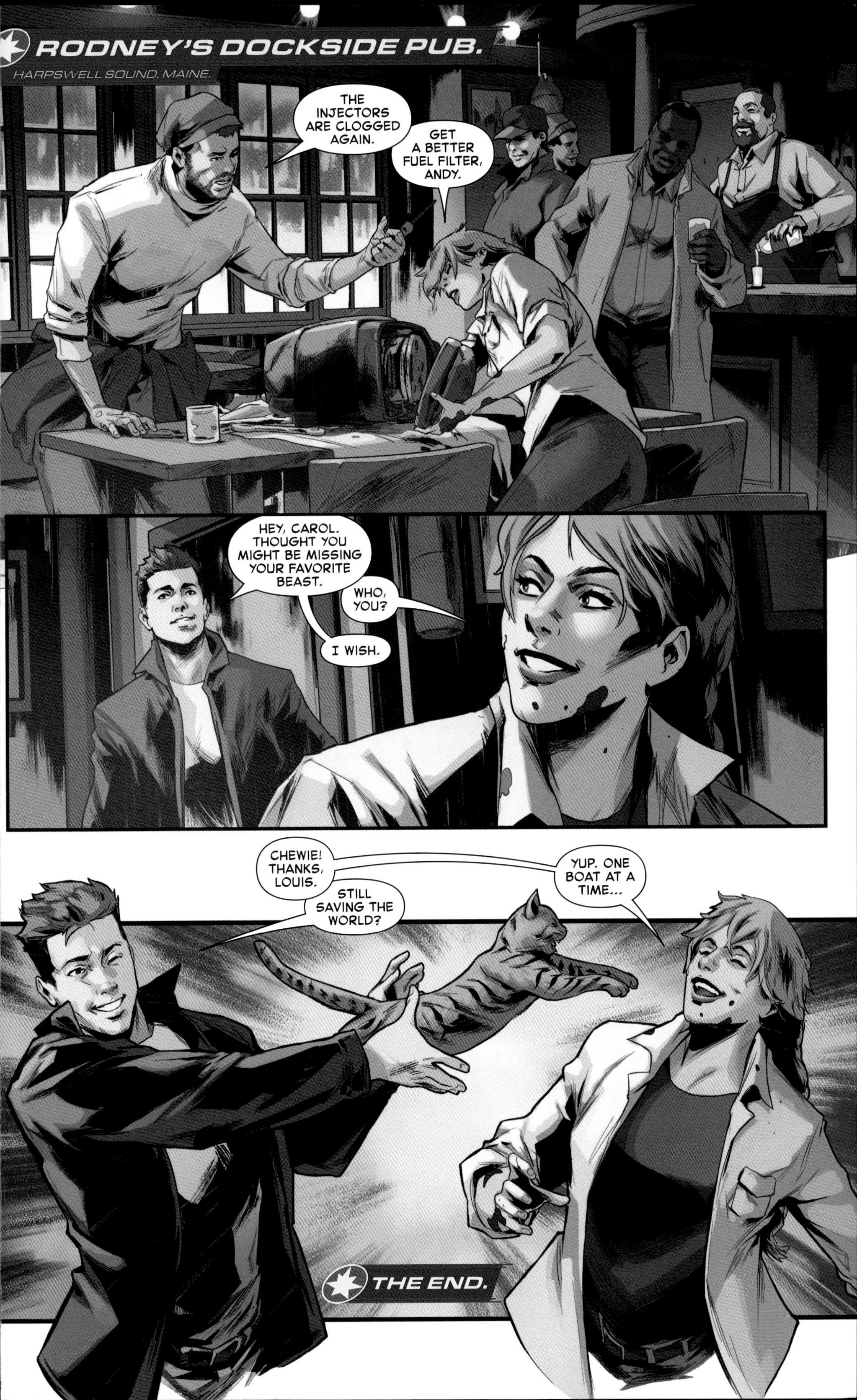
RODNEY'S DOCKSIDE PUB.
HARPSWELL SOUND, MAINE.
THE INJECTORS ARE CLOGGED AGAIN.
GET A BETTER FUEL FILTER, ANDY.
HEY, CAROL. THOUGHT YOU MIGHT BE MISSING YOUR FAVORITE BEAST.
WHO, YOU?
I WISH.
CHEWIE! THANKS, LOUIS.
STILL SAVING THE WORLD?
YUP. ONE BOAT AT A TIME...
THE END.

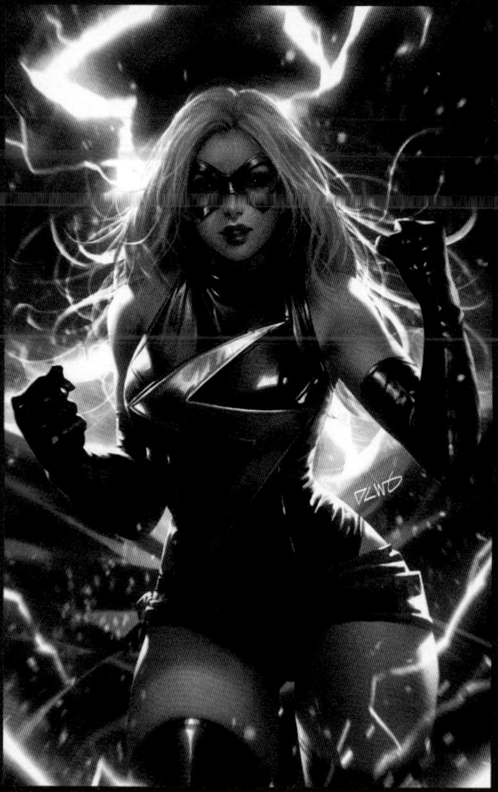

DERRICK CHEW
#1 VARIANT

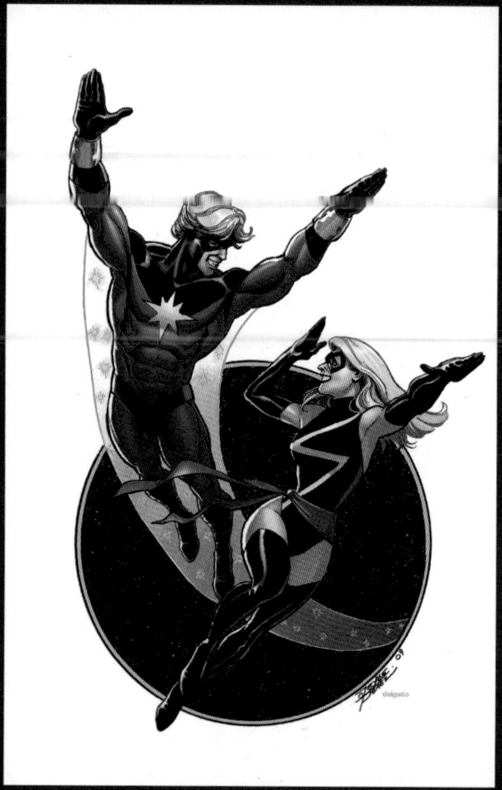

GEORGE PÉREZ & EDGAR DELGADO
#1 VARIANT

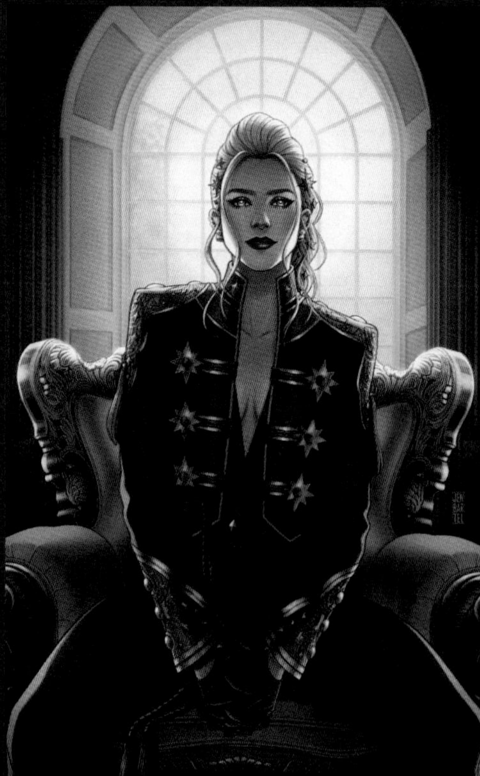

JEN BARTEL
#1 HELLFIRE GALA VARIANT

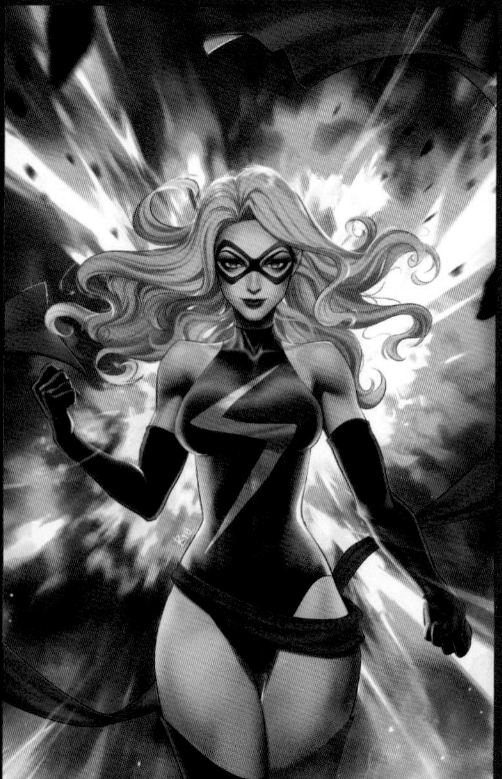

R1C0
#1 VARIANT

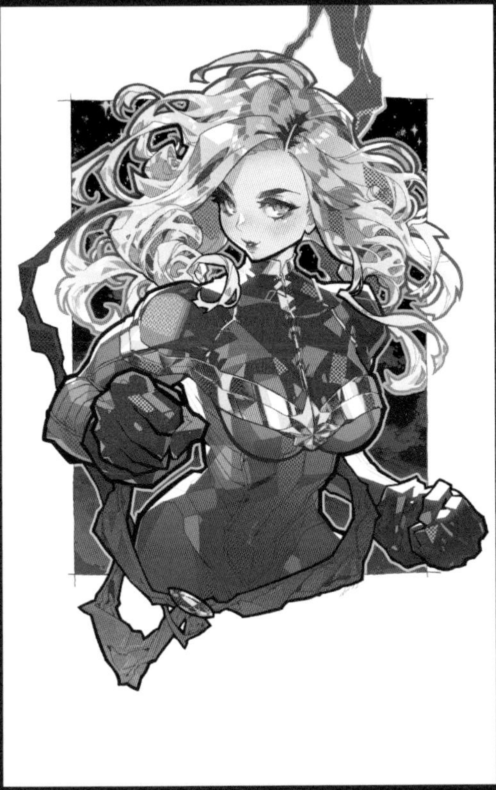

ROSE BESCH
#1 VARIANT

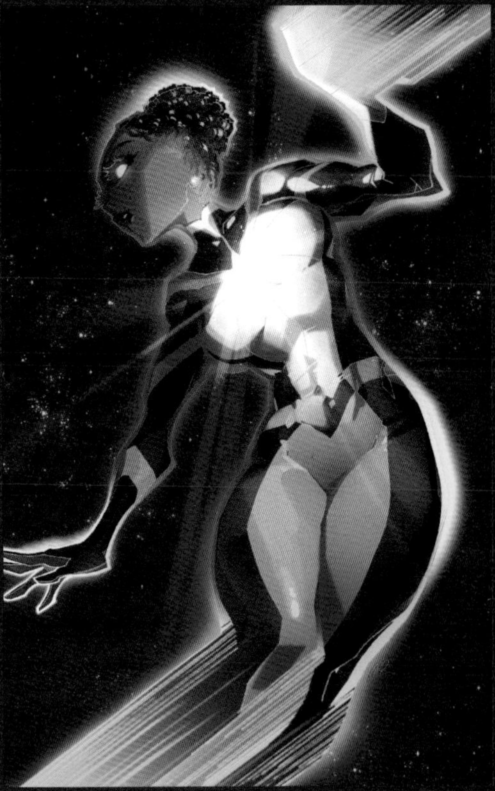

ROSE BESCH
#2 VARIANT

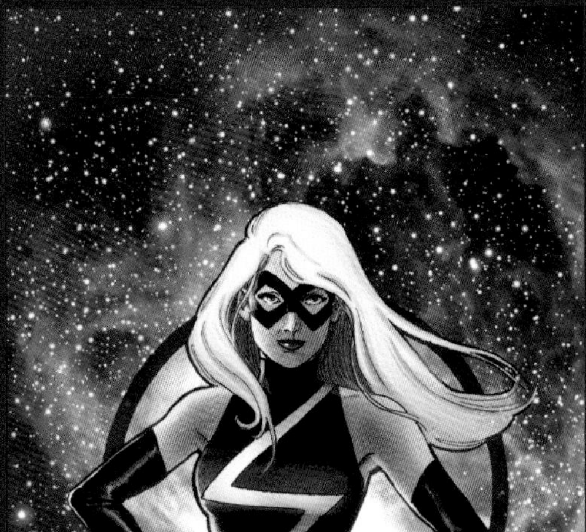

GEORGE PÉREZ & RICHARD ISANOVE
#2 VARIANT

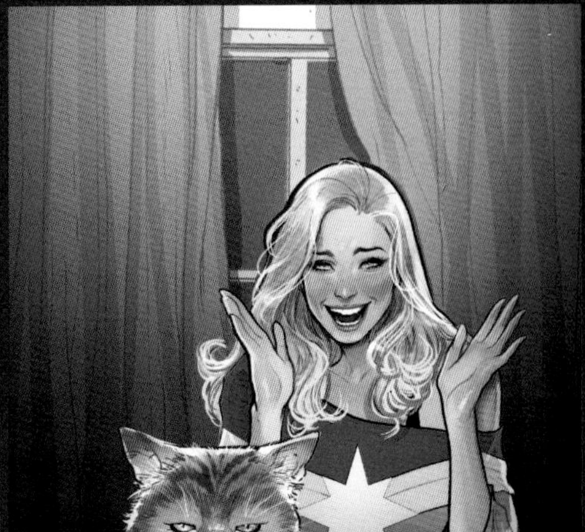

LUCAS WERNECK
#2 STORMBREAKERS VARIANT

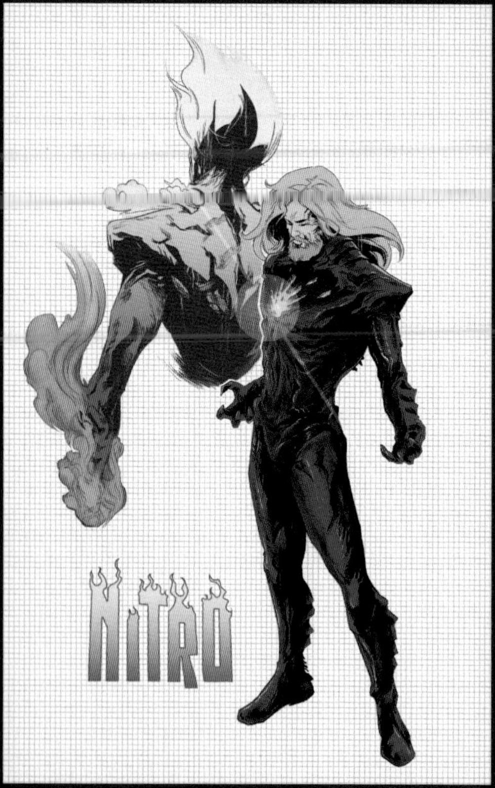
NITRO

PAOLO VILLANELLI
#2 DESIGN VARIANT

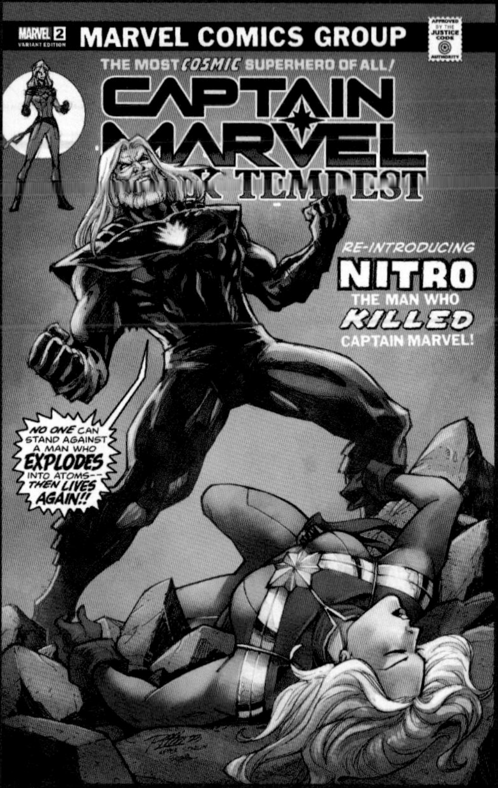
MARVEL 2
VARIANT EDITION
MARVEL COMICS GROUP
THE MOST COSMIC SUPERHERO OF ALL!
CAPTAIN MARVEL
RE-INTRODUCING
NITRO
THE MAN WHO
KILLED
CAPTAIN MARVEL!
NO ONE CAN STAND AGAINST A MAN WHO EXPLODES INTO ATOMS-- THEN LIVES AGAIN!!

RON LIM & RACHELLE ROSENBERG
#2 VARIANT

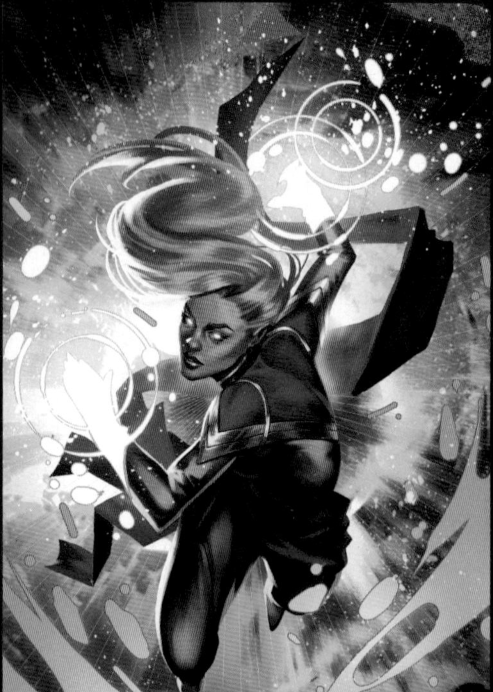

MATEUS MANHANINI
#3 VARIANT

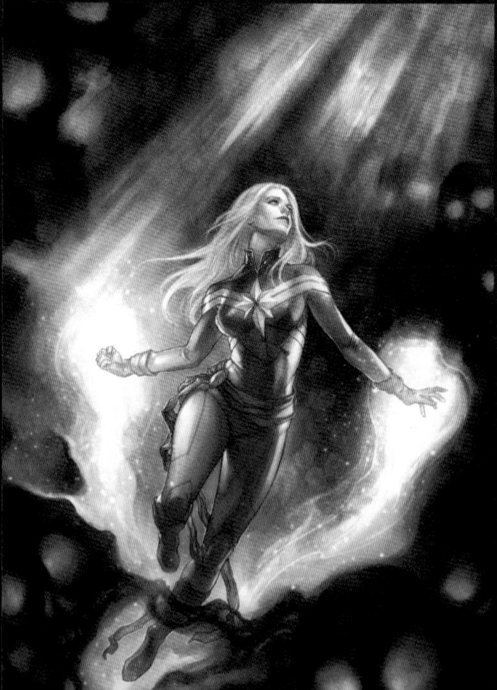

MEGHAN HETRICK
#4 VARIANT